ITALIAN FALSE FRIENDS

R. FERGUSON

Italian
False Friends

University of Toronto Press

TORONTO BUFFALO LONDON

© University of Toronto Press Incorporated 1994
Toronto   Buffalo   London
Printed in Canada

ISBN 0-8020-6948-7

Printed on acid-free paper

Toronto Italian Studies

Canadian Cataloguing in Publication Data

Ferguson, Ronnie.
Italian false friends

(Toronto Italian studies)
Includes bibliographical references.
ISBN 0-8020-6948-7

1. Italian language – Paronyms – Dictionaries.
2. English language – Paronyms – Dictionaries.
3. Italian language – Translating into English –
Handbooks, manuals, etc.   I. Title.   II. Series

PC1593.F47 1994   453'.21   C94-932218-0

For

Annie, Stefan and Nathalie

Contents

Preface

It is only in the past decade or so that 'false friends' have begun to be properly explored. French-English *faux amis* have, inevitably, been fairly extensively treated.* Italian-English *falsi amici* have received some attention in Italian but very little in English.**

From the practical and pedagogical viewpoints this neglect appears particularly surprising. The amusing pitfalls of such unreliables as *casino* (brothel or mess, not casino), *costipazione* (blocked nose more often than constipation), *intossicazione* (food poisoning, not intoxication) and *preservativo* (condom, but never preservative) are well known to most Italianists, and can be attested to by anecdotes both personal and apocryphal. Teachers of the language and students progressing beyond the basics feel, intuitively, that these are only the tip of an insidious and largely uncharted iceberg.

On the survival level, signs, menus, brochures and posters bristle with the treacherous attractions of *abusivo* (not abusive but illegal), *caratteristico* (picturesque as well as characteristic), *coincidenza* (a coincidence, but also a travel connection), *prezzi convenienti* (value-for-money, not convenient, prices), *genuino* (wholesome instead of genuine), *suggestivo* (not suggestive but evocative), and many more. Innocuous-looking headlines turn out to be subtly misleading. The main story in *La Repubblica* (16/9/93) was headed: *Assassinati due parà. Facevano footing ... I soldati erano disarmati. 'Tragica fatalità'*. To avoid misreading it one had to be aware that *assassinare*, here, meant to murder, not assassinate; that the two paratroopers had been jogging (*il footing* is a false anglicism rapidly being supplanted by *il jogging*); that these unfortunate soldiers were unarmed (*disarmati*) not disarmed; and that while *una fatalità* looks like a fatality it actually means a misfortune.

Accurate translation, essay and comprehension work, as well as the proper appreciation of advanced Italian texts, hinge on the confident handling of key words like *abilità* (skill or shrewdness, not just ability), *argomento* (not argument but topic or subject), *attuale* (present/topical, never actual), *attualmente* (resembles actually but means: at present), *discussione* (either discussion or argument), *casuale* (fortuitous, not casual), and *eventuale* (not eventual but possible).

Owing to the passing or only haphazard treatment of *falsi amici* in language texts, in conjunction with the regrettable silence of even the best bilingual dictionaries, it is probably seldom appreciated just how widespread the phenomenon is. My own analyses, based on ten years of collecting and sifting material, suggest, for instance, that in extended journalistic articles it is not unusual for around 10% of nouns, adjectives, verbs and adverbs to be false friends. What is more they tend, as the above examples illustrate, to be important, recurring items. One function of the present book is to make available to anyone interested — from beginners to scholars — this rich seam of potential lexical confusion, providing

---

*   See, e.g., C. W. E. Kirk-Greene, *French False Friends*, Routledge and Kegan Paul, London, 1981; P. Thody and H. Evans, *Faux Amis and Key Words*, Athlone, London, 1985; and J. Van Roey, S. Granger and H. Swallow, *Dictionnaire des faux amis français-anglais*, Duculot, Paris, 1988.

**   See the SELECTIVE BIBLIOGRAPHY, below, p. 121.

clear, readable guidance backed by helpful examples with accompanying translations.

In some ways it is equally odd that unreliables have not attracted the attention of socio-linguists for the fascinating insights which they provide into those impalpable links between a society and its language. It is perhaps worth pointing out the obvious at this juncture. Accidental lookalikes are not the object of this investigation. Chance resemblances, for example, pane and *pane* (bread), are of negligible interest, and only one, the irresistible crook versus *crucco*, has been included. False friends are correctly defined as deceptive cognates. This means that they share a common etymological origin. In the majority of words studied this origin is Latin, the parent of all Romance languages, including Italian, but also a huge contributor, through the Norman conquest and later deliberate borrowing, to the vocabulary of English — originally a Germanic language, but now sometimes described as semi-Romance. In a minority of cases the shared root is, on account of more recent two-way exchanges, Italian or English.

Under a host of influences, internal and external, languages evolve inexorably. The same root planted in different soils will develop in more or less diverse directions. In some cases, only the etymologist perceives the connection. *Un pupillo* (from Latin, little doll) is a cognate of pupil but means a ward of court. *Dislocare* (from Latin, to displace) is not to dislocate but to post troops or employees in Italian. *Concussione* (from Latin, shaking about) has a common source with concussion but is now embezzlement. A continued, partially shared, meaning which is most frequently the outcome, is often more confusing still. *Crisi, fiscale*, and *raccomandazione* are crisis, fiscal and recommendation, but they have acquired very different cultural connotations. *Eccellente* may sometimes translate unproblematically as excellent; however, due to the historical associations of *Eccellenza* (Your Excellency), newspaper headlines of the type *arresti eccellenti* do not mean excellent but celebrity or V.I.P. arrests (a common meaning not recorded in any Italian-English dictionary). Tangible evidence of language evolution in action is provided by the disconcerting semantic changes already undergone by some recent English loan-words in Italian: *big, box, basket, gadget, pocket, ticket* and *tight* are part of a new, expanding vein of *falsi amici*. This branching off parallels the shifts in meaning undergone by an earlier series of Italian words, such as alfresco, ballerina, bimbo, bravura and furore, borrowed by English from Italian.

I have, consequently, endeavoured to stress the link between word and society. Frequent references are made to Italian life and culture, and my examples are drawn, where possible, from Italian authors, as well as from daily newspapers, periodicals and advertising.

A word about justification and limitation. I have felt impelled to carry out this study by my (partly) bilingual origins, by fourteen years of teaching Italian to young adults, from beginners to finalists, and by the frustrating neglect of the topic to which I have alluded. I am confident of having included all the common deceptive cognates and of having examined the core ones adequately, within the practical constraints of space. However, ambitions of completeness in this area are an illusion. Even descriptive dictionaries involve exclusion and judgement. All the more so in a work on false friends. Ultimately subjective decisions have constantly had to be made about what constitutes a useful entry (I have rejected, for example, the pair filibuster/*filibustiere* — buccaneer or rogue — on the grounds that each is rather uncommon and mix-ups are highly unlikely), and even about what constitutes a false friend (would *asilo* be taken for asylum?). Finally, it was not an aim of this work to examine every possible meaning of each headword, only to concentrate on areas of possible misunderstanding.

Some acknowledgements are in order. I have had fruitful discussions on cognates with colleagues, notably Michela Masci-Gore, and also Davina Chaplin, with whom I collaborated on an earlier, very different false-friend project. Alison Grant has contributed immaculate word-processing skills but also sound advice. I am grateful to Sandy Grant for his computing expertise, and to Elena Tognini-Bonelli for providing me with access to, and materials from, the *Corpus of Modern Italian* at the University of Birmingham. Stefan Ferguson has read my entries critically, pointing up the verbose or unconvincing. Above all, I owe a debt of thanks to my family for their patience and encouragement.

Signs, Abbreviations and Translations

Cross references to headwords are indicated by an asterisk (*) or by an arrow (———→). The English translation of headword examples often follows a colon, to avoid awkwardness and ambiguities. The equals sign (=) is followed by the correct translation of the English cognate. *Italics* are reserved for Italian words and phrases.

The following conventional abbreviations have been employed:

ad.	- advertisement
adj.	- adjective
adv.	- adverb
coll.	- colloquialism
interj.	- interjection
lit.	- literally
n.f.	- noun, feminine
n.f.pl.	- noun, feminine, plural
n.m.	- noun, masculine
n.m.pl.	- noun, masculine, plural
U.S.	- American English
v.	- verb

Translations of illustrative examples are my own. I have likewise used my own renderings of Italian book titles where no widely-established English equivalent exists.

A

abbondante, adj. — abundant, but also a generous or good amount, e.g. *una porzione abbondante di pastasciutta*, a generous helping of pasta. Shopkeepers weighing out food for you will ask if *un chilo abbondante*, just over a kg., is too much for you.
———→ GENEROSO, PASTA, SCARSO

abilità, n.f. — can simply mean: ability (= *la capacità*), but sometimes the emphasis is on astuteness of brain or skill of hand or mind. So *è apprezzato per le sue abilità come amministratore** may best be rendered: he is appreciated for his shrewdness as an administrator. *È apprezzato per le sue capacità come amministratore* is, unambiguously: he is appreciated for his abilities as an administrator. *L'abilità del prestidigitatore* is the conjurer's sleight of hand, *l'abilità del falegname* is the carpenter's skill, and *la sua abilità nel dirigere gli attori* is: his skill in directing the actors. Consequently, while *abile* is able (= *capace*), it can be manually skilful or mentally shrewd: former Prime Minister Bettino Craxi has been described, e.g., as *un abile manovratore*, a cunning tactician. *Abile per il servizio* militare*, however, means: fit for military service (———→ RIFORMARE), and someone qualified to teach is *abile all'insegnamento* in that they have obtained *il diploma d'abilitazione*, the teaching certificate (———→ DIPLOMATO), in the examination called *l'esame d'abilitazione*.
———→ BRAVURA, COMPETENTE, INABILITÀ, MANEGGIARE, QUALIFICATO

aborigeni, n.m. pl. — not restricted to the Aborigines of Australia but applied to any native population. *L'Espresso* (13/6/93) described the heroine of Jane Campion's film 'The Piano' (1993) *che trascina fra gli aborigeni un pianoforte in piena età vittoriana*, dragging a piano among the natives [= Maoris], in the heart of the Victorian period.

abusivo, adj. — means: illegal, unlawful or illicit but can easily be mistaken for abusive (= *ingiurioso*, *insultante*, or *osceno*). *Un tassista abusivo*, an unlicensed taxi-driver, is therefore very different from an abusive taxi-driver = *un tassista villano**, *maleducato* or *cafone*. Similarly, *una chiamata abusiva* is an unauthorised 'phone-call while an abusive 'phone call is *una chiamata oscena*. Parts of Italy's coastline have been spoilt by *costruzioni abusive*, buildings put up without planning permission. *Inquilini abusivi* (lit. unlawful tenants) are squatters, and *posteggiatori abusivi* are the unauthorised car-park attendants who sometimes pester tourists at holiday resorts.
———→ IRREGOLARE

accidente, n.m. — is not to be confused with an accident (= *un incidente**). *Gli accidenti della vita* are life's unforeseen events/occurrences. However, it usually means: a stroke (*è morto d'un accidente*, he died of a stroke) or else is employed pejoratively in expressions such as *non capisce un accidente*, he doesn't understand a damn thing, and *gli venga un accidente*, I hope he drops dead. The interjection *accidenti!* is the equivalent of Good Heavens!

acconto, n.m. — looks like an account but is, in fact, an advance, down payment or deposit. *Chiedere un acconto sullo stipendio* is: to ask for an advance on one's salary, and *versare un acconto* is: to make a down payment. A bank account, on the other hand = *un conto in banca*, and a current account = *un conto corrente**, from which you can obtain

money via the cash-dispenser, *il bancomat*. To have a savings account = *avere un conto/un libretto* di risparmio*, while the accounts of a company = *la contabilità*.
─────→ ANTICIPARE, BILANCIA, LIQUIDAZIONE, RETRIBUZIONE

accostare, v. — *accostare una persona* is only to approach a person, while to accost somebody = *abbordare qualcuno*. Also to place alongside, as in *un'architettura che accosta l'antico* e il nuovo*, a type of architecture which brings together the old and the new.

accurato, adj. — easily confused with accurate, but it means: careful or thorough, so that *un'analisi accurata del problema* is a careful analysis of the problem, and *uno studente accurato* is a thorough or conscientious student. Accurate = *preciso* or *esatto*.
─────→ CURARE, PUNTUALE, SCRUPOLO

accusare, v. — to accuse, of course, but beware of the following. In the medical context *l'ammalato accusa un forte mal di testa* means that the patient is complaining of, or suffering from, a bad headache. Can mean: to feel, e.g. *accusa il colpo*, he's feeling the effects, or to reveal/show/betray signs of; *dopo lo sforzo il suo viso accusò stanchezza*, after the effort his face showed signs of fatigue. The set expression for: to acknowledge receipt of a letter is *accusare ricevuta di una lettera*.

acquedotto, n.m. — can be an aqueduct, though usually it is a water main. This explains the curious headlines *Fluoro nell'acquedotto comunale**, Fluoride in the town's water-supply system, and *acquedotti in tilt**, water mains out of action or commission.

aderire, v. — occasionally to adhere, in the sense of to stick to. More often to join an organisation or party, or else to support, e.g. *il politico ha deciso di aderire al partito socialista*, the politician decided to join the Socialist Party, and *la Gran Bretagna non aderisce ancora all' Europa monetaria*, G.B. has still to join the European Exchange Rate Mechanism. Contrast *aderire a un programma*, to support a plan, and to adhere to a plan = *rimanere fedele a un programma* (─────→ PROGRAMMARE).

affare, n.m. — is often affair (although a love affair = *un'avventura**), as in foreign affairs, *gli affari esteri*, or *l'affare Moro*, the Moro affair. However, you may come across *un affare* in the sense of a bargain (─────→ OCCASIONE), and you are bound to encounter its commonest meaning, business, e.g. *un uomo d'affari*, a business man, *gli affari sono gli affari*, business is business, and *un negozio che fa affari*, a shop doing good business. *Piazza Affari*, lit. Business Square, is the expression used for the Italian money markets centred on *la borsa*, the stock exchange in Milan.
─────→ AZIONE, COMMERCIO

affascinante, adj. — is not always a straightforward equivalent of fascinating, so that while a fascinating story could be translated as *una storia affascinante*, it may be just as appropriate to use *suggestiva* (─────→ SUGGESTIVO), *avvincente, appassionante* or even *interessantissima*. In the main, however, *affascinante* has stronger sensual connotations. Thus, *un'attrice affascinante* is a charming, seductive, glamorous, attractive, captivating or bewitching actress. It follows that *il fascino* is glamour and charm as often as it is fascination.
─────→ INTRIGANTE

affermazione, n.f. — affirmation but also, surprisingly, success or emergence. Thus *l'affermazione recente di un'idea*, the recent success of an idea, and *l'affermazione di una nuova generazione di politici*, the success, emergence or coming of age of a new generation of politicians.

affezionato, adj. — close to/attached to, but not affectionate. *È molto affezionato alla sorella* means: he's very attached to his sister, as opposed to *è molto affettuoso con lei*, he's very affectionate with her. For affection use *l'affetto* in preference to *l'affezione*, although note that *il prezzo d'affezione* of an object is its sentimental value. Disconcertingly, *un'affezione* is also an infection, e.g. *un'affezione dell'apparato respiratorio*, a chest infection.

affluenza, n.f. — not affluence (= *il benessere* or *la ricchezza*) but crowd(s) or an influx of people. *Il sabato di Pasqua c'è sempre molta affluenza nei centri storici delle città italiane* means, therefore, that the old city centres in Italy are always busy/crowded on Easter Saturday, and *c'è la solita affluenza di turisti a Firenze quest'anno* means: there is the usual influx of tourists to Florence this year. The most affluent city in Italy in the early 1990s was Modena, *la città più benestante/ricca d'Italia nei primi anni novanta era Modena*. The affluent society is *la civiltà del benessere* (————→ CIVILIZZAZIONE).
————→ INFLUSSO, STORICO

affrontare, v. — not to affront but to face up to, confront or deal with. *Ho paura di affrontare i miei genitori* therefore means: I am afraid of facing up to my parents (————→ PARENTE), whereas I am afraid of affronting them = *ho paura di offenderli. I problemi affrontati in questo libro* are the problems tackled in this book, but *lo sforzo finanziario affrontato dalla nuova ditta* is the financial cost shouldered or borne by the new firm.
————→ CONFRONTARE

agenda, n.f. — often used, like agenda, in the business context, and consequently open to confusion. It may occasionally be an agenda (*l'ordine del giorno* is more usual). Normally, though, it is a diary or engagement book, e.g. *la 'mitica' Filofax, un'agenda … che è diventata una sorta di status symbol* (*Noidonne*, Jan. 1991), the legendary Filofax, a diary that has become a kind of status symbol. The Lediberg company have advertised their desk diaries with the rhyming slogan *Le agende per le aziende*, the diaries for companies. The political agenda can be *l'agenda politica*.
————→ MITICO, RIUNIONE, SOCIETÀ

agente, n.m. — in most cases, including James Bond *agente segreto 007*, it translates unproblematically as agent, although on the stock exchange *un agente di cambio* is a stockbroker. You will probably come across it, however, meaning a policeman, i.e. *un agente (di polizia)*, also called *un poliziotto*. The Italian police are, bewilderingly, not one but many separate forces as you will see if you consult *i numeri utili*, the useful telephone numbers, in a newspaper. *La polizia* proper, for instance, enforce law and order in main towns. *I carabinieri*, with their flambuoyant ceremonial uniforms, are, like the French *gendarmerie*, a military corps with nation-wide jurisdiction. *Le Guardie di Finanza* are the frontier and customs police, while the ordinary local policeman on the beat or on traffic duty is *il vigile (urbano)*.
————→ CUSTODIA, EFFETTIVO, FINANZIERE

aggiornamento, n.m. — adjournment, but also updating or renewal, so that *l'aggiornamento di una proposta* could be either the deferral or the updating of a proposal. In a firm, *l'aggiornamento dei registri* is the updating of the books, and in any organisation *l'aggiornamento delle attrezzature* is the modernisation of the equipment. Note *un corso d'aggiornamento*, a refresher course. The word achieved a certain international notoriety in the 1960s when it was applied to the renewal of the Catholic Church carried out by the Vatican II council (1962–65) under Pope John XXIII.

aggiudicare, v. — confusable with adjudicate (= *guidicare, fare da arbitro** or *pronunciare un guidizio*, according to context). It actually means: to award, e.g. *aggiudicare un premio* or *un contratto*, to award a prize or contract, or else to sell/knock down for at an auction, so that auctioneers cry *aggiudicato!* gone! when they bring down their hammer.

aggiustare, v. — not to adjust (= *regolare*) but to repair, mend or fix, so that *aggiustare la T.V.* is: to repair, not to adjust, the T.V. Also to arrange or set right, e.g. *aggiustare i mobili*, to arrange the furniture, or *aggiustarsi i capelli*, to arrange one's hair. Note *ti aggiusto io!* I'll fix you!
———→ RIPARARE

aggressione, n.f. — not aggression (= *l'aggressività*), except in the military sense. Otherwise it means: attack or assault, so that *essere vittima di un'aggressione* is: to be the victim of an assault or mugging, and *l'aggressione a mano armata* is armed assault. *Assalto*, on the other hand, is restricted to military-type assaults.

agile, adj. — agile but, rather oddly, also applied to books where it means: handy or compact, e.g. *un'agile edizione** *scolastica* (———→ SCOLASTICO), a handy edition for schools, and the Garzanti ad. for their mini encyclopedias: *in un solo volume agile e maneggevole il sapere di una grande enciclopedia*, in a single compact and easy-to-handle (———→ MANEGGIARE) volume all the knowledge of a major encyclopedia. *Uno stile agile* is a clear and concise writing style. An organisation with *strutture agili* has flexible structures.
———→ PRATICO, SINTETICO

agitazione, n.f. — political and personal agitation, but also unrest, e.g. *l'agitazione sindacale*, labour unrest, or *l'agitazione di piazza*, social unrest. Particularly common in industrial relations where it means stoppages or industrial action, as in the headlines *aumenta il caos per le agitazioni nei trasporti pubblici*, increasing confusion caused by industrial action on public transport/U.S. transportation, and *i metalmeccanici in agitazione*, steel workers take industrial action. *Agitazioni* can take the form of *lo sciopero*, the strike, *lo sciopero selvaggio*, the wildcat strike, *lo sciopero a scacchiera*, the selective strike, *lo sciopero a singhiozzo* (lit. hiccup), the on-off strike, or *lo sciopero bianco*, the work-to-rule.
———→ ASTENZIONE, CATEGORIA, LICENZA, MILITANTE, OCCUPAZIONE, SINDACATO

agonia, n.f. — never means agony in the sense of extreme physical pain (I'm in agony = *soffro dolori atroci*). Occasionally you may find it used figuratively as in English, e.g. *il periodo prima degli esami è stato una vera e propria* (———→ PROPRIO) *agonia*, the period prior to the exams was really agony. However, it is mainly used for death throes. Thus *essere in agonia*, to be at death's door, *la sua agonia è stata molto lunga*, his death came very slowly, and *è morta dopo lunga agonia*, she died after a protracted struggle. Here it can be employed figuratively, too: commenting on the financial troubles of Italy's traditional language watchdog, the Accademia della Crusca, *Il Venerdì della Repubblica* (19/4/91) noted: *Un anno fa la sottoscrizione lanciata dal 'Giornale' ha salvato la Crusca dall'agonia in cui l'aveva ridotta l'esiguo assegno dello stato*, A year ago the subscription got up by the *Giornale* newspaper saved the Crusca from the terminal illness brought on by its meagre state subsidy. Beware of the noun *l'agonismo* which means sporting or competitive spirit, and its adjective *agonistico*, often found in sports columns or broadcasts: *L'Espresso* (12/5/91), discussing the popularity of tennis in Italy, complained that *a livello agonistico internazionale i risultati non si vedono*, at the competitive international level results have not been forthcoming.

al fresco, adv. — is not an adjective, and does not mean alfresco. *Tenere in* or *al fresco* of food is: to keep it in a cool place, and *mettere al fresco* (coll.) of a person is to put them away (i.e. in jail). You could say *mangiare un pasto al fresco* but it would mean: to eat a meal in the (cool) shade; an alfresco meal, on the other hand = *un pasto all'aperto*. Note that a fresco painting is *un affresco*.

alterare, v. — particularly tricky as it always implies alteration for the worse, so that *alterare un documento* is: to falsify a document, *l'alcol altera l'organismo* means: drink adversely affects the body, and *il caldo altera il cibo* means that heat makes food go off/spoils food. Also tampered with, of food and drink: *un vino alterato*, e.g., may be a doctored wine (———→ SOFISTICATO). To alter is *cambiare* or *modificare*. *Alterazione* carries the same implication of deterioration, as in *la minaccia principale alla sopravvivenza della lontra è l'alterazione dei corsi d'acqua*, the main threat to the survival of the otter is the deterioration of water courses. Note its commonest use as a mild fever: *il bambino ha un po' d'alterazione*, the child is running a slight temperature.

amabile, adj. — amiable, kind or sweet of a person, but also sweet of wine (synonym, *abboccato*). The best-known Italian *vino amabile* is the slightly fizzy Lambrusco from Emilia Romagna described, in its export version, by critics as having the appearance and taste of pink bubblegum.
———→ DENOMINAZIONE, SOFISTICATO

amatore, n.m. — is not an amateur but an enthusiast, lover or connoisseur, with no suggestion of lack of expertise, e.g. *un amatore di musica*, a music lover, *un amatore di corse di cavalli*, a horse-racing enthusiast, and *un amatore di vini pregiati*, a connoisseur of fine wines (———→ DENOMINAZIONE). An amateur is, confusingly, *un dilettante**, so that *un pittore dilettante* is someone who paints in their spare time, or as a hobby.

amministrativo, adj. — administrative, but *le elezioni amministrative* (or simply *le amministrative*) are local elections, *l'anno amministrativo* is the financial year, and in a bank *le spese amministrative* are handling charges.
———→ AMMINISTRATORE, AMMINISTRAZIONE

amministratore, n.m. — an administrator, but also a company director. The managing director is *l'amministratore delegato*.
———→ AMMINISTRATIVO, AMMINISTRAZIONE, SOCIETÀ

amministrazione, n.f. — administration, of course, but also where it is housed, e.g. *l'amministrazione si trova al primo piano*, the administrative offices are on the first floor, and *andare in amministrazione*, to go over to the administration building or offices. Do not be misled by the term *l'amministrazione comunale** (or *regionale*): it is the local (or regional) authority/government. *Il consiglio d'amministrazione* is the board of directors. Note, also, the expressions *problemi/affari/cose di ordinaria amministrazione*, routine problems/business/matters (———→ ORDINARIO). The notoriously bureaucratic Italian civil service is called *la pubblica amministrazione*; its staff, known as *gli statali*, are widely held to have a cushy job, *una pacchia*.
———→ AMMINISTRATIVO, AMMINISTRATORE, ASSESSORE, GIUNTA, PRESIDENTE, PROTOCOLLO

analisi, n.f. — analysis, but in a medical context it is often a test, as in *l'analisi del sangue/delle urine*, blood or urine test.

annoiare, v. — not to annoy but to bore. *L'ho annoiato con le mie lamentele* is: I bored him with my complaints, while I annoyed him with my complaints would be *l'ho seccato/ l'ho disturbato/l'ho scocciato* (coll.)/*gli ho dato fastidio con le mie lamentele*. *Annoiato* is therefore bored, and the title of Alberto Moravia's novel *La noia* (1960) means: boredom.
———→ PERTURBARE

anticipare, v. — not to anticipate but to bring forward in time, e.g. *ho dovuto anticipare la data di partenza* or *l'ora della riunione**, I have had to bring forward the date of departure, or the time of the meeting (the opposite, to put back or postpone, is *posticipare*). Also to pay in advance, e.g. *la ditta gli ha anticipato la metà dello stipendio*, the firm advanced him half of his salary (———→ ACCONTO, RETRIBUZIONE). I anticipate problems = *prevedo problemi*, and I anticipated that something like this would happen = *m'aspettavo che sarebbe successo una cosa simile*. *Anticipato*, therefore, is not anticipated (= *previsto*) but early, brought forward or paid in advance; note in particular, *una prenotazione anticipata*, an advance booking, *il pagamento anticipato*, advance payment, *la pensione anticipata*, early retirement (———→ RITIRARE), and *un'elezione anticipata*, an early election — Italy's general elections of 1972, 1976, 1979 and 1983 were all *anticipate*. Similarly, *l'anticipazione di una data* is the bringing forward of a date, and *un' anticipazione* is an advance payment but also a preview (*Anticipazioni: il nuovo libro di Giorgio Bocca*, G.B.'s new book previewed). The anticipation of something pleasurable = *la pregustazione*.

antico, adj. — antique, as in *un mobile antico*, a piece of antique furniture but, more commonly, old or ancient. Examples are *il mondo antico*, the ancient world, *l'Antico Testamento*, the Old Testament, *l'arte antica*, ancient art, and *la storia antica*, ancient history. Antiques are *pezzi d'antiquariato*, and should not be confused with *gli antichi* = the ancients.
———→ ANZIANO

anziano, adj. and n.m. — looks like ancient (= *antico**) but means elderly, so that *gli anziani*, the elderly, are not to be confused with *gli antichi*, the ancients. *L'anzianità* is seniority.

apparenza, n.f. — can only be safely used as the equivalent of appearances in the common expressions *l'apparenza inganna*, appearances are deceptive, *giudicare dalle apparenze*, to

go/judge by appearances, and *salvare le apparenze*, to save face. Otherwise, tread carefully. Someone's or something's physical appearance is best rendered by *l'aspetto*, as in *gli italiani sono ben noti per curare* il loro aspetto*, the Italians are well known for taking care over their appearance, and *l'aspetto severo dei palazzi fiorentini*, the austere appearance of Florentine palaces. When someone or something makes an appearance, *fare una comparsa* or *un'apparizione* are used. However, an appearance in court = *una comparizione*, the appearance of a publication = *l'uscita*, the unexpected appearance of a ghost, a vision or a U.F.O. = *l'apparizione*, and in order of appearance is: *in ordine d'apparizione*.
———→ ESTETICA, PRESENZA

applicazione, n.f. — application in all cases except a job application, *una domanda di lavoro* (———→ DOMANDARE), and an application form, *un modulo**.

appuntamento, n.m. — appointment, as in *fissare un appuntamento*, to make an appointment, but *ho un appuntamento* may mean: I have an appointment, engagement, rendez-vous or date, depending on context. *Darsi appuntamento*, to arrange to meet, is much used at the end of television programmes: *vi diamo appuntamento per la settimana prossima*, see you same time next week. In a newspaper, the column called *Appuntamenti* will list what is on in town, and the advice *l'appuntamento è veramente da non perdere* means: the event is not to be missed.

arbitro, n.m. — an arbiter or arbitrator, but usually encountered meaning referee or umpire (Italian makes no distinction), as in the expression *l'arbitro non tifa*, referees are neutral. Not used for an academic referee, though. 'Could you be my referee?' has to be paraphrased as *Potrebbe scrivermi una referenza o una lettera di raccomandazione*?* Arbitration in Italy is handled at a regional level by the *T.a.r.* (*Tribunale* amministrativo* regionale*), a court which combines the functions of an ombudsman and an industrial tribunal.

archivio, n.m. — archive(s) but also (computer) file, record office or even filing cabinet, so that *archiviare*, to place in the archives, means to file (away), too. Canon advertisements (———→ PUBBLICITÀ) claim that their fax machines *danno documenti facili da leggere, da evidenziare, da archiviare*, provide documents that are easy to read, highlight and file. *Un archivista* is, therefore, a filing clerk as well as an archivist. *Il materiale* d'archivio* is the records.

argomento, n.m. — a classic deceptive cognate. It only overlaps with argument in sentences like *l'argomento più forte in favore della riforma è il suo costo*, the strongest argument for the reform is its cost. Otherwise it means: topic, subject (matter) or issue, e.g. *l'argomento di un saggio/libro/film*, the subject or subject matter of an essay, book or film, *l'argomento che ho scelto per la mia tesi di laurea*, the topic I have chosen for my degree dissertation (which all Italian university students must complete in order to graduate), and *la sicurezza: un argomento sempre attuale**, security: an ever-topical issue/question. An argument, on the other hand = *una discussione**, e.g. *una discussione accesa*, a heated argument, but a convincing argument = *una tesi/un'argomentazione/un ragionamento convincente*.
———→ LITIGARE, SOGGETTO

aroma, n.f. — aroma (*l'aroma del caffè**, the aroma of coffee), but can, surprisingly, mean: flavour, e.g. in an ice-cream parlour (*una gelateria* ⟶ BAR) you might request *aroma fragola e pistacchio*, strawberry and pistachio flavour.
⟶ CLASSICO, PROFUMO

arrangiare, v. — not to arrange (= *sistemare, organizzare, provvedere* or *combinare**, according to context) but to fix up or improvise, e.g. *le arrangerò un buon pasto*, I'll rustle up a good meal for her. Compare *ha arrangiato tutto*, he's patched up the whole thing, with he's arranged the whole thing = *ha organizzato tutto*. Italians are proud of their ability (⟶ ABILITÀ) to *arrangiarsi*, get by, manage or make do, in the face of *lo stato*, the state, seen as ineffectual at government level, and obstructively inefficient at the administrative level, and described as *l'Italia che non funziona*, the Italy that does not work. The individual dynamism of *arrangiarsi* explains, on the one hand, the survival of a chaotic city like Naples, and, on the other hand, the entrepreneurial success which, according to many economic indicators, has made Italy the world's fifth industrial power: *l'Italia che funziona*.
⟶ AMMINISTRAZIONE, MANEGGIARE

arsenale, n.m. — an arsenal or weapons store/cache, but if linked to the name of a city, e.g. *l'arsenale di Taranto*, it is a naval dockyard/U.S. navy yard. The most famous, historically, is *l'arsenale di Venezia* in Venice. The hub of the Venetian republic's military and commercial power, and the greatest manufacturing complex in the world before the industrial revolution, the *arsenale*'s bustling activity is vividly described by Dante in *Inferno* XXI (7–18). Jocularly, *un arsenale* is a mess, e.g. *la tua camera è un arsenale*, your room is a junk yard (⟶ CASINO). The word itself, of Arabic origin, came through to English via the dialect of Venice. Probably the most prestigious dialect in Italy, and still employed by all social classes in the city, Venetian has also given to the world: lagoon, lido, gondola, regatta, scampi, pantaloon, zany, sequin, doge, ghetto, ballot, and the universal *ciao*!

articolato, adj. — means structured, but is deceptively like articulate, especially as both are used in the context of language. Take care, therefore, not to mistake *un discorso* articolato*, a well-structured or well-organised speech, for an articulate speech = *un discorso chiaro/ben espresso/eloquente. Un libro articolato in cinque sezioni* is a book made up of/structured in five sections. An articulate speaker = *un oratore* che si esprime con facilità/che ha facilità di parola*. An articulated vehicle is *un articolato*.

artigiano, n.m. — an artisan, but with none of the 'olde worlde' connotations of the English term. Independent, skilled craftsmen employing only a few people, *gli artigiani* are a mainstay of Italy's economy, and the breeding ground for the small and medium-sized family businesses, *le piccole e medie industrie*, which power Italian economic success. They include leather-workers, glass-makers, silversmiths, potters and watch-makers. The importance accorded to craft work, *l'artigianato*, by the government explains the official title of the Italian Minister for Trade and Industry, *il Ministro dell'industria*, del commercio* e dell'artigianato*.

asilo, n.m. — this sign on a building does not indicate a (lunatic) asylum (= *un manicomio*), but a nursery school or kindergarten. Also known as *scuole materne*, the *asili* — some

state-run, most private — cater for children between ages three and six when primary/U.S. elementary school, *la scuola elementare**, begins. Until they are three children may attend *un asilo nido*, a crêche or playgroup, often laid on by companies for their female employees. Some 85% of Italian children are in nursery education from age three. The common thread linking asylum and *asilo* is the idea of safe haven which appears explicitly in *l'asilo politico*, political asylum, and *il diritto d'asilo*, the right of asylum.
———→ ATTENDERE, FREQUENTARE, LUNATICO, MANIACO

assassino, n.m. — an assassin, but more commonly a murderer (there is no distinction in Italian between the concepts of assassination and murder). Note, though, that the anglicism *un killer* is often used for a hired assassin or hit man. *Assassinare* is, therefore: to murder or assassinate.

assessore, n.m. — is not connected with assessor. He or she is the chairman of a town, county or regional council committee, e.g. *l'assessore allo sport/alla cultura/al commercio**, the chairman of the committees on sport, culture, and trade and industry. In Italian local politics *l'assessorato*, chairmanship of a committee, is a high-profile post. An assessor is either *un perito* or, if a tax assessor, *un ispettore delle tasse/un funzionario del fisco*.
———→ AMMINISTRAZIONE, COMUNALE, FISCALE, GIUNTA

assistente, n.m. or n.f. — assistant. However, *un assistente sociale** is a social worker, and *un assistente sanitario* (———→ SANITÀ) is a health visitor. A shop assistant = *un commesso/ una commessa*.
———→ ASSISTENZA

assistenza, n.f. — sometimes translates straightforwardly as assistance, e.g. *prestare assistenza*, to give assistance, although note that *l'assistenza tecnica* is after-sales service, and *un servizio di assistenza* is a back-up/information service or help-line. Often, however, the emphasis is on aid or care, as in *l'assistenza umanitaria internazionale*, international humanitarian aid, and in the 1991 advertisement for the Catholic Church's charity activities: *per la cura, l'assistenza ai malati di AIDS, per l'assistenza alle famiglie, agli anziani* (———→ ANZIANO), for the treatment and care of AIDS victims, for aid to families and the elderly. The following usages are worth noting: *l'assistenza sanitaria*, health care, and *l'assistenza sociale**, social work. *Lo stato assistenziale* is the welfare state. Occasionally, *l'assistenza* means presence, as in *l'interrogatorio* (———→ INTERROGAZIONE) *dell'accusato si è svolto con l'assistenza di un avvocato*, the questioning of the accused took place in the presence of a lawyer, where 'with the assistance of a lawyer' would have been rendered as *con l'aiuto* or *l'ausilio di un avvocato*. *Assistere a uno spettacolo** is not, therefore, to assist (= *collaborare* or *aiutare* ———→ COLLABORATORE) in a show, but to be present at it, and *assistiamo all'agonia* del regime* means: we are witnessing the death throes of the regime.
———→ ASSISTENTE, CURARE, INTERVENTO, PACCHETTO, SANITÀ

assoluto, adj. — usually means absolute, but beware of it in sporting contexts: *il campione* assoluto dei pesi massimi* is the undisputed heavyweight champion, and *il Campionato Italiano Assoluto di Pentathlon Moderno* is the all-comers'/undisputed/overall Italian Modern Pentathlon Championship. Can be used figuratively, too, in this sense, e.g. *L'Italia detiene un record assoluto, quello della più bassa natalità tra i paesi del mondo* (*La*

Repubblica, 26/1/93), Italy holds an undisputed record: the lowest birthrate in the world (1.3 children per woman, compared, for instance, to the U.K. figure of around 2.0).

assoluzione, n.f. — acquittal as well as absolution. Italian, like Scottish, law has acquittal on a verdict of not proven, *l'assoluzione per insufficienza di prove*.
———→ EVIDENZA, PROCESSO

assumere, v. — to assume importance, a pseudonym, responsibility or an expression. However, I assume it is true = *do per scontato/suppongo/immagino che sia vero*. By and large, you will come across *assumere* meaning: to engage, hire or take on staff, e.g. *assumere un operaio* or *una segretaria*, to employ a worker or secretary, and *lo stato dell'economia non consente alle società* di assumere personale*, the state of the economy does not permit companies to take on staff. Its opposite, to make redundant or fire, is *licenziare* (———→ LICENZA). *Assumere farmaci/droghe* (———→ DROGA), though, means to take medicines or drugs. Similarly, *le assunzioni* are not assumptions (= *le premesse* or *i presupposti*) but the hiring or employment of personnel.
———→ DIPENDENTE, OCCUPAZIONE

astemio, adj. — *una persona astemia* is a teetotaller and, therefore, not quite the same as an abstemious person = *una persona sobria, moderata* or *temperata*.
———→ ASTENZIONE, INTOSSICAZIONE

astenzione, n.f. — abstension from alcohol, work or voting, but, less predictably, also the observance of a strike or labour dispute, e.g. *nel trasporto aereo l'astenzione dal lavoro andrà dalle 9 alle 11*, on the airline side, the strike will be observed from 9 till 11.
———→ AGITAZIONE, ASTEMIO

attaccare, v. — to attack (or attach), but also to launch into something, e.g. *l'orchestra attaccò la sinfonia*, the orchestra struck up the symphony, and *ha attaccato discorso* col vicino di casa*, he struck up a conversation with his neighbour.

attendere, v. — is neither to attend a school, university or course (= *frequentare**), nor to attend to something (= *accudire a* or *occuparsi di qualcosa*). *Attendere* is: to await, e.g. Alfa Romeo claim that in their latest model *vi attendono sedili rivestiti in pregiato velluto persiano*, seats upholstered in finest Persian velvet await you. Italo Calvino wrote of the hero of his 1960 novel *Il visconte dimezzato* ['The Cloven Viscount'], before he was split down the middle by a cannonball: *Se avesse potuto prevedere la terribile sorte che l'attendeva, forse avrebbe trovato anch'essa naturale e compiuta, pur in tutto il suo dolore*, If he could have foreseen the dreadful fate which awaited him, perhaps he would have found it, too, natural and right, even in all its painfulness.

attico, n.m. — beware, when searching through the classified ads. (*gli annunci economici* ———→ ECONOMICO) for accommodation: *un attico* is a top-floor flat or penthouse, and therefore much more expensive than an attic (= *una soffitta, un sottotetto* or *una mansarda*). *La Repubblica* (19/1/91) carried the picturesque ad. *attico mq 170 centralissimo panoramissimo*, very roughly translatable as penthouse, 17m × 10m, bang-in-the-middle-of-town, vistas-a-plenty.
———→ LUMINOSO

attitudine, n.f. — an aptitude not an attitude (= *un atteggiamento*), e.g. *avere un'attitudine per le lingue*, to have a bent or aptitude for languages. An aptitude test is *un test attitudinale*. You have the wrong attitude, or you have an attitude problem = *hai un atteggiamento sbagliato*.

attività, n.f. — activity, but also a commercial asset, so that *attività fisse* are fixed assets, and *attività immateriali* are intangible assets.

attuale, adj. — a very common false friend meaning not: actual but present, current or topical. *L'attuale presidente* del consiglio* is the present Prime Minister, whereas the actual P.M. would be *il presidente del consiglio in persona*. The assertion that *i problemi attuali richiedono soluzioni attuali* means: present-day/today's problems need present-day/up-to-date solutions. A topical question/issue is *un argomento** or *un tema attuale*. The actual circulation of a newspaper = *la diffusione effettiva* (⟶ DIFFUSO, EFFETTIVO) *di un giornale*. *Attualmente* is: at the present time or currently, so that *attualmente non ho progetti*, I've no plans at present, should not be taken for: actually, I've no plans = *infatti/a dire il vero/in realtà non ho progetti*. *L'attualità* is current affairs, and *l'attualità politica* or *sportiva* is the latest political or sports news.

audience, n.f. — not audience (= *il pubblico*) but the viewing public or viewing figures for a T.V. programme. An audience (with, e.g., the Pope) = *un'udienza*.
⟶ PUBBLICITÀ

auditore, n.m. — not a financial auditor (= *un revisore dei conti*) but an unregistered student allowed to attend lectures/U.S. auditor, e.g. *ho frequentato* (⟶ FREQUENTARE, FREQUENZA) *come auditore alcuni corsi presso la New York University*, I attended some courses at N.Y. Univ. as an unregistered student.
⟶ LEZIONE

audizione, n.f. — audition, but beware: it is also the examination of witnesses in court. So the headline *Audizioni per politici e pentiti* (*La Repubblica*, 25/10/92) means that politicians and those who turned state's evidence are to be cross-examined.
⟶ INTERROGAZIONE

autografo, n.m. — autograph, but also a manuscript (in the author's hand), e.g. *gli autografi di molte opere del Cinquecento sono andati dispersi*, the manuscripts of many 16th-century works have been lost. By extension, *un'opera* autografa di Giorgione* is not a signed work (= *un'opera firmata*) by G., but an original G. (⟶ ORIGINALE) or a work in his hand.
⟶ AUTORE, DISPERSO

autonomia, n.f. — autonomy, but can be confusing, especially when applied to vehicles, where it means range, e.g. *un aereo con un autonomia di 1000 km*, a plane with a range of 1000 km. If a lap-top computer is described as having *un'autonomia di 4 ore* then it has a 4-hour battery life. Note that *i lavoratori autonomi* are the self-employed (⟶ DIPENDENTE), although *gli autonomi* are the members of independent trade unions (⟶ SINDACATO).

autore, n.m. — presents no problem in expressions such as *l'autore del progetto*, the author of the scheme, but note that *l'autore del delitto/dell'attentato* is the perpetrator or person responsible for the crime/terrorist attack. Remember, too, that *un autore* is not only a writer; he or she (*un'autrice*) may sometimes be a painter, sculptor or musician, e.g. *Michelangelo è l'autore degli affreschi della Capella Sistina*, M. painted the frescoes in the Sistine Chapel. *Verdi è l'autore di numerose opere liriche* means not that V. wrote the libretti (————→ LIBRETTO) of many operas (————→ LIRICO, OPERA), but that he composed them. *Un quadro d'autore* is an original (painting): the publicity for the Taviani brothers' film *La notte di San Lorenzo* (1982) described it as *un film d'autore*, a classic or quality film, a recent compact disc collection of hits by famous singer-songwriters, *cantautori*, described their songs as *canzoni d'autore*, classic songs or standards, and the headline *Quel master è d'autore* (*Campus*, Dec. 1991) means: That is a top quality M.A.
————→ EDITORE, LIBRERIA

aviazione, n.f. — is not only the abstract concept of aviation but also the actual air-force, *l'aviazione* (or *l'aeronautica*) *militare*. The navy is *la marina*, and the army *l'esercito*.
————→ RIFORMARE

avventura, n.f. — an adventure, but sometimes a love-affair (————→ AFFARE), as in Antonioni's film *Avventura* (1959).

avvisare, v. — rarely to advise (= *consigliare* or *raccomandare* ————→ RACCOMANDAZIONE), usually to inform or let someone know, e.g. *avvisami quando sei pronto*, let me know when you are ready.

azione, n.f. — although it means (stockmarket) share/U.S. stock as well as action, confusion is unlikely except perhaps in *una Società* per Azioni* (*S.p.A.*), a Public Limited Company (P.L.C.). A shareholder/U.S. stockholder is *un azionista*.
————→ OBBLIGAZIONE, QUOTAZIONE, TITOLO

B

ballerina, n.f. — unlike ballerina, is not restricted to classical dance. *Una ballerina* is simply any female dancer, the male equivalent being *un ballerino*. *La Repubblica* (23/6/87) announced Fred Astaire's death with the headline *È morto Fred, il ballerino del secolo*, Fred, the dancer of the century, is dead. Earthquake-prone Southern Italy is sometimes called, with grim humour by Northerners, *la terra ballerina*, the dancing land.

banale, adj. — banal, but sometimes also trivial (——→ TRIVIALE), ordinary, everyday, mundane (——→ MONDANO) or commonplace. *Motivi banali* (——→ MOTIVO) are, therefore, trivial reasons, *un banale raffreddore* is nothing but a common cold, *un banale viaggio in macchina** is an ordinary, everyday car journey, and *un'esistenza banale* is a mundane existence.
——→ FUTILE, ORDINARIO

bar, n.m. — neither a bar in the British or American sense (its nearest Italian equivalent is *la birreria*, where the main drink served is beer), nor the actual bar-counter where you are served (= *il banco*). *Il bar* is the ubiquitous and totally typical Italian café (——→ CAFFÈ). Open from 7 a.m. through to late at night and staffed by *il barista* and *i camerieri*, it provides its customers with coffee, tea, beer, wine, aperitifs and digestifs either at tables outside, which is more expensive, or often — especially in the smaller establishments — simply standing up at the counter, especially during a break from work (*una pausa*). Snacks are always available. *Il bar gelateria* specialises in *il gelato*, ice-cream, *il bar pasticceria* in cakes. In the home, though, *il bar* is the cocktail-cabinet.

baracca, n.f. — could be mistaken for barracks (= *una caserma*) but is in fact a shed, hut, cabin, shack or shanty, according to context. Figuratively it means: a dump or hovel, and the idiom *mandar avanti la baracca* is: to make ends meet or to keep the pot boiling.

basket, n.m. — may puzzle you in sports headlines. It is not a basket (= *un cesto, una cesta* or *un canestro*) but basketball, also known as *la pallacanestro*, one of Italy's most popular spectator-sports. As in many languages, sporting terminology in Italian is heavily influenced by English. Note, however, that Italians are probably unique in using a native-word for football, *il calcio*, due to Mussolini's policy of discouraging foreign borrowings. For other truncated English words in Italian ——→ BIG, GOLF, NIGHT, PERSONAL.

bastardo, adj. or n.m. — corresponds to all the meanings of bastard but, in addition, is used of animal crosses or plant hybrids, so that a mongrel is *un cane bastardo*, as opposed to *un cane di razza*, a pedigree dog.

batteria, n.f. — covers all the uses of battery, with the proviso that an individual battery for an electrical applicance is *una pila*. Surprisingly, *una batteria* is also a drum-kit or the drums in a band, and a heat in a sporting event. In a kitchen, *la batteria di cucina* is the pots and pans.

bestiale, adj. — bestial but, most commonly, huge, terrible or tremendous, e.g. *un lavoro bestiale*, a massive amount of work, or *un peso bestiale*, a tremendous weight. Note the

14

expressions *fa un freddo bestiale*, it's freezing cold, *che tempo bestiale!* what dreadful weather! and *ho una fame bestiale*, I could eat a horse.

big, n.m. — always a noun and never an adjective, this curious false anglicism means: a big-name or big-wig/U.S. big-shot. *I big della politica* are, therefore, the political heavy-weights, and *tutti i big della canzone italiana si riuniscono ogni anno per il festival di San Remo* means that all the big names in Italian music gather every year for the San Remo song festival (Italy's great pop music institution). The big four Italian industrial magnates of the early 1990s, Gianni Agnelli, Silvio Berlusconi, Carlo De Benedetti and Raul Gardini could have been described as *i big dell'industria* italiana*.
———→ PERSONAGGIO, PROTAGONISTA

bilancia, n.f. — not balance (= *l'equilibrio*) but scales for weighing. The balance of payments, though, is *la bilancia dei pagamenti*. A balance sheet = *un bilancio*, and a bank balance = *un saldo* (*in banca*).
———→ ACCONTO

bimbo, n.m. — a perfectly innocent word in Italian. *Un bimbo/una bimba* is a baby or, sometimes, a child. The American and, lately, British use of bimbo meaning an attractive but empty-headed girl (= *una ragazza bella ma stupidella*) may stem from Italian Americans using *bimba* to mean doll or baby, as in the popular song *Come balli bene bella bimba*, How well you dance pretty baby.
———→ BOX

biologico, adj. — biological, but watch out for it meaning: organic, as in the ad. for the magazine *La Nuova Ecologia* (Jan. 1993) *gli spaghetti: normali, integrali e biologici: a confronto le 19 marche più diffuse*, spaghetti: plain, wholemeal and organic: the 19 most popular (or best-known) brands compared.
———→ CONFRONTARE, DIETA, DIFFUSO, INTEGRALE

bitter, n.m. — is not, of course, a bitter beer (the nearest Italian equivalent would be *una birra scura*) but bitters, a typical flavouring of many Italian aperitifs such as *bitter San Pellegrino* and *bitter Campari*. The adjective bitter is *amaro* which is also the generic name for the numerous brands of bitter-tasting digestifs, like *Amaro Averna* from Sicily, which Italians are particularly fond of.
———→ BAR

blando, adj. — bland, but never with pejorative connotations. Bland food and music are, therefore, best rendered as *cibo e musica insipidi*. Note *una reazione blanda*, a mild reaction, *un avvertimento blando*, a gentle warning (———→ GENTILE), and *una luce blanda*, (a) soft light(ing).

bloccare, v. — to block is often an inappropriate translation. Potentially misleading are statements such as *la società* ha bloccato tutti i posti e tutte le assunzioni*, the company has frozen all posts and all hiring of staff (———→ ASSUMERE), and *i grandi magazzini hanno bloccato l'acquisto di salmone delle Shetland*, department stores have suspended purchases of salmon from the Shetlands. *Bloccare il motore* is to stall the engine, *tutto s'è improvvisamente bloccato* is: everything suddenly ground to a halt, *gli automobilisti bloccati dal traffico* are

motorists stuck/held up in the traffic, and *sono rimasto bloccato* will often mean: I was left speechless or I couldn't utter a word.
————→ TILT

blusa, n.f. — a blouse, but also a smock.

bombardiere, n.m. — not a bombardier (= *un sottufficiale d'artiglieria*) but a bomber aircraft. Remember that *bombardare* can be: to bomb, as well as to bombard.

box, n.m. — is never a box (= *una scatola*). A couple seeking *un box* or *un box bimbo** for their child want a play-pen, while a sign or advertisement displaying the words *affitasi box* indicates that there is a lock-up garage to let. It also means: a horse-box, the pits in motor racing and a shower unit. On the other hand, *la boxe* (pronounced box) is boxing, also known as *il pugilato*, while wrestling is *il catch*, from English catch-as-catch can. Curiously, *un boxer* is not a boxer (= *un pugile*) but boxer shorts (————→ SLIP).

bravo, adj. or interj. — not brave (= *coraggioso*) but clever or good. *Un bravo ragazzo* is simply a good or clever boy whereas *un ragazzo bravo* is, more specifically, an intelligent boy. *Un bravo cantante* means: a good singer, and *un bravo medico*: an able doctor. The exclamation *bravo!* (well done!) is shouted not only at the end of opera performances in Italy but often after well-known arias too (————→ OPERA). Remember that its ending varies according to who is being praised, e.g. *brava!* for the soprano, but *bravi!* for the entire cast. Sometimes *bravo!* has the ironic connotations of well done! as in *ah, hai lasciato cadere il vaso*? Bravo!* So you dropped the vase? Well done!
————→ BRAVURA, CORAGGIO

bravura, n.f. — is bravura in the musical expression *un pezzo di bravura*, a bravura passage. Usually, though, the emphasis is on outstanding skill or excellence rather than flashiness. Contrast *la bravura del pianista*, the pianist's great skill or ability (————→ ABILITÀ), and the pianist's bravura, *il virtuosismo del pianista*. *Panorama* (5/9/93) asked, of Placido Domingo: *Come può ... il grande tenore dominare tutte le situazioni con tanta bravura?* How can the great tenor dominate every situation with so much outstanding ability? Also bravery (sometimes with the suggestion of foolhardiness), e.g. *la bravura del poliziotto nell'affrontare* i banditi armati*, the policeman's bravery in confronting or dealing with the gunmen.
————→ BRAVO

brigadiere, n.m. — resembles brigadier (= *un comandante di brigata*) but is a sergeant-major in the *carabinieri* (————→ AGENTE). A sergeant-major in the regular army is, however, *un sergente maggiore*.
————→ BOMBARDIERE, GRADUATO, MARESCIALLO, UFFICIALE

brillante, adj. — is sometimes brilliant (e.g. *una carriera/un risultato/un futuro/un successo brillante*, a brilliant career, result, future or success), but do not take it for granted. *Colori brillanti* are bright rather than brilliant colours (= *colori molto vivaci*), and *un'idea brillante* is a bright rather than a brilliant idea (= *un'idea geniale**). Also means shiny, sparkling, lively or vivacious, as in *i capelli brillanti*, shiny hair, *una conversazione brillante*, a sparkling conversation, *una guida brillante*, lively driving/handling, of a vehicle (————→ GUIDARE), *un temperamento/uno stile brillante*, a lively temperament or style, and *Isabella* *d'Este, la brillante e affascinante* marchesa di Mantova*, I. d'E., the vivacious and glamorous marquise of Mantua. Beware also of *una commedia* brillante*, a light comedy, and of *acqua brillante*, tonic water.

———→ LUMINOSO, SCINTILLANTE, VIVACE

buscare, v. — like to busk, is derived from the Spanish *buscar*, to seek. However, do not be misled by *buscarsi da vivere* and *buscarsi del pane*; they mean not to busk for a living or for one's bread, but to scrape a living and to earn a crust. Busking has to be paraphrased as *cantare/dare spettacolo* per le strade*. The often negative connotations of catching or getting in *buscare* are apparent in *buscare una multa*, to receive or 'cop' a fine, and *buscarsi un raffreddore*, to catch a cold.

busto, n.m. — not bust (= *il petto* or *il seno*), other than in sculpture, but the trunk or the body from the waist up. *Un ritratto a mezzo busto* is a half-length portrait, and Italian newsreaders are jocularly known as *i mezzibusti*, both because they are always seen from the waist up and on account of their sculptural solemnity. *Un busto* is also a corset.

C

cabina, n.f. — a plane or boat cabin (but a log cabin is *una capanna*, as in Beecher-Stowe's 'Uncle Tom's Cabin' (1852) translated as *La capanna dello zio Tom*). However, note that *una cabina (telefonica)* is a 'phone-booth/box/kiosk, and *una cabina elettorale* is a polling-booth (———→ URNA).

caffè, n.m. — coffee and café. Remember, though, that the ordinary café is *il bar**. *Il caffè* is an elegant, higher class establishment, often with links going back to 18th- or 19th-century café society, such as *il Pedrocchi* in Padua or the *Florian* in St Mark's square, Venice, which features in Henry James's 'The Aspern Papers' (1888).
———→ CORRETTO

campare, v. — looks like to camp (= *fare il campeggio* or *campeggiare*) but means: to get by or survive, so that *campare alla giornata* is: to live from hand-to-mouth, and *campare alla meglio* is: to get by as best one can. A camp-site is *un campeggio* or *un camping*. *Un camper* refers to the vehicle; the person is *un campeggiatore*.

campione, n.m. — is deceptive on two counts. In the first place, it is not only a champion but also simply a great sportsman/woman. Outstanding competitors are commonly referred to as *grandi campioni*. Secondly, it also means a sample of any kind, e.g. *un campione di stoffa**, a sample of fabric. A trade-fair is called *una fiera campionaria* because samples are on display.

candela, n.f. — candle, but also spark-plug.

candido, adj. — of a person's character or utterances is pure, innocent or even naive rather than candid (= *franco, onesto* or *schietto*). Also pure white, as in travel-brochure statements like *le candide spiagge della Giamaica*, the spotless sands of Jamaica. A favourite word in soap-powder ads. where it means whiter-than-white.

cantina, n.f. — not a canteen (= *una mensa*) but a cellar, whether for wine, food or anything else. Almost all Italians have *una cantina* in the basement of their home or block of flats (———→ PALAZZO). Note the potentially misleading *cantina sociale**, wine co-operative. *Le mense universitarie*, university refectories, are excellent value for money in Italy, as English-speaking year-abroad students are well aware.
———→ DENOMINAZIONE

capsula, n.f. — a capsule of all kinds but also a bottle-top, cap or jar-lid.
———→ TAPPO, VASO

caramella, n.f. — is not confined to (a) caramel. It is a sweet/U.S. candy of any kind. *Una caramella al liquore* has a liqueur centre, and *una caramella alla frutta* is a fruit pastille.

carattere, n.m. — character, but not in a book, film or play (= *un personaggio**), e.g. the title of Pirandello's best-known play *Sei personaggi in cerca d'autore** (1921) translates as 'Six Characters in Search of an Author'. Sometimes, confusingly, it means characteristic,

as in *la poesia di Dante ha certi caratteri inconfondibili*, Dante's poetry has certain unmistakable characteristics.
————→ PROTAGONISTA

caratteristico, adj. — characteristic. However, if the medieval streets of San Gimignano in Tuscany are described in your guide-book as *caratteristiche* it is best rendered as picturesque. If you wish, in a restaurant, to know what the house speciality is, one way to put the question is: *Qual è il vostro piatto caratteristico?* When asked on a document for your *segni caratteristici*, give your distinguishing marks.
————→ TIPICO.

carbone, n.m. — is coal, whereas the element carbon is *il carbonio*, e.g. *l'ossido di carbonio*, carbon monoxide, *il diossido* or *biossido di carbonio*, carbon dioxide, and *il ciclo del carbonio*, the carbon cycle. Carbon paper, however, is *la carta carbone*, and hydrocarbons are *gli idrocarburi*. Italy has negligible reserves of coal.
————→ ENERGETICO, PETROLIO

cargo, n.m. — is easy to confuse with cargo (= *il carico*) but is actually a cargo ship or plane.

casino, n.m. — asking where *il casino* (= the brothel) is could be embarrassing. If your interest is in gambling what you want is *il casinò*. These treacherous twins provide a fascinating insight into false friend development. Originally the diminutive of *casa*, house, *un casino* was, in the 16th century, a noble or country residence. By the 17th it had become a salon, especially for gambling (a small palace called *casin dei nobili* still stands in the San Barnaba district of Venice). With the meaning of gaming-house the word was borrowed by French which has given it to the world. In Italy, though, it had evolved by the 18th century to whorehouse. When, therefore, it required a term for casino Italian borrowed back *casinò* (the accent indicates the normal French stress on the final syllable). Since the closing down of brothels (*i postriboli*, or euphemistically, *le case di tolleranza*) in Italy in 1958, *casino* has become an old fashioned word. Figuratively, though, it has gained a new lease of life meaning a mess or shambles, e.g. *che casino dopo la festa!* what a mess after the party! (————→ CONFUSIONE). A call-girl is *una ragazza squillo* (————→ SQUILLARE) and solliciting, *adescare*, is widely practised.
————→ PRESERVATIVO, RUFFIANO

castigare, v. — to castigate or punish, but when applied to books it means: to expurgate or bowdlerise, so that *un'edizione* castigata del Decameron* is an expurgated version of Boccaccio's masterpiece.

castrato, n.m. — is not only the high-voiced singer but also, incongruously, lamb (meat), as in the dish *castrato in umido**, lamb stew.

casuale, adj. — not usually casual but fortuitous, as in *un incontro casuale*, a chance meeting, or in the usual disclaimer in works of fiction: *ogni riferimento a persone esistenti in questo libro è puramente casuale*, any resemblance between characters in this book and living persons is purely coincidental (————→ COINCIDENZA). Note *un controllo casuale* (————→ CONTROLLARE), a spot-check. A casual attitude = *un atteggiamento noncurante* or *disinvolto*, casual work = *il lavoro saltuario*, a casual suggestion = *una proposta poco*

meditata or *spontanea*, while to make casual conversation = *parlare del più e del meno*. Casual clothes, though, are *gli abiti casual*, and casual fashions are *la moda casual*. *Casualmente*, therefore, means: by chance — compare *sono entrato casualmente nella stanza*, I entered the room by chance, and I entered the room casually = *sono entrato nella stanza con disinvoltura/noncuranza*.
———→ OCCASIONALE

categoria, n.f. — category or class (*un albergo di seconda categoria* is a second class hotel), but also a section of the workforce. During the annual round of industrial wage-bargaining in the autumn known as *il rinnovo dei contratti*, the renewal of (labour) contracts, newspapers commonly carry headlines like *molte categorie in sciopero: dai metalmeccanici ai bancari*, many groups of workers on strike: from steel-workers to bank staff. *Categorico* can be categorical, but if the Yellow Pages, *le Pagine Gialle*, in the 'phone book are described as *un elenco telefonico categorico* it means that they are a classified telephone directory.
———→ AGITAZIONE, DIPENDENTE, LICENZA, SINDACATO

cauzione, n.f. — not caution (= *la precauzione/la cautela* or, of an offender, *l'ammonimento*) but bail, surety or deposit. *L'accusato è stato rilasciato* (———→ RILASCIARE) *dietro cauzione* means, therefore, that the accused was released on bail, and not after a caution. *Versare una cauzione* is: to put down or pay a deposit.

cava, n.f. — not a cave but a quarry, e.g. *una cava di marmo*, a marble quarry, of which the best known are those at Carrara in north west Tuscany which supplied Michelangelo with his stone. A cave = *una caverna* or, if very deep, *una grotta*.

cavalleria, n.f. — cavalry but chivalry too (the horse, *il cavallo*, being the common factor). The title of Giovanni Verga's short story (1880) and play (1884) *Cavalleria rusticana* ['Rustic Chivalry'], made world-famous by Mascagni's operatic adaptation, was an ironic comment on the bloody ritual of the Southern Italian crime of passion, revealingly known as *il delitto d'onore*, the crime of honour, and partly condoned (———→ CONDONARE) by the Italian Criminal Code until the reform of family law in 1975.

celebrare, v. — to celebrate, of course, but beware of the expression *celebrare un processo**, to hold a trial.
———→ CONCILIATORE, MAGISTRATO, TRIBUNALE

celibe, adj. — not celibate (= *casto*) but unmarried or single. Usually applied to a bachelor, *uno scapolo*, who uses the term to answer the question about marital status, *lo stato civile*, on the Italians' compulsory identity card, *la carta d'identità*. The equivalent term used of a single woman is the even falser friend *nubile**! As the unmarried lifestyle becomes commoner in Italy it is fashionable to talk of *un(a) single*.
———→ MATRIMONIO, SINGOLO

centrifuga, n.f. — a centrifuge, but also those useful household conveniences (———→ COMODITÀ), the spin-dryer and the salad spinner.

cilindro, n.m. — a top-hat as well as a cylinder. The Italian for bowler-hat/U.S. derby comes from another amusing analogy, for *la bombetta* literally means: a small bomb.

circolare, v. — to circulate, but on train noticeboards and timetables a statement such as *circola tutti i giorni escluso il sabato* means: this train runs every day except Saturdays.
———→ CIRCOLAZIONE, COMPARTIMENTO, ESPRESSO

circolazione, n.f. — has all the meanings of circulation but is also traffic (flow) or sometimes, driving, e.g. *la circolazione è stata bloccata* (———→ BLOCCARE) *da un incidente**, the traffic has been held up by an accident, and *la circolazione a sinistra è vietata in Italia*, driving on the left is illegal in Italy. The sign *divieto di circolazione/di transito* means: no thoroughfare.
———→ CIRCOLARE, GUIDARE, PRECEDENZA, SEMAFORO, VIABILITÀ

circolo, n.m. — does mean: a geometric circle (although *il cerchio* is commoner). More often used figuratively, especially to mean: a club, as in *un circolo sportivo*, a sports club, or *un circolo ufficiali* (———→ UFFICIALE), an officers' club. *Come fare per attirare i giovani nei circoli cattolici?* is likely to mean: what can we do to get young people to join Catholic clubs? Catholic circles, in this context, = *gli ambienti cattolici*. A vicious circle is *un circolo vizioso**, but an inner circle = *un cerchio ristretto*. Watch out, too, for *un angolo*: as well as a geometric angle, it is also a corner, e.g. *il bar* d'angolo*, the corner or local café (———→ CAFFÈ).

citazione, n.f. — a citation, military or scholarly, but also simply a quotation, so that a student's essay which is full of useful quotations is *un saggio ricco di citazioni*. A legal summons as well, as in *una citazione a comparire davanti al giudice*, a summons to appear before the judge (———→ TRIBUNALE).
———→ QUOTATO, QUOTAZIONE

civilizzazione, n.f. — not civilisation (= *la civiltà*) but the civilising process, so that, e.g., *la civilizzazione dei barbari* is not barbarian civilisation (= *la civiltà dei barbari*) but their civilising, as carried out by Roman civilisation, *la civiltà romana*. A civilised country/society is *un paese/una società* civile*.

clamoroso, adj. — can occasionally mean clamorous but is invariably used figuratively. Typical examples are *uno scandalo clamoroso*, a shocking or dreadful scandal, *una vittoria clamorosa*, a sensational victory, and *una sconfitta clamorosa*, a resounding or crushing defeat.

classico, adj. — classic, but often traditional, as in *il classico tè inglese*, the traditional English tea. In Dario Fo's play *La signora è da buttare* (1968) ['The Lady is for Throwing Away'] a stage-direction explains the photographers' cry 'cheese!' as *classica espressione americana impiegata per poter meglio atteggiarsi al sorriso*, traditional American expression used to help one put on a smile better. Of flavours, *classico* is regular, as in *aroma* classico, limone o menta*, regular, lemon or mint flavour. *Un vino classico*, a classic wine, must be made from grapes grown in a strictly delimited central area, *la zona* d'origine*. Hence, *un Chianti classico* (———→ DENOMINAZIONE). *Un liceo classico* is the nearest Italian equivalent to the traditional British grammar school (———→ GINNASIO, INFERIORE, MATURO, SUPERIORE).

clergyman, n.m. — refers not to the man of the cloth (= *un prete* or *un sacerdote* if Catholic, *un pastore* if Protestant) but to the cloth itself. *Un clergyman* is the dark suit, shirt and dog-collar outfit which has spread to Italy from Britain and America.

cocomero, n.m. — shares the same etymology as the cucumber (= *il cetriolo*) but is, in fact, the watermelon, sold at stalls, *le bancarelle*, throughout Italy during the summer. Also known as *l'anguria* in the North and *il mel(l)one d'acqua* in the South.

coerente, adj. — coherent of a theory or style but, otherwise, consistent. *Un comportamento coerente* is, therefore, consistent behaviour, *adottare una posizione coerente rispetto al problema* is: to adopt a consistent position vis-à-vis the problem, and *durante i negoziati la condotta del governo è stata coerente* means: during the negotiations the government's conduct was consistent.
———→ CONSISTENTE, INCOERENTE, INCONSISTENTE

coincidenza, n.f. — a coincidence (also *una combinazione**) but very commonly encountered meaning: a train, plane or bus connection, e.g. *ho perso la coincidenza*, I missed the connection. Typical disclaimers state: *non assumiamo alcuna responsabilità per eventuali* (———→ EVENTUALE) *ritardi, sospensioni, modifiche di orario o mancate coincidenze*, we accept no responsibility for trains (or planes or buses) running late or cancelled, for timetable changes or for missed connections. Also used figuratively, so that *la coincidenza è puramente casuale** means, confusingly, that the connection is purely coincidental.
———→ NAZIONALE

collaboratore, n.m. — only collaborator in the sense of colleague or partner (———→ GOLF). The traitorous kind = *un collaborazionista*, e.g. *L'Ira … ha dichiarato di essere responsibile dell'uccisione di tre collaborazionisti dell'esercito inglese* (*La Repubblica*, 3/7/92), the I.R.A. claimed responsibility for the killing of three British army collaborators. *Collaborare col nemico* is: to collaborate with the enemy, but the verb also means: to contribute or co-operate (e.g. *collaborare a un giornale*, to contribute to/write for a newspaper), and *grazie della Sua collaborazione* is: thanks for your contribution. The 'Appointments Wanted' section of the classified ads. is called *Offerte di collaborazione*, whereas the 'Situations' section is headed *Ricerche di collaboratori*.

collegio, n.m. — is never a college, either in the sense of University (= *un'università* or *un ateneo*) or any higher education institution (= *un istituto* d'istruzione superiore**). It is a boarding school, to which Italians sometimes send their children out of necessity or because of difficult behaviour but rarely, unlike the English, out of choice.

colonizzare, v. — to colonise, but also to reclaim land. A number of land-reclamation boards/U.S. agencies, *enti di colonizzazione*, were set up in Italy after the Second World War to reclaim parts of the Po delta and the Maremma, the marshy coastal strip of Tuscany and Lazio.

colonna, n.f. — column, in most senses, but watch out for its figurative use as a pillar or mainstay, as in *David Bellamy, colonna e guru del conservazionismo internazionale*, D.B., mainstay and guru of international conservation. Note, too, that *la colonna (sonora)* of a film is its soundtrack. A newspaper column = *una rubrica*.

combinare, v. — to combine, but also to arrange, so that *combinare un incontro* or *una gita* is: to arrange a meeting or an outing, and *hanno combinato d'uscire insieme* is: they've arranged to go out together. Needs to be handled with care in idioms such as: *cos'hai combinato?* what have you been up to?, *oggi non riesco a combinare niente*, I can't do a thing today, and *ne ha combinato di tutti i colori*, he's been up to all kinds of mischief. The odd-looking *un matrimonio* combinato* means: an arranged marriage.
———→ ARRANGIARE

combinazione, n.f. — combination (*una combinazione di colori diversi* ———→ DIVERSO, a combination of different colours), but is often encountered meaning a (sheer) coincidence (———→ COINCIDENZA), so *l'ho incontrata per combinazione*, I met her by sheer chance, and *che combinazione trovarti qui!* what a coincidence meeting you here!

comma, n.m. — not a comma (= *una virgola*) but a sub-section or paragraph of a law, as in *il terzo comma dell'articolo 2 del Codice penale*, the third paragraph of article 2 of the Italian Criminal Code.

commando, n.m. — commando, but also a terrorist unit, as in *un commando delle Br* or *dell'Ira*, a Red Brigade or I.R.A. hit squad.

commedia, n.f. — is, confusingly, both a comedy and a play, so that *Tutte le commedie di Shakespeare* is 'S. : the Complete Plays' (whereas 'Shakespeare: the Complete Comedies' would have to be *Tutto il teatro comico di S.*). *C'è una bella commedia a teatro stasera* is: there's a good play on this evening, and *abbiamo tre commedie in programma** means: we have three plays on the bill. However, since the term is not as neutral as play, Italians often have recourse to *un dramma** if the play is serious in tone, or *una tragedia* if a tragedy. A light comedy is *una commedia brillante**.
———→ MELODRAMMA, PROSA

commento, n.m. — comment, but also literary or philological commentary, as in *l'autore* di un fortunato* (———→ FORTUNA) *commento alla 'Divina Commedia'*, the author of a successful/best-selling commentary on the 'Divine Comedy'. In *Inferno* IV (144) Dante sees *Averrois che il gran commento feo*, Averroës who wrote the great commentary (i.e. on Aristotle). A television commentary is *una telecronaca*.
———→ PUNTUALE

commercio, n.m. — commerce in general but also trade in particular, as in *il commercio della carne/all'ingrosso/al dettaglio* (or *al minuto*), the meat, wholesale and retail trades. *Mettere un articolo in commercio* means: to put an article on the market or on sale, and *un catalogo dei libri in commercio* is a catalogue of books in print. The Italian equivalent of a degree in Business Studies is *una laurea in economia e commercio*, the holder of which may wish to set up as a business consultant, *un commercialista*.
———→ AFFARE, ARTIGIANO, SOCIETÀ

commissione, n.f. — commission (e.g. *la Commissione europea dei diritti dell'uomo*, the European Commission on Human Rights), but often best rendered by committee (also *un comitato*). *Una commissione d'inchiesta** is, therefore, a committee of enquiry, *una commissione permanente* is a standing committee, and *una commissione parlamentare* is a parliamentary committee. Note *una commissione esaminatrice*, a board of examiners (———→ MATURO). To receive a commission in the armed forces, however = *recevere la nomina di ufficiale**, 5% commission on a sale = *una provvigione del 5%*, while out of commission = *in tilt**.

commozione, n.f. — not commotion (= *la confusione*, l'agitazione** or *il tumulto*) but emotion, as in *il disastro ha destato una viva commozione nella popolazione*, the disaster moved/stirred the population deeply, and *aveva la voce rauca dalla commozione*, her voice was hoarse/choked with emotion. However, *una commozione cerebrale* is concussion.
———→ CONCUSSIONE, EMOZIONE

comodità, n.f. — resembles commodity (= *un prodotto, un articolo* or *una derrata*) but is, in fact, a household convenience or modern comfort. *Una casa in campagna senza comodità* is, therefore, a house in the country without household conveniences, and *gli piacciono le sue comodità* means: he likes his home comforts. Also used figuratively, as when Delta Airlines, in their advertising, stress *orari e comodità, elementi di primaria importanza per ciascun viaggiatore*, flight schedules and convenience, factors of fundamental importance to every passenger.
———→ CONVENIENTE

compartimento, n.m. — a compartment (also *uno scompartimento*) on a train, but an administrative area, too, so beware of *un compartimento ferroviario* which is, confusingly, a region of the Italian railway network. Similarly, *un compartimento telefonico* is a subdivision of the Italian telephone system.
———→ CIRCOLARE, ESPRESSO

compasso, n.m. — is limited to (a pair of) compasses. The navigational compass = *la bussola*.

compatto, adj. — compact, but used of groups of people it means: united or tightly-knit, so that *un partito compatto nella sua opposizione alle reforme* is a party united in its opposition to the reforms, and *una comunità compatta* is a tightly-knit community. Noteworthy is its use in expressions like *gli italiani del nord votarono compatti per la Repubblica nel referendum del 1946*, northern Italians voted overwhelmingly for the Republic in the 1946 referendum, and *gli operai aderirono compatti allo sciopero*, the workers obeyed the strike-call to a man.

competente, adj. — sometimes competent, but frequently qualified/expert on, or else concerned/relevant/appropriate. *Non sono competente in materia* means: I am not an expert on this/I am not qualified to speak on this matter, and *le autorità competenti* are the authorities concerned/in charge, or the relevant/appropriate/responsible authorities. Competent authorities = *autorità qualificate* (———→ QUALIFICATO). While *la competenza* is competence, it can also be skill or ability (———→ ABILITÀ), as in *acquisire nuove competenze*, to acquire new skills, or *hanno messo in dubbio le mie competenze*, they called my abilities into question.
———→ INCOMPETENTE, INTENDERE

compilare, v. — to compile, but remember that *compilare un modulo*, un coupon* or *una scheda* is: to fill in a form, coupon or record-card.

complementare, adj. — complementary, except in schools and universities where *le materie complementari* are subsidiary or minor subjects, as opposed to the main subjects, *le materie fondamentali* or *principali*.

complessione, n.f. — is not complexion (= *la carnagione*) but (physical) constitution. Compare *è di complessione delicata*, she has a delicate or weak constitution, with she has a delicate complexion, *ha una carnagione delicata*.

completo, adj. — complete, but full up too, so that *il teatro/cinema è completo* is: there's a full house. If you ring a hotel in Italy and are told that *l'albergo è completo*, then it is fully booked. If you receive the response *il nostro personale è al completo*, when applying for a job, it means: we are fully staffed.

complimenti, n.m. pl. and interj. — although used for compliment in the singular, the plural form is tricky. *Complimenti per il tuo successo!* means: congratulations on your success! When you refuse a second helping at table you will be asked pointedly *senza complimenti?* are you sure? (i.e. that you are not just being polite). If you make too much of a fuss over someone they may say *non fare complimenti!* don't stand on ceremony, or *quanti complimenti!* what a fuss/to do! However, my compliments to your wife = *riverisco Sua moglie/ossequi alla signora*, while send him a copy of the book with our compliments = *mandagli una copia del libro in omaggio**.

composta, n.f. — garden compost, but do not be deceived: a menu listing *composta* among the puddings is offering fruit compote or stewed fruit, e.g. *la composta di pesche*, peach compote. Beware, too, of *un composto chimico* (a chemical compound) and of *un composto omogeneo* (a smooth mix or mixture in cooking).

comprensivo, adj. — is understanding rather than comprehensive (= *esauriente, globale* or *completo**), so that *un approccio comprensivo*, an understanding approach, contrasts with a comprehensive approach = *un approccio globale*. *Una persona comprensiva* is a sympathetic person and is, thus, more than *una persona simpatica* (⟶ SIMPATIA), a nice person. A comprehensive study of the Italian language = *uno studio completo/ esauriente/globale della lingua italiana*. The British comprehensive school has no equivalent in Italy but might be crudely paraphrased as *una scuola secondaria unificata* (⟶ COLLEGIO, GINNASIO, INFERIORE, MATURO, SUPERIORE). The hotel brochure statement *il prezzo è comprensivo della piccola colazione* means: the price of your room includes breakfast.

comunale, adj. — do not be misled by the sign *comunale* often seen in public places. It is not communal (variously = *pubblico, comune* or *in comune*) but municipal. Typical are *teatro/biblioteca/stadio comunale*, municipal theatre, library and stadium (in large towns *lo stadio comunale*, like the famous San Siro stadium in Milan, is leased out to the major football clubs). *Il consiglio comunale* is the town, local or borough council — *il comune* being the basic unit of local government in Italy (⟶ GIUNTA) — and its town clerk is *il segretario comunale*.
⟶ AMMINISTRAZIONE, ASSESSORE, FRAZIONE

concetto, n.m. — concept, but frequently idea. Thus *un articolo pieno di concetti* is simply an article that is full of ideas, and *lo studente ha espresso i suoi concetti chiaramente*

means: the student expressed his ideas clearly. Occasionally means: opinion, e.g. *avete un alto concetto di voi stessi*, you've a high opinion of yourselves.
———→ NOZIONE

conciliatore, n.m. — a conciliator in general but also, specifically, the Italian equivalent of a Justice of the Peace. The majority of Civil Law cases are handled by *il conciliatore* who arranges settlements on a friendly basis but has no power to send people to prison. Unlike the magistrate, *il pretore*, and the judge, *il giudice*, the unpaid *conciliatore* is not a law professional.
———→ MAGISTRATO, PROCESSO, TRIBUNALE

conclusivo, adj. — can be conclusive (also *decisivo*), but means: final or concluding too, so that *il quinto e conclusivo volume della serie* is the fifth and final volume of the series.

concussione, n.f. — is a cognate of concussion (*una commozione* cerebrale*), but surprisingly it means: graft, embezzlement or misappropriation of public funds, e.g. *A Milano i magistrati stanno per incriminare* funzionari, imprenditori e uomini politici imputati di corruzione e di concussione* (*La Repubblica* 5–6/4/92), In Milan the judges are about to charge officials, entrepreneurs and politicians accused of corruption and graft. A word persistently associated with the scandals which shook the Italian political establishment in the 1980s and 90s. These exposed *Tangentopoli* (lit. Briberyville) with its *tangenti* (bribes, kick-backs, pay-offs) oiling the all-pervasive Italian patron-client system, *il clientelismo*, the spoils system, *la lotizzazione*, and the network of corrupt party patronage at all levels, *il sottogoverno*. The common factor originally shared by concussion and *concussione* is shaking: this became linked in English with health, in Italian with extortion.
———→ RACCOMANDAZIONE

condannare, v. — to condemn, but also to sentence or find guilty, e.g. *condannare a dieci anni di reclusione*, to sentence to ten years' imprisonment, *condannare all'ergastolo*, to sentence to life imprisonment (Italy has never had the death-sentence), and *i giudici hanno condannato l'imputato*, the judges found the accused guilty. In Dario Fo's political farce *Morte accidentale di un anarchico* (1970) ['Accidental Death of an Anarchist'], the Suspect (*l'Indiziato*), though arrested twelve times, retorts *Sì, dodici arresti ... ma le faccio notare, signor commissario, che non sono mai stato condannato*, yes, twelve arrests ... but let me point out, superintendent, that I have never been found guilty. Can mean: to denounce, as in *condannare la politica* del governo*, to denounce the government's policy.
———→ CONCILIATORE, DENUNCIARE, PROCESSO, SENTENZA, TRIBUNALE

condiscendente, adj. — can be either condescending (*gli parlarono con aria condiscendente*, they spoke to him in a condescending manner) or willing/obliging/ compliant. In Italo Calvino's version of the good sister—bad sister tale from his *Fiabe Italiane* (1956) ['Italian Fairy Tales'], the good sister is *sempre condiscendente*, always willing to oblige.

condonare, v. — not to condone an action (= *trovare una scusa per* or *passare sopra un'azione**) but to forgive it. So *condonare un'offesa*, to forgive an insult, is not the same as condoning an insult = *passare sopra un'offesa*. Legally it means: to remit a penalty, as in *gli sono stati condonati cinque anni di carcere*, he had five years taken off his sentence.
———→ CONDANNARE

conduttore, n.m. — despite appearances, is not the conductor of an orchestra (= *il direttore* d'orchestra*) but a television presenter or host. The following is a typical T.V. listing: *'OK il prezzo è giusto' gioco condotto da* …, 'The Price is Right', game-show hosted (lit. conducted) by …

conferenza, n.f. — occasionally the equivalent of conference, e.g. *una conferenza al vertice*, a summit conference, *una conferenza stampa**, a press conference and *una conferenza di pace*, a peace conference. Often, though, a lecture or talk, e.g. *tenere/dare una conferenza su Machiavelli*, to give a lecture or talk on M. If the conference is academic, use *il convegno*, if business, *il colloquio*, and if party-political, *il congresso*.
───────→ LETTURA, LEZIONE, RELAZIONE

confessione, n.f. — (a) confession, of the religious type too, but also, confusingly, a religious denomination (───────→ DENOMINAZIONE), e.g. in April 1993 the Prime Minister (───────→ PRESIDENTE) Giuliano Amato spoke of *l'opportunità* di un disegno* di legge che tratti le materie relevanti* (───────→ RILEVANTE) *per le confessioni religiose*, the appropriateness of a parliamentary bill dealing with matters of significance for religious denominations.
───────→ CULTO

confetti, n.m. pl. — are part of Italian weddings but are not confetti (= *i coriandoli*). They are, instead, the traditional sugared almonds wrapped in net and ribbon and given to guests at christenings, communions and weddings in *la bomboniera*, the bonbonnière. Confetti comes from the Italian *confetti (di coriandolo)*, coriander-flavoured sweets originally thrown at festivities but now replaced by discs of coloured paper.
───────→ CARAMELLA, MATRIMONIO

confezione, n.f. — is neither a sartorial confection (= *una creazione*) nor an elaborately decorated cake or dessert (= *una torta/un dolce ornati con gran cura per una festa*). It is a packet, pack(age), packaging or wrapper, so that *vuole una confezione regalo?* is: would you like a gift pack/it gift wrapped? and the request *mi faccia una confezione robusta* means: please wrap it well. *Una confezione da sei* is a six pack. Sometimes, by extension, a (packaged) item, e.g. *ogni confezione costa £.5.000*, each item costs 5,000 lire. Also clothing or wear, as in the sign *confezioni uomo/bambino*, men's/children's wear in shops, and in the expression *confezioni su misura*, made-to-measure/U.S. custom clothes. An ad. which stresses *la confezione elegante* of a garment, though, is praising its elegant cut or tailoring.
───────→ PACCHETTO

confidenza, n.f. — occasionally corresponds to confidence, e.g. *avere confidenza nella propria* (───────→ PROPRIO) *forza*, to have confidence in one's own strength (more commonly = *la fiducia* or *la sicurezza*), but in most cases means: familiarity, intimacy or trust. Contrast *ho confidenza con lui*, I'm intimate with him, and I'm confident in him = *ho fiducia in lui*. *Ha molta confidenza col padre* means: he is very close to his father, but *si è preso delle confidenze col padre* is: he took liberties with his father. *Un rapporto* di assoluta confidenza e di grande amicizia* is a relationship of absolute trust and great friendship. Note *non dà molta confidenza*, he keeps his distance, and *ho preso confidenza col computer*, I've got the hang of the computer. Self-confidence = *la sicurezza di sè* or *la fiducia/confidenza in se stessi*, while confidence in the sense of a secret piece of information that you tell somebody is *una confidenza*.

la fiducia/confidenza in se stessi, while confidence in the sense of a secret piece of information that you tell somebody is *una confidenza*.
———→ DIFFIDENTE

confine, n.m. — confine, but also border or frontier between countries. Both senses are present in the title of Giorgio Napolitano's book *Oltre i vecchi confini — Il futuro della sinistra e l'Europa* (1989) ['Beyond the old frontiers/confines — the future of the Left and Europe'].

confortare, v. — to comfort, but look out for it in the sense of to back up or confirm in sentences like *ho confortato la mia ipotesi* con elementi nuovi* (———→ ELEMENTO), I backed up my theory with new facts, and *le sue scoperte confortano la mia tesi*, his discoveries confirm my thesis.

confrontare, v. — not to confront (= *affrontare**) but to compare or contrast (———→ CONTRASTO), as in *confrontare i due personaggi principali del romanzo**, to compare the two main characters of the novel.
———→ CARATTERE, PARAGONE, PERSONAGGIO

confusione, n.f. — aside from confusion, also means disorder or mess, e.g. *nel suo ufficio c'è una confusione inimmaginabile*, there's an unbelievable mess in his office. On looking into such an office, one would exclaim *che confusione!* which can also, in other situations, translate as what a din/crowd/commotion (———→ CASINO). *Confuso* usually means: confused, but it can be: embarrassed, e.g. *con l'aria confusa, si scusò*, looking embarrassed, he apologised.
———→ INTRICATO

congelare, v. — shares the same Latin root with congeal (= *coagulare*) but retains the original meaning of to freeze, so that *congelare gli alimenti* is: to deep freeze food, and *L'Onu si prepara a congelare i beni di Ghedaffi* means: the U.N. is about to freeze G.'s assets.

congregazione, n.f. — is used in the field of religion but is not the congregation (= *l'assemblea dei fedeli*, lit. the gathering of the faithful). *Le sacre congregazioni* are the permanent committees (———→ COMMISSIONE) of the Roman Catholic College of Cardinals, the best known being the *Congregazione de propaganda* fide*, the Commission for the Dissemination of the Faith, from which the word propaganda is derived. Also used for any body of Christians living according to a set of rules.

conoscente, n.m. — do not take the views of acquaintances, *l'opinione dei conoscenti*, for those of the cognoscenti (= *gli intenditori* or *i conoscitori*). It is sometimes said that the highly serious Italian daily press (———→ STAMPA) is aimed at a readership of cognoscenti, *è rivolto a un pubblico d'intenditori*. Cognoscente is from Latin not Italian.

consenso, n.m. — consensus and consent, but also critical praise or acclaim, e.g. *la commedia* ha riscosso un vivo consenso*, the play was highly acclaimed.

conservare, v. — sometimes to conserve (although to conserve one's energies = *risparmiare le proprie energie*) but usually to preserve or keep, as in *conservare documenti essenziali*, to preserve vital documents, *conservare la propria integrità*, to preserve one's integrity (⟶ PROPRIO), and *conservare il tonno in olio*, to preserve tuna fish in oil. *La Repubblica* (13–14/10/91), in an article on the latest Italian attitudes to virginity, carried the headline *La verginità? Meglio conservarla*, Virginity? Best preserve it. *Conserva sempre la calma* means that he always keeps his calm, and *ha conservato tutte le lettere che ha ricevuto* means: he kept all the letters he received. On a food package, the advice *conservare in luogo fresco/asciutto* is: store or keep in a cool/dry place.

conservativo, adj. — is not politically conservative (= *conservatore*, so that the British Conservative Party is *il partito conservatore*). Instead it means preventive, precautionary or for conservation, e.g. *un sequestro conservativo* (⟶ SEQUESTRARE) is a preventive or precautionary seizure (of property or funds), and *il restauro conservativo di un palazzo** is the conservation and restoration of a building (⟶ EDIFICIO, RISTORAZIONE).

considerato, adj. — is never considerate. It means: cautious, prudent or careful. So do not confuse *una persona considerata*, a prudent person, with a considerate one (= *una persona premurosa* or *piena di riguardi*). *Prendere in considerazione* is: to take into consideration, and after careful consideration is: *dopo attenta considerazione*. However, *la considerazione* is also prudence, as in *agire con la massima considerazione*, to act with the utmost caution, as well as esteem, e.g. *è tenuto in ottima considerazione*, he is held in very high esteem or regard (⟶ RIGUARDO).
⟶ CAUZIONE

consistente, adj. — not consistent (= *coerente**) but considerable, substantial, well-founded, solid or thick, e.g. *una somma consistente*, a considerable or substantial sum, *ragionamenti consistenti*, well-founded or solid arguments, and *una salsa consistente*, a thick sauce. *Il gruppo di verbi irregolari più consistente* would translate as the biggest, or most important, group of irregular verbs. Consistency = *la coerenza* or *la costanza* or, of food, *la consistenza*. The latter also means: (considerable) size, extent or substance (*la consistenza delle pensioni italiane*, the size or sizeable level of Italian pensions) or else basis/validity (*un'idea priva di consistenza* is, therefore, a flimsy idea and not one lacking in consistency = *priva di coerenza*).
⟶ INCOERENTE, INCONSISTENTE

consultazione, n.f. — consultation, but often used as a synonym for election (i.e. a consultation of the people's will), e.g. *Per le politiche '92, le norme di comportamento sono parzialmente diverse* (⟶ DIVERSO) *da quelle delle precedenti consultazioni*, For the '92 general election the procedures differ, in some respects, from those in previous elections.
⟶ URNA

consumare, v. — to consume (or consumate) but also, commonly, to wear out, get through, or even to squander, e.g. *i bambini consumano le scarpe rapidamente*, children wear out their shoes fast, *ho consumato i gomiti della giacca*, I've worn my jacket through at the elbows, *consumiamo 5 litri di vino alla settimana*, we get through 5 litres of wine a week, and *ha consumato un patrimonio*, he squandered a fortune. *Un tappeto consumato* is a worn carpet.

conflict, dispute or disagreement, so that the headline *Contrasto tra Bonn e Washington* (*La Repubblica*, 8/5/93) actually means: Disagreement between Bonn and Washington. To avoid ambiguity, the contrast between the two capitals = *la disparità* or *la grande differenza tra i due capitali*. *Contrastare* is rarely to contrast (= *confrontare*, mettere in confronto* or *fare il raffronto*). Usually it means: to confict or clash (*le tue opinioni contrastano con le mie*, your opinions conflict with mine), or else to combat, as in *contrastare l'ingiustizia e l'inuguaglianza*, to combat injustice and inequality, and *medicinali che contrastano i sintomi dell'influenza*, medicines which fight 'flu symptoms.

controllare, v. — to control (as in *controllare i mari* or *i nervi*, to control the seas or one's nerves), but also to check, e.g. *controllare un passaporto/i documenti/la posta*, to check a passport, identity (papers) or the mail. Amplifon advertise their hearing aids with the slogan *Controllare l'udito come controllare la vista non vi costa niente*, Having your hearing tested, just like having your eyesight tested, costs you nothing. As well as control, *un controllo* is also a check, as in *un controllo di polizia/dogana*, a police or customs check. *Il controllore* is the ticket inspector on a bus or train.
———→ CASUALE, INFLESSIBILE

conveniente, adj. — is rarely convenient (= *comodo, opportuno*, or *pratico**) but, rather, appropriate or suitable. Compare *una risposta conveniente*, a suitable answer, with a convenient answer = *una risposta che fa comodo*. Also likely to cause confusion when it means: economically advantageous in the expression *un prezzo conveniente*, an attractive or reasonable price. The sign *prodotti di grande qualità* a prezzi convenienti* is, therefore, offering you high quality products at the right price, the advert *Con Alitalia la tariffa* più conveniente è la Superpex* informs you that the best value fare with Alitalia is Superpex, and the travel brochure claim that *un sogno può diventare una conveniente realtà* means that a dream can turn into an attractively-priced reality. *Convenienza* presents the same pitfalls, so that if a magazine highlights *la convenienza di un abbonamento* it is referring not to the convenience (= *la comodità**) of a subscription but to its cheapness or financial advantageousness. Remember that *le convenienze* is etiquette (———→ DECORO, ETICHETTA): *Epoca* (30/11/93) wrote of the Princess of Wales's *Gran rifiuto ... delle convenienze di corte*, great refusal of court etiquette.
———→ INTERESSANTE, LIQUIDAZIONE, OCCASIONE, PROPOSTA

convento, n.m. — can be a monastery as well as a convent so that, confusingly, the pugnacious Capuchin (*Cappuccino*) Fra Cristoforo in Alessandro Manzoni's great novel *I Promessi Sposi* (1840–42) ['The Betrothed'] lives in *un convento*, while the wayward Nun of Monza is shut away in *un monastero* (which has both meanings too!). Cappuccino coffee (———→ BAR, CAFFÈ, CORRETTO) takes its name from the colour of the Capuchin habit.

coppa, n.f. — comes from the same Latin root as cup (= *una tazza*) but only shares the same meaning in sporting trophy, e.g. *la coppa Davis*, the Davis cup. Otherwise it is a champagne-glass, *una coppa da champagne*, a cocktail-glass, *una coppa da cocktail*, or a sundae dish for fruit or ice-cream.

coraggio, n.m. and interj. — courage, daring or bravery (———→ BRAVO), but sometimes impudence, e.g. *che coraggio!* what a nerve! and *hai un bel coraggio!* you've got a nerve! The exhortation *coraggio!* means: take heart! but also: come on! as in *Coraggio! Com'è successo?* Speak up/out with it/come on! How did it happen?

coraggio, n.m. and interj. — courage, daring or bravery (——→ BRAVO), but sometimes impudence, e.g. *che coraggio!* what a nerve! and *hai un bel coraggio!* you've got a nerve! The exhortation *coraggio!* means: take heart! but also: come on! as in *Coraggio! Com'è successo?* Speak up/out with it/come on! How did it happen?

corda, n.f. — not cord for tying (= *grosso spago*) but rope, as in *una corda per saltare*, a skipping rope/U.S. jump rope, and *le corde del ring*, the ropes in a boxing ring. Electrical cord or flex = *il cavo*. String is *lo spago* (so that *spaghetti* translates literally as little strings), although of an instrument it is *la corda*. Do not mistake *una stringa* for string; it is a shoelace. Useful idioms are *tagliare la corda*, to sling your hook, *essere giù di corda*, to feel low or blue, and *avere la corda al collo*, to be in dire straits.

corrente, adj. — current (e.g. *un conto corrente*, a current account, and *prezzi correnti*, current prices), but often means: common or normal. *Idee correnti*, commonly-held ideas are, therefore, not the same as current ideas, *idee attuali*. *Il linguaggio* corrente* is everyday language, *le operazioni correnti* in a bank are routine transactions, and of a commercial product *la qualità* corrente* is standard quality.
——→ ATTUALE

corretto, adj. — correct, right or proper (a correct answer may be *una risposta corretta, giusta* or *esatta*), but it often means: honest, fair, above-board, decent, even-handed or even polite, e.g. *il direttore* è sempre corretto nei confronti dei suoi colleghi*, the manager is always fair to/with his colleagues, *un prezzo molto corretto*, a very fair price, the 1985 Communist Party poster (——→ MANIFESTO) in Florence which maintained punningly *ci sono atti corretti e uomini corrotti*, there are honest deeds and corrupt men, and *un saluto* corretto*, a polite greeting. Of coffee, it means, surprisingly: laced with alcohol, *il caffè corretto*, e.g. with cognac (*corretto col cognac*) or with grappa, the northern Italian version of brandy. As well as being 'corrected', coffee in Italy is sometimes 'restricted', *ristretto*, i.e. strong and concentrated. *Una corretta alimentazione* is a balanced diet.
——→ BAR, CAFFÈ, DIETA, INFORMATIVO

correzione, n.f. — correction, but can also mean punishment, e.g. *un bambino che ha bisogno di correzione*, a child who needs punishing, and *una casa di correzione*, a borstal or young offenders' institution. Also reproof, as in *una correzione fraterna*, a friendly rebuke. *La correzione delle bozze*, though, is proof-reading.
——→ CORRETTO

coscienza, n.f. — conscience, as in the expressions *avere la coscienza sporca/pulita*, to have a guilty/clear conscience. Be careful, though. It also means consciousness (physical or mental), conscientiousness and awareness, so that *perdere coscienza* is: to lose consciousness, *avere coscienza dei propri difetti* is: to be conscious of one's own faults, *fare un lavoro con coscienza* is: to do a job conscientiously, and *la coscienza politica* is political awareness. Any of these meanings can be read into the title of Italo Svevo's novel *La coscienza di Zeno* (1923), whose English translation, 'The Confessions of Zeno', avoids the issue. Remember that the adjective *incosciente*, as well as meaning unconscious or unaware, is also thoughtless. Note, too, that although a conscientious objector is *un obiettore di coscienza*, a prisoner of conscience = *un detenuto per motivi* (——→ MOTIVO) *di opinione*.

cospicuo, adj. — occasionally means: conspicuous (e.g. *un cospicuo successo*, a conspicuous success), but if you are offered *un cospicuo pacchetto* assicurativo*, it is a sizeable insurance package, and if you inherit *una somma cospicua*, you get a considerable sum of money. The poster is conspicuous = *il manifesto* è vistoso* or *attira gli sguardi*.

costa, n.f. — coast (as in *la costa azzurra*, the Côte d'Azur, and *la costa smeralda*, the Emerald Coast in Sardinia), but also hillside or mountain-side. In Cesare Pavese's novel *La luna e i falò* (1950) ['The Moon and the Bonfires'], the narrator's best friend Nuto has his house *a mezza costa sul Salto*, half-way up the side of the Salto mountain.
———→ MARINA, RIVIERA

costipazione, n.f. — comes dangerously close to constipation in both appearance and meaning. However, in Italian the blockage applies, in the main, to the head, nose or throat, so that the statements *ho un po' di costipazione* or *sono un po' costipato* mean: I've a slight head-cold/stuffy nose, or I'm a bit choked up. Constipation is, invariably, *la stitichezza*, and I'm constipated is: *sono stitico*. The Spanish *constipación* is equally unreliable.
———→ INTOSSICAZIONE, PUNTUALE

costume, n.m. — costume but also customs, ways, habits, manners or morals. So although *i costumi tradizionali* are traditional costumes, *l'Europa tiene più che mai ai suoi costumi* means that Europe is more than ever attached to its local customs. *Conoscere gli usi e costumi di un paese* is: to know the customs and ways of a country, *l'evolversi del costume linguistico nazionale* means: the changing speech-habits of the nation, *la vita e i costumi del Rinascimento* is likely to be Renaissance life and manners, and *una donna di facili costumi* is a woman of loose morals. Noteworthy are the expressions *un esperto di costume*, an expert on social change, *la squadra del buon costume* (*il buon costume* for short), the vice squad, and *il mal costume governativo*, governmental corruption or corruption in high places (———→ CONCUSSIONE).

crack or *crac*, n.m. — not a crack (= *una crepa, una spaccatura, una fenditura* or *un' incrinatura*, according to context) but a financial, economic or company crash. Examples in the 1980s were *il crack del Banco Ambrosiano*, the collapse of Italy's largest private bank with its embarrassing Vatican connections, and *il crack del ticket**, the débâcle over the introduction of state medical charges. *Il crack della borsa*, the stock-exchange crash of October 1987, had little effect on the Italian economy which, at the time, was enjoying a boom, *un boom*. *Il crack* is also the cocaine-based drug, crack.
———→ AZIONE

crauti, n.m. pl. — not a rude word for Germans (= *crucco**), *i crauti* is sauerkraut (from German *kraut*, cabbage), a dish found in north-east Italy which was once part of the Austro-Hungarian Empire. Also eaten there are *il gulasch, i wurstel, i frankfurters, i krapfen* (creme-filled doughnuts), and *lo strudel*.

crema, n.f. — do not use for cream (= *la panna*, e.g. whipped cream = *la panna montata*). *La crema* is (egg) custard and creme-filling. Used, too, for certain smooth, soft cheeses such as *crema Bel Paese* and for non-culinary creams, e.g. *la crema idratante*, moisturising cream, and *la crema da/per barba*, shaving cream. Cream is little used in Italian cooking except in the notoriously rich cuisine of Bologna. Ice-cream is, of course, *il gelato*.
———→ ZUPPA INGLESE

crisi, n.f. — crisis, but often less strong than in English. Beware, for instance, of taking the frequent, dramatic headline *crisi (di governo)*, government crisis, literally. First of all, *la crisi di governo* is simply the technical term for the period between a government's resignation after a vote of no confidence, and the appointment of its successor. Secondly, although Italy, with some fifty cabinets since the Second World War, has a reputation for governmental instability, the reverse has been the case. *Crisi* have been provoked by disputes within the multi-party coalitions dominated until the early 1990s by the Christian Democrats (*il pentapartito*, the five-party coalition, being the usual format in the 1980s) and are basically cabinet reshuffles, *rimpasti*, with the same faces reappearing in different ministries. *Una crisi economica* (————➤ ECONOMICO) is really a slump or recession, while *una crisi degli alloggi/di insegnanti* is only a housing/teacher shortage. *Una crisi di nervi*, on the other hand, is an attack of nerves.

cristallo, n.m. — as well as crystal, can mean car or train window. FIAT boast that on their Tempra *i cristalli Solar control sono di serie*, 'Solar control' windows are standard. *Il tergicristallo* is the windscreen/U.S.windshield wiper.

cristianità, n.f. — is not Christianity (= *il cristianesimo*) but Christendom.
————➤ CRISTIANO

cristiano, n.m. — obviously a Christian but also used for human being or soul, as in *non c'è un cristiano in giro*, there isn't a soul about, and *non vedeva un cristiano da tre giorni*, he hadn't seen a living soul for three days. *Comportarsi da cristiano* is: to behave in a decent or civilised way.
————➤ CRISTIANITÀ

criterio, n.m. — criterion but also, surprisingly, common sense or even opinion. *Un uomo di criterio* is, therefore, a sensible man (————➤ SENSIBILE), *hai agito con poco criterio* means: you did not act very sensibly, and *secondo il mio criterio* is one way of saying: in my opinion/as I see it.

crosta, n.f. — crust but remember that it can be cheese-rind, *la crosta del formaggio*, or even a scab.

crucco, n.m. — not a crook (= *un malfattore, un ladro* or *un delinquente*) but the pejorative term for a German, *un tedesco*, or a German-speaker. While it is, thus, the equivalent of Hun, Jerry or Kraut, the Italian word emphasises Germanic dull-wittedness rather than wickedness. Originally it designated the Slavs living on Italy's north eastern border whose word for bread is *kruch* (compare the French *baragouin*, gibberish, the first element of which is the Breton *bara*, bread). It became army slang for a German in the Second World War. Do not be misled either by *un cugino germano*: this is not a German cousin (= *un cugino tedesco*) but a first cousin.
————➤ CRAUTI, DELINQUENZA

crudo, adj. — *un linguaggio* crudo* (blunt language, rough talking) is not quite the same as crude language (= *un linguaggio volgare* or *triviale**). Of food it means: raw, as in *il prosciutto crudo*, raw or Parma ham, uncooked or unripe, e.g. *frutta cruda*, unripe fruit (————➤ MATURO), and of weather it is: harsh. Note the expression *la verità nuda e*

culto, freedom of worship, is guaranteed to Italy's religious minorities, belonging in the main to the small Protestant and Jewish communities. Over 90% of Italians are Catholic, although those practising, *i praticanti*, make up, at most, 30% of the population, with particularly high concentrations in the South (*il Mezzogiorno*) and the North East.
————→ CONFESSIONE, CRISTIANITÀ, CRISTIANO, DENOMINAZIONE, DEVOZIONE

culturista, n.m. or f. — not someone involved in the culture industry (= *un operatore* culturale*) but a body-builder. The magazine *Epoca* highlighted the pun in 1987 when it captioned a photograph of Chinese women working out in a gymnasium (————→ GINNASIO) with: *la rivoluzione culturista*. Body-building is *il culturismo*, although the Italian Championships are called *Il campionato italiano di body-building*. Bear in mind that while *la cultura* is culture, *la coltura* — from the same root — means: crop (growing).

curare, v. — not to cure (= *guarire*) but to treat someone. A notoriously tricky pair because they occur in the same context. Do not, therefore, confuse *il medico cura il paziente*, the doctor is treating the patient, with the doctor is curing the patient (= *il medico guarisce il paziente*), or *la curano con gli antibiotici*, they are treating her with antibiotics, with they are curing her with antibiotics (= *la guariscono con gli antibiotici*). You will come across it meaning: to look after, as in the Black & Decker ad.: *Il piacere di curare il giardino*, the pleasure of looking after your garden, to be responsible for, as in *i ricercatori che hanno curato la parte italiana dell'inchiesta**, the researchers who carried out the Italian part of the enquiry, and to edit, e.g. *sta curando un nuovo volume*, he's bringing out/preparing/editing a new volume (————→ CURATORE). The latter will have on its title-page *a cura di* (edited by) followed by the editor's name. Similarly *la cura* is treatment or care (————→ CUSTODIA) rather than cure (= *la guarigione* or *il rimedio*), so that *una cura di bellezza dall'estetista* is beauty treatment at the beautician's (————→ ESTETICA), but *una cura dimagrante* is a slimming diet (————→ DIETA).
————→ RICOVERARE, SANITÀ

curatore, n.m. — not the curator of a museum, library or buildings (= *il conservatore* or *il soprintendente/sovrintendente*) but, variously, the official receiver or liquidator/U.S. trustee in bankruptcy (*il curatore fallimentare*), the editor of a literary work (————→ EDITORE) or, in general, the person in charge or director: *il curatore della Biennale di Venezia* is, therefore, the person in charge or the organiser of the Venice Biennale.
————→ CURARE, LIQUIDAZIONE

curva, n.f. — a curve of any kind, but also a turn or bend in a road, so that *una curva pericolosa* is a dangerous corner, and *una strada piena di curve* is a winding road. Also used for the terraces in a sports stadium.
————→ SORPASSARE

cuscino, n.m. — depending on context, may be a cushion or a pillow (also *un guanciale*).

custodia, n.f. — legal custody but also, simply, care of people or things, as in *le ho affidato la custodia dei figli mentre ero al lavoro*, I entrusted her with the care of my children while I was at work, and in the carpet advertisement *Per saperne di più sui tappeti: custodia, pulizia e mantenimento*, Know more about carpets: care, cleaning and upkeep. Also, oddly, a case, as in *la custodia del violino*, the violin case, and *una custodia per occhiali*, a spectacle case. Note that *un agente* di custodia* is a prison warder.

———→ CURARE

D

dancing, n.m. — not the activity (= *il ballo* or *la danza*) but the dance-hall. A false anglicism.
———→ BALLERINA, NIGHT

debito, n.m. — is a debt not a debit (= *un addebito*).

decadenza, n.f. — decadence, but decline or deterioration as well, so that Gibbon's 'Decline and Fall of the Roman Empire' (1776–88) is translated as *La decadenza e la caduta dell'Impero Romano*, and *la decadenza di un centro storico* is the deterioration/deteriorating condition of an old town-centre. As well as decadent, *decadente* also means: deteriorating, crumbling or falling to bits, as in *le decadenti infrastrutture dell'industria* inglese*, the crumbling infrastructure of Britain's (heavy) industries.

decoro, n.m. — is seldom decorum (= *il rispetto/il senso* delle convenienze* or else *la correttezza* ———→ CORRETTO). Usually it is subtly different and means: personal dignity or good name/honour, as in *comportarsi con decoro*, to behave in a dignified manner. When the rector of Venice University complained, in July 1993, that his students' degree celebrations were at times *non compatibili con il decoro dell'università*, he meant that they were not compatible with the institution's good name. Can also mean: motif, as in *regaliamo le due tazze dal decoro esclusivo*, we are giving away the two cups with the exclusive motif. Decor, on the other hand = *lo scenario**.
———→ CONVENIENTE, ETICHETTA

dedicare, v. — to dedicate, in all senses, but often simply means: to devote, so that *un volume dedicato a Cristoforo Colombo* will almost always be a book or volume devoted to C.C. *Dedicare tutto il tempo libero allo sport* is: to devote all one's free time to sport, and the notice *Il Museo del Cinema di Torino dedica una retrospettiva a Pasolini* means that the Turin Museum of Cinema is devoting a retrospective to P.

defunto, adj. — looks like defunct (= *caduto in disuso, sciolto* or *liquidato*, according to context) but means: dead, deceased or late, as in *le truffe del defunto editore* Robert Maxwell* (*La Repubblica*, 10/3/93), the swindles/scams of the late publisher R.M.

degradare, v. — can be to degrade (also *umiliare* or *avvilire*), but most frequently means: to demote or break of someone in the armed forces, e.g. *il tenente è stato degradato*, the lieutenant was demoted/broken. *La degradazione* is usually, therefore, the breaking or demotion of an officer (———→ UFFICIALE). *Degradato* also means: delapidated, as in *i quartieri degradati di Napoli e Palermo*, the run-down or slum districts of Naples and Palermo (———→ DILAPIDATO). *Il degrado dell'ambiente* is the deterioration of the environment.
———→ DESTITUZIONE, DISLOCARE

deliberare, v. — goes further than to deliberate (= *ponderare, riflettere* or *considerare*). Always used of official bodies, it means: to take a decision upon reflexion, as in *il consiglio dei ministri ha deliberato un aumento del tasso d'interesse*, the cabinet has decided on a rise in interest rates, and *la Corte costituzionale ha deliberato sulla questione**, the Constitutional Court has pronounced judgement on the matter.

———→ PRESIDENTE

delinquenza, n.f. — delinquency, as in *la delinquenza minorile*, juvenile delinquency, but also crime or criminality in general, e.g. *la piccola delinquenza*, petty crime, and *la delinquenza è in aumento*, crime is rising. *La delinquenza organizzata*, organised crime, in Southern Italy takes the form of the Mafia in Sicily, the 'Ndrangheta in Calabria and the Camorra in Campania. *Delinquente* is, consequently, most often used for a criminal, crook or wrong-doer and sometimes, jocularly, for rascally children.

———→ CRUCCO, ECCELLENTE, GIOVANILE

delizioso, adj. — delicious, but note *un sorriso delizioso*, a charming smile. *Una bambina deliziosa* is only a delightful child.

delusione, n.f. — tantalisingly similar to delusion, but it actually means: a disappointment or let-down. *Che delusione!* is, therefore: How disappointing! and the headline *La delusione di Bush: è lenta la ripresa* (*La Repubblica*, 3/7/92) means: B. disappointed: the economic upturn is slow in coming. To have delusions of grandeur = *avere manie di grandezza*, to suffer from delusions = *soffrire di allucinazioni*, and they are only delusions of his sick mind = *sono solo fantasmi della sua mente malata*. Don't delude yourself is: *non illuderti*.

democratico, adj. — democratic. Note, however, that *una persona democratica* is someone in authority who is unpretentious and unaffected (on the other hand, a democratic person = *un sostenitore/proponente della democrazia*). This is a much-appreciated quality in Italy where the governing class has traditionally been remote. It explains why personalities like Pope John XXIII and President Sandro Pertini (1978–85) who had the common touch, *erano democratici*, attracted much affection (———→ AFFEZIONATO) from Italians. A Democrat, in the American party-political sense = *un membro/esponente* del partito democratico*.

———→ PRESIDENTE

denominazione, n.f. — very occasionally a religious denomination (———→ CONFESSIONE). Usually, though, a formal word for a name, heading or designation, as in *la denominazione scientifica*, the scientific name, and *'fromento indiano', l'antica denominazione del mais*, 'Indian corn', the old name for maize/U.S. corn. Most often encountered on the label (———→ ETICHETTA) of wine-bottles where the designation *Denominazione di origine controllata* (D.O.C.), the equivalent of the French *Appellation Contrôlée*, indicates a wine made from grapes grown in particular conditions in a specific area (———→ CLASSICO). Only since D.O.C. was introduced in 1963 has Italy, the world's biggest wine producer, acquired a reputation for quality and reliability. More recently, the designation D.O.C.G. (G. = *garantita*, guaranteed) has been applied to the most stringently controlled wine like the Vino Nobile di Montepulciano, the best Chianti, and Barolo from Piedmont.

———→ CONTROLLARE, ESERCIZIO, SOFISTICATO, STRINGENTE

denunciare, v. — this versatile verb is rarely to denounce (usually = *condannare**). *Denunciare uno scandalo politico*, e.g., is either: to expose, condemn or denounce a political scandal, but *il suo comportamento denuncia disagio* means: his behaviour betrays unease. Often used in the context of crime. Thus *denunciare un furto* or *uno scippo* is: to report a theft or mugging, while *denunciare un complice* is to inform on an accomplice. Note that *denunciare il reddito* is: declaring your taxable income, which Italians do annually in May, and *denunciare la nascita dei figli* is: to register the birth of your children (————➔ REGISTRARE).

destituzione, n.f. — not destitution (= *l'indigenza* or *l'estrema miseria**/*povertà*) but dismissal from office. Thus *la destituzione di un funzionario/del direttore*/della commissione* d'inchiesta**, the dismissal of an official, of the manager, and of the committee of enquiry.
————➔ DEGRADARE, UFFICIALE

detenzione, n.f. — detention but also illegal possession, so that someone charged with *la detenzione d'armi* is being accused of unauthorised possession of firearms.
————➔ CONDANNARE, DISARMARE

determinato, adj. — determined, but also given or certain, so do not confuse *una persona determinata*, a determined person, and *una determinata persona*, a given person. *In determinate circostanze* is: in certain circumstances. Note that *un contratto a tempo determinato* is a fixed-term contract.

dettaglio, n.m. — detail but also retail, so that *il prezzo al dettaglio* is the retail price, and *vendere al dettaglio* is to retail. To sell wholesale is: *vendere all'ingrosso*.
————➔ COMMERCIO

deviazione, n.f. — deviation, but a road-sign, *un cartello stradale*, carrying the warning *deviazione* indicates that there is a diversion ahead. However, travelling from Pisa to Florence one might make a detour through Lucca, *fare una deviazione per Lucca*. Italy has an excellent network of trunk roads/U.S. federal highways, *le statali*, of motorways/U.S. freeways or turnpikes, *le autostrade*, as well as of ring roads, *le circonvallazioni* and by-passes, *le tangenziali*.
————➔ CIRCOLAZIONE, DIGRESSIONE, GUIDARE, PATENTE

devozione, n.f. — devotion, but sometimes devoutness, piety or worship, as in *inginocchiarsi con devozione*, to kneel devoutly, and *opere d'arte destinate alla pubblica devozione*, works of art intended for public worship.
————➔ CULTO, OPERA, PIETÀ

didattico, adj. — does not have the negative connotations of didactic (= *pedante*). It simply means educational or teaching, e.g. *metodi didattici*, teaching methods, *un film didattico*, an educational film, and *un centro didattico*, a teachers' centre. *Un corso autodidattico per imparare l'italiano* is a teach-yourself Italian course.
————➔ EDUCAZIONE, MAESTRO, MANSIONE, PROFESSORE, SCOLASTICO

dieta, n.f. — diet, whether of the slimming, medical or health kind. Note, however, that *un regime (alimentare)* may also be used, especially of specialised diets: thus a vegetarian or vegan diet = *un regime vegetariano* or *vegetaliano*. Otherwise *l'alimentazione* is employed, as in Barilla's claim that its crispbread provides *le fibre necessarie per una sana e corretta alimentazione* (————➔ CORRETTO), the fibre required for a healthy and balanced diet, and in the well-known fact that *l'alimentazione dell'Europa è stata modificata dalla scoperta*

dell'America, the European diet was altered (———→ ALTERARE) by the discovery of America. The now-fashionable Mediterranean diet, though, is *la dieta mediterranea*.
———→ BIOLOGICO, GENUINO, INTEGRALE, SANO

diffidente, adj. — *una persona diffidente*, a suspicious or mistrustful person, is very different from a diffident person = *una persona timida/eccessivamente modesta/che manca di sicurezza in sè*. The same distinction applies to *la diffidenza* and diffidence.
———→ CONFIDENZA

diffuso, adj. — means widespread, not diffuse, so beware of constructions such as *un giornale molto diffuso/idee molto diffuse* meaning: a widely-read newspaper, and widely-held ideas. *La diffusione di un giornale*, therefore, is a newspaper's circulation. Diffuse of style, speech or ideas = *prolisso, vago* or *indefinito*.
———→ BIOLOGICO

digressione, n.f. — a digression but also a detour, so that *un'interessante* digressione storica* (———→ STORICO) could be an interesting historical digression, but it might well be an interesting historical detour which you undertake during a journey.
———→ DEVIAZIONE

dilapidato, adj. — surprisingly, means not: dilapidated (a dilapidated building = *un edificio* in rovina*) but squandered of money or possessions. Thus *un patrimonio dilapidato/ un'eredità* dilapidata*, a squandered fortune or inheritance. Similarly, *la dilapidazione del denaro pubblico* is the squandering of public money or funds. Dilapidated has remained closer to the original Latin meaning of scattered stones; *dilapidato* retains a later figurative sense which English once had.
———→ DEGRADARE

dilettante, n.m. and adj. — is occasionally as negative as dilettante, e.g. *in questo campo lui è solo un dilettante*, in this field he is only a dilettante or dabbler, and *un lavoro mediocre, da dilettante*, amateurish work. For the most part, though, it is simply: amateur with absolutely no pejorative overtones. Thus *una recita* (———→ RECITARE) *della compagnia di dilettanti*, a performance by the amateur theatrical group, *un campionato di dilettanti*, an amateur championship (the opposite is *un campionato di professionisti*), and *una mostra di pittori dilettanti*, an exhibition of amateur painters.
———→ AMATORE

dimostrare, v. — is not a problem when it means: to demonstrate, show, display or prove. However, of age it is: to look, as in *Ha 40 anni? Ne dimostra 50*, He's 40? He looks 50. To demonstrate politically = *manifestare* (———→ MANIFESTAZIONE).

dipendente, n.m. — not a dependent (= *una persona a carico*) but an employee. *La ditta ha licenziato 50 dipendenti* therefore means that the company (has) laid off 50 workers.
———→ ASSUMERE, LICENZA, OCCUPAZIONE

diplomato, n.m. — looks like a diplomat but is in fact someone in possession of *il diploma di maturità* (*la maturità* for short) or equivalent, the Italian high-school leaving certificate.

Advertisements for jobs aimed at *laureati e diplomati* are, therefore, read by university and high-school graduates.
———→ LICENZA, MATURO, SUPERIORE

direttore, n.m. — director is not the right translation in every case. Note, e.g., *un direttore di produzione* or *di vendite*, a production/sales manager, *un direttore di banca*, a bank manager, *un direttore d'orchestra*, a conductor (———→ CONDUTTORE), *un direttore di prigione*, a prison governor, and *un direttore di giornale*, a newspaper editor-in-chief (———→ EDITORE). A company director = *un consigliere d'amministrazione**, a managing director = *un amministratore*/consigliere delegato*, and a film director = *un regista*.
———→ DIREZIONE, PRESIDENTE

direzione, n.f. — direction, of course, but remember its very common meanings of management (*la nuova direzione della società**, the company's new management) and the boss's office or head office (e.g. *è stato convocato in direzione*, he's been summoned to see the director or manager). The director's personal or private secretary is *la segretaria di direzione*. Also leadership, so *la direzione di un partito* may turn out to be the leadership of a political party.
———→ DIRETTORE

disarmare, v. — to disarm, but take care with the following usages: *disarmare una costruzione*, to dismantle the scaffolding from a building and, even more confusingly, *disarmare una nave* which, depending on context, can mean: to lay a ship up/put it in dry dock or else to disarm it. Even in the area of firearms *disarmato* is tricky: it can be unarmed as well as disarmed. *I soldati erano disarmati* is, therefore, likely to mean: the soldiers were unarmed. *Armare* is equally slippery. As well as to arm it may mean: to fit out or man a ship, or else to reinforce a building (*armare una nave/un edificio**). *Un armatore* is not an arms dealer (= *un trafficante d'armi*) but a ship owner.
———→ ARSENALE, DETENZIONE

discorso, n.m. — can be a discourse, and discourse analysis in linguistics is *l'analisi del discorso*. However, as its range is much wider it needs to be treated with care. *Il discorso pronunciato dal presidente* della Repubblica* is the speech made by the President, and *un discorso elettorale* is an election speech. *Non capisco il suo discorso*, on the other hand, means: I don't follow his reasoning or his (line of) argument (———→ ARGOMENTO). *Attaccare discorso* is: to strike up a conversation, *cambiare discorso* is: to change the subject, *questo è un altro discorso* means: this is another matter, and the indignant *che discorsi sono?* means: what kind of talk is that? In grammar *le parti del discorso* are the parts of speech, and *il discorso indiretto* is indirect speech.
———→ INTERVENTO

discreto, adj. — discreet, but also reasonable, moderate or quite good. Thus *un risultato discreto* is a fair result, *un discreto cantante* is quite a good singer, and *prezzi discreti* are reasonable prices. Much used by teachers as a comment on work which is quite good. A discrete discipline = *una materia di studio* distinta/separata* (———→ DISTINTO).
———→ INSUFFICIENTE, SUFFICIENZA, VOTO

discussione, n.f. — handle with care: while it is usually discussion, sometimes it is argument (in Italian the two concepts shade imperceptibly into one another). So in *questa*

famiglia abbiamo discussioni in continuazione is likely to mean: in this family we argue (or quarrel) constantly. Similarly, *si sono bastonati in seguito a una violenta discussione*, they came to blows after a violent argument, and *niente discussioni, vi prego!* no arguments, please! To avoid ambiguity discussion is sometimes best rendered by the verbal form *discutere*, e.g. there has been much discussion of disarmament = *si è discusso molto del disarmo*, and we have had discussions about the changes = *abbiamo discusso dei cambiamenti*. Note that *(ri)mettere in discussione* is: to call into question.
———→ ARGOMENTO, DISCUSSO, LITIGARE

discusso, adj. — occasionally discussed, but almost always controversial, e.g. *Esce finalmente 'Candide' una delle opere più discusse di Leonard Bernstein*, At last 'Candide' is coming out — one of L.B.'s most controversial works (———→ OPERA). Do not, therefore, take *un argomento* discusso*, a controversial topic, for a topic already discussed = *un argomento già trattato/di cui si è già parlato*.
———→ DISCUSSIONE, POLEMICA

disegno, n.m. — design, but also drawing (———→ INCISIONE). On the one hand, then, Olivetti can claim that their M20 P.C. (———→ PERSONAL) is *di magnifico disegno*, splendidly designed, and Saffa describe *la funzionalità del disegno a tutto tondo*, the functional overall rounded design, of one of their lighters. On the other hand, *il disegno del bambino/di Leonardo* is the child's's/Leonardo's drawing, *il disegno precede la pittura* is: drawing comes before painting, and *il disegno industriale* is technical drawing. Note *il disegno pubblicitario*, commercial art (———→ PUBBLICITÀ). However, Italian design is famous = *il design italiano è rinomato*, the designs for the new building = *i progetti del nuovo edificio**, faulty design = *la costruzione difettosa*, and interior design = *la progettazione d'interni/d'arredamento*. Similarly, *disegnare* is to design or draw but bear in mind that a statement like: household appliances designed for the 1990s is rendered as *elettrodomestici pensati/ideati/concepiti/studiati per gli anni novanta*, while she designed the new art gallery/ship can be: *ha disegnato* or *ha progettato la nuova pinacoteca/nave*.
———→ MOTIVO, STUDIARE

disertare, v. — to desert but also, curiously, to fail to attend or not turn up. Thus *disertare una riunione*/un'udienza*, to fail to attend a meeting or hearing, and *disertare le lezioni*, to play truant (———→ LEZIONE). In these contexts, to desert = *abbandonare*. Similarly, *una riunione deserta* is a meeting no-one attended (note the change of spelling).

disgrazia, n.f. — looks like disgrace but actually means misfortune, tragedy or calamity, except in the expression *in disgrazia*, in disgrace/out of favour. Thus *l'eruzione dell'Etna è stata una vera disgrazia per il paese*, the eruption of Etna was a real disaster for the village, *una disgrazia sull'autostrada*, a tragic accident on the motorway, and *ha la disgrazia di essere cieco*, he has the misfortune to be blind. It's a disgrace = *è una vergogna*, a child in disgrace = *un bambino in castigo*, and he's a disgrace to his parents = *è il disonore dei genitori*. *Un disgraziato* is not, therefore, someone who is disgraced (= *disonorato* or *svergognato*) but a person who is wretched or a victim of misfortune.
———→ ACCIDENTE, INCIDENTE

dislocare, v. — a genuine cognate of dislocate (= *slogare*) but with no medical connections whatsoever. It means: to station of the armed forces and to post of officials, employees or journalists. Thus *il giornale sta dislocando molti suoi corrispondenti esteri nell'Europa dell'est*, the newspaper is posting many of its correspondents to Eastern Europe, and *dislocare le reclute*, to station recruits. Traditionally, Italian conscripts (⟶ RIFORMARE) have been stationed, *dislocati*, far from their home town to ensure loyalties are not divided between family or local patriotism (*il campanilismo*) and the state, and to break down Italy's deeply-rooted dialects in favour of the national language (⟶ LINGUAGGIO). Of buildings or facilities, *dislocare* is: to site or locate, as when holiday clubs boast of their *villaggi dislocati in oasi* incantevoli vicino al mare*, villages sited in dream havens near the sea. *La dislocazione delle scuole nella regione Lombardia* is not, therefore, the dislocation (= *la perturbazione*) of schools in the Lombardy region, but their siting, location or distribution.

dismesso, adj. — not dismissed (= *rifiutato, licenziato* or *congedato*, according to context) but disused or disaffected, so that *una strada dismessa* is a disused road, and *mettere i profughi nelle scuole dismesse* is: to house the refugees in disaffected schools.
⟶ LICENZA

disperso, adj. — occasionally dispersed, but usually means: missing or lost, especially of troops in action or victims in an accident. Thus *soldati dispersi*, soldiers missing in action and presumed dead, and *disperso in aereo l'amministratore* della Primigi* (*La Repubblica*, 5–6/4/92), the managing director (⟶ DIRETTORE) of P. missing, presumed dead, in his aircraft.

disposizione, n.f. — has all the meanings of disposition, but note *è a tua disposizione*, it is at your disposal. Can also be an official order, instruction or provision, e.g. *una nuova disposizione ministeriale sul porto d'armi*, a new ministerial order on carrying firearms.

disputare, v. — to dispute but also, in sport, to take part in, compete, contest, play or fight for, e.g. *chi disputerà la finale di Wimbledon?* who will be in the Wimbledon final?, *il pilota* non disputerà il Gran Premio d'Italia*, the racing driver won't compete/take part in the Italian Grand Prix, *in Italia le partite di calcio si disputano la domenica*, in Italy football games/matches are played on Sundays, and *i pugili si disputano il titolo dei pesi massimi*, the boxers are fighting for the heavyweight title.

disservizio, n.m. — not a disservice (= *un torto, un danno* or *un brutto servizio**) but inefficiency, bad service or a malfunction. *Il disservizio postale* is, therefore, the inefficiency of the postal services, and *il disservizio Sip è un elemento* quasi peculiare* (⟶ PECULIARITÀ) *della nostra storia contemporanea* (*L'Espresso*, 15/9/91) means that the bad service or malfunctioning of the S.I.P. (the Italian telephone service) is an almost typical feature of our recent history.

distinto, adj. — can be distinct, although a distinct advantage = *un notevole/netto vantaggio*, and I have a distinct feeling = *ho la netta impressione*. Usually, it means: distinguished, as in *una signora distinta*, a distinguished lady, or in the expression *distinti saluti*, best wishes (lit. distinguished greetings) at the end of a letter. A distinguished scholar, however = *uno studioso eminente/di fama* internazionale*, and a distinguished guest = *un ospite di riguardo**. Distinguishing features or marks are *segni particolari* (⟶ CARATTERISTICO).
⟶ DISCRETO, INDISTINTAMENTE

distributore, n.m. — distributor (both of trade and in an engine), but also any kind of dispensing, slot or vending machine, e.g. *un distributore automatico di sigarette*, a cigarette vending machine. Note *un distributore di benzina*, a petrol/U.S. gas pump (⟶ PETROLIO).

diverso, adj. — occasionally the equivalent of diverse, as in *cavarsela nelle situazioni più diverse*, coping in the most diverse situations, and *mode prese in prestito dalle più diverse civiltà*, fashions borrowed from the most diverse civilisations (⟶ CIVILIZZAZIONE). However, diverse interests = *interessi svariati*. Usually, though, if placed after a noun, *diverso* means: different, if before it means: various/several. Compare *abbiamo interessi diversi*, we have different interests, and *abbiamo diversi interessi in comune*, we have a number of interests in common.

divulgare, v. — sometimes to divulge information, but often more neutral than its English equivalent. Thus *il testo del trattato sarà ufficialmente divulgato a Natale* could mean, according to context: the text of the treaty will be made public, published or even broadcast at Christmas. More surprisingly, it also means: to vulgarise or popularise. The well-known journalist Indro Montanelli has, for instance, popularised Italian history with his books = *ha divulgato la storia italiana con i suoi libri*. Popular science writing is *gli scritti scientifici divulgativi*, and Stephen Hawking's 'A Brief History of Time' (1988) could be described as *un'opera* divulgativa di fisica teorica*, a work on theoretical physics for the layman.
⟶ SCIENTIFICO

dizione, n.f. — diction, but also reading aloud or recitation (⟶ RECITARE), e.g. *uno strumento musicale per accompagnare il canto o la dizione*, a musical instrument to accompany singing or recitation.

dolcevita, n.m. — the success of Fellini's 1960 film *La Dolce Vita* gave a name to the sweet life but also to the polo-neck sweater, as worn by Marcello Mastroianni.
⟶ GOLF

domandare, v. — to ask or request, of course, but never to demand (= *esigere*). Do not confuse *domandare una risposta*, to ask for an answer, with to demand an answer = *esigere una risposta*. *La domanda* is only demand in the sense of supply and demand, *la domanda e l'offerta*. Otherwise it means question, request or application, as in *una domanda facile**, an easy question, and *una domanda d'iscrizione**, an application to enrol or join (⟶ APPLICAZIONE). A demand = *una richiesta* or, sometimes, *un'esigenza*.
⟶ INTERROGAZIONE, QUESTIONE

dottore, n.m. — doctor. A title applied not only to M.D.s or Ph.D.s in Italy but to any university graduate (= *un laureato*), so that *un dottore in lettere* is the equivalent of a B.A., and *un dottore in scienze* is a B.Sc. The doctorate by research, *il dottorato di ricerca*, was still, at time of writing, in its infancy, with many Italian graduates doing Ph.D.s abroad. In Southern Italy *dottore* is often heard as a term of deference employed by such as waiters and parking attendants.

dramma, n.m. — is a drama or play (⟶ COMMEDIA), but drama as a subject or activity is *l'arte drammatica, la drammatica, la prosa** or *il teatro*. However, *il dramma dei Palestinesi/dei profughi albanesi* should be translated as the plight of the Palestinians or of the Albanian refugees, and the headline *un dramma familiare*: il suicidio di una coppia* means: a family tragedy — a couple commit suicide. In such contexts *drammatico* is often urgent, acute, desperate, critical or tragic, rather than dramatic, e.g. *il problema della droga* è ormai drammatico in certe città italiane*, the drugs problem has now become acute/desperate/critical in some Italian cities.

————→ SCENA

droga, n.f. — is, of course, a drug, literally and metaphorically. More surprisingly it is also a spice, especially in the plural form. Umberto Saba's poem 'Tre Vie' in *Trieste e una donna* (1910–12) ['Trieste and a Woman'] describes a city street as *Odorata di droghe e di catrame dei magazzini desolati a fronte*, Scented with spices and pitch from the deserted warehouses opposite. Possible misunderstandings (nowadays avoided by invariably using *le spezie* for spices) are neatly illustrated by the dialogue between doctor and headache-sufferer in Giovanni Guereschi's *Lo Zibaldino* (1948) ['Little Notebook']. Puzzled doctor at a loss to understand what is provoking the pain: *Droghe allora?* So it's drugs? Patient's reply: *No. Niente pepe e solo un po' di noce moscata*, No, no pepper and only a little nutmeg. Doctor: *Intendevo* (————→ INTENDERE) *droghe nel senso* di stupefacenti*, I meant drugs in the sense of narcotics. Drugs are therefore, more formally, *stupefacenti*, but medical drugs are *farmaci*. A drug addict is *un tossicodipendente* or, in everyday parlance, *un drogato*. Do not take *una drogheria* for a drugstore (= *una farmacia*, very approximately): it is a general store.

duomo, n.m. — is not the dome of a building (= *la cupola*) but a cathedral. Well-known *duomi* are found in Milan, Florence and Pisa. The guide-book statement *La cupola del duomo di Firenze fu costruita dal Brunelleschi tra il 1420 e il 1436* therefore means that the dome of Florence cathedral was built by B. between these dates.

————→ LESIONE

duplex, n.m. — if an Italian suggests sharing *un duplex* he is referring not to a duplex or semi-detached house (= *una villetta familiare**) but to a telephone party-line.

————→ CABINA, PHON, VILLA

E

eccellente, adj. — excellent, but sometimes, disconcertingly, it means: distinguished or celebrity. At election time, for instance, newspapers discuss *candidati eccellenti*, V.I.P. or celebrity candidates, i.e. well-known personalities from outside politics standing on a party ticket. A famous example from the late 1970s was the art historian Giulio Carlo Argan who became mayor of Rome for the Communist Party. More infamous (⟶ NOTORIETÀ) was the election in the 1980s of the country's best-known stripper, Cicciolina, as a Radical Party M.P. *Eccellente* also crops up in the context of Mafia crime and political corruption, as in the headlines *I 'delitti eccellenti' alla vigilia del voto** (*La Repubblica*, 5–6/4/92), 'Crimes against top people' on the eve of the elections, and *Arresto 'eccellente'* (*La Repubblica*, 11/3/93), Arrest of a prominent personality. Hence the title of Francesco Rosi's powerful film about Mafia and right-wing destabilisation, *Cadaveri eccellenti* (1975) ['Distinguished Corpses']. Originally the adjective applied to those with the title *Eccellenza*, Your Excellency.
⟶ DELINQUENZA

eccitante, adj. — exciting, but use sparingly. It tends to apply to sexual arousal or to the over excitement caused by stimulants. Strong coffee is therefore described as (*un*) *eccitante*, a stimulant, and *un pornovideo eccitante* would be an exciting pornographic video. Can, by extension, be used of anything procuring strong sensations. Thus Honda maintain that when driving their Accord *potrete distintamente sentire 133 cavalli e l'eccitante presenza di un'iniezione computerizzata*, you will distinctly feel 133 horsepower and the thrilling or rousing presence of its computerised fuel-injection. Usually, though, exciting in the sense of thrilling = *appassionante* or *emozionante*, e.g. *un giallo appassionante* (⟶ ROMANZA), an exciting detective story or thriller, and *una partita appassionante*, an exciting game or match. If this game were exciting enough to stir your emotions it might become *una partita emozionante*. Italian airforce ads. offer graduates *una carriera emozionante e moderna*, an exciting, modern career. However, working abroad was an exciting experience could be rendered as *vivere all'estero è stata un'esperienza stimolante* or *entusiasmante*.
⟶ EMOZIONE

economico, adj. — economic or economical (*un'edizione** *economica* is a cheap edition) but classified ads. are *gli annunci economici*, and in such an ad. *la nostra offerta economica* means: we offer the following terms or package (⟶ PACCHETTO).

edificio, n.m. — not as impressive as an edifice (= *un edificio imponente*, e.g. St Peter's in Rome, or the monumental Central Station in Milan). It is simply a middle-sized building such as a block of flats, hospital, school or station. The most general term, applicable to any building large or small, is *una costruzione*.
⟶ MONUMENTO, PALAZZO

edito, adj. — not edited but published, so *un romanzo** *edito dalla Mondadori*, a novel published by M., is different from a novel edited by Mondadori = *un romanzo a cura della/curato dalla M.* (⟶ CURARE). Beware of its negative, *inedito*; *un libro/documento inedito* is an unpublished book or document, but *un film inedito* is a film as yet unreleased, and *idee artistiche inedite* are absolutely new or unheard of artistic ideas.
⟶ EDITORE, EDIZIONE

editore, n.m. — genuinely confusable with editor, it is actually a newspaper or book publisher. Well-known Italian *editori* are Mondadori, Einaudi and Rizzoli. A publishing house is *una casa editrice*. On the other hand, a newspaper editor = *un redattore* or *un direttore** (if editor-in-chief), and the editor of a scholarly work = *il curatore** (————➔ CURARE).
————➔ EDITO, EDIZIONE

edizione, n.f. — exactly like edition where published material is concerned, but *la terza edizione di una mostra/una manifestazione*/un convegno*, is the third time an exhibition, event or conference has been held. Also means: version, as in *il festival propone una promettente edizione in inglese del 'Barbiere di Seviglia' di Rossini*, the festival presents a promising English version of Rossini's 'Barber of Seville'.
————➔ EDITO, EDITORE

educazione, n.f. — sometimes education but often upbringing, so that *ricevere una buona/cattiva educazione* is: to receive a good or bad upbringing. Susanna Agnelli, in *Vestivamo alla marinara* (1975) ['We dressed in Sailor Suits'], wrote: *ci davano da mangiare sempre quello che più odiavamo; credo che facesse parte della nostra educazione britannica*, they always used to feed us the things we hated most; I think it was part of our British upbringing. If an action is impolite Italians say: *non è educazione*. *Educato* is therefore: polite or well-mannered, definitely not educated (= *colto* or *istruito*), and *maleducato* means: rude (————➔ RUDE). To receive a good education = *ricevere un'ottima istruzione*, the education(al) system is *il sistema d'istruzione (educativo)*, and the Ministry of Education = *il Ministero della Pubblica Istruzione*. Sex education, though, is *l'educazione sessuale*.
————➔ DIDATTICO, ISTITUTO, MAESTRO, PROFESSORE

effettivo, adj. — sometimes corresponds to effective (e.g. *avere il controllo effettivo del paese*, to be in effective control of the country, and *il valore effettivo del dollaro*, the effective value of the dollar). On occasion, though, it means real, genuine (————➔ GENUINO), concrete or actual (————➔ ATTUALE). Thus *misure effettive* are concrete measures, whereas effective measures = *misure efficaci*. *Un progetto che presenta vantaggi effettivi* is a plan presenting real or genuine advantages, and *un'effettiva necessità* is a real need. Of a sporting event, *il tempo effettivo* is the actual (as opposed to the theoretical) time played. Note that, of the armed forces, it means: active-service, as in the potentially misleading *carabinieri effettivi*. To become effective of a law or measure = *entrare in vigore*. Very common is the adverbial form *effettivamente* meaning not: effectively (= *efficacemente* or *in modo efficace*) but indeed, in fact, really or it's true, e.g. *effettivamente ho sbagliato strada*, it's true I've taken/I have indeed taken a wrong turning.

elaborare, v. — never means: to elaborate (on) = *approfondire* or *spiegare in modo (più) dettagliato*. It is: to formulate, draw up or devise (e.g. *elaborare un piano/un sistema/idee/materiali*, to devise a new plan, system, ideas or materials) or else to process, as in *i computer elaborano i dati*, computers process the data. Data processing is *l'elaborazione dei dati* (————➔ PERSONAL). *Rielaborare* is, therefore: to reformulate but it also means: to re-master a recording, as in *Sony Classical si è proposta di rielaborare tutte le registrazioni di Glen Gould*, S.C. has undertaken to re-master all of G.G.'s recordings (————➔ REGISTRARE).

elementare, adj. — elementary or basic, but also elemental, as in *le violenze elementari della natura e dell'ambiente*, the elemental violence (or assaults) of nature and the environment.

elemento, n.m. — an element of any kind, but sometimes encountered unexpectedly in expressions such as *è il miglior elemento della squadra/della scuola/della società**, where it can be rendered by: the best member or player in the team/pupil in the school/employee or man in the company. The periodic table (of elements) is *il sistema periodico*, as in the eponymous collection of short stories by Primo Levi (1975).

elevato, adj. — elevated (e.g. *sentimenti elevati*, elevated sentiments), but usually only means: high, so do not take *una posizione elevata*, a vantage point, for an elevated position = *una posizione (molto) prestigiosa*. *Prezzi elevati* are high prices, *un prodotto di elevata qualità* is a high-quality product, *uno schermo T.V. ad elevato contrasto** is a high-contrast T.V. screen, and *una montagna elevata* is a lofty mountain.
──────→ ESALTARE

emissione, n.f. — emission in all senses, but remember that the sign *banco/sportello emissione biglietti* indicates a ticket-issuing counter, and *una nuova emissione di francobolli* is a new stamp issue.

emotivo, adj. — can be emotive (*servirsi di un linguaggio emotivo* is: to use emotive language, but an emotive issue = *una questione che suscita forti reazioni*), though not always. *Un bambino/un temperamento emotivo* is an excitable, impressionable or emotional child/temperament, *l'impatto emotivo* is the emotional impact, and *un ricatto emotivo* is emotional blackmail.
──────→ EMOZIONE

emozione, n.f. — sometimes corresponds to emotion or feeling (e.g. *il divario tra la ragione e l'emozione*, the gap between reason and emotion, *esprimere una forte emozione*, to express a strong emotion, and *la dolce emozione di essere liberi*, the sweet feeling of being free), but at times means: excitement or thrill. Thus you may be advised by a doctor to *evitare le emozioni*, avoid excitement. This explains why Honda describe driving their Prelude as *un'emozione rara*, a rare thrill, going on to ask *Può ancora una macchina dare emozioni?* Can a car still be exciting? Note that to appeal to the emotions = *fare appello ai sentimenti* (──────→ SENTIMENTO), and a voice choked with emotion = *una voce rotta dalla commozione**.
──────→ ECCITANTE, EMOTIVO

energetico, adj. — temptingly similar to energetic (an energetic person, though = *una persona energica*), but it actually means: to do with energy. Thus *una crisi* energetica*, an energy shortage or crisis. Greenpeace advertise their *nuove lampadine a risparmio energetico*, new, energy-saving light bulbs, and Italy's energy-development agency E.N.E.A. claims to guarantee *uno sviluppo energetico in armonia con l'ambiente*, energy development that respects the environment.
──────→ CARBONE, ILLUMINAZIONE, LUMINOSO, PETROLIO

entità, n.f. — entity, but beware of its commoner meanings of extent, size or amount. Thus *l'entità del problema*, the extent of the problem, *l'entità dello scandolo ha stupito*

l'opinione pubblica, the size of the scandal surprised public opinion, and *danni di lieve entità*, a slight amount of damage.
———→ ESTENSIONE

equanimità, n.f. — resembles equanimity (= *la serenità** or *la tranquillità d'animo*) but means: fairmindedness. Compare *giudicare la situazione con equanimità*, to judge the situation impartially, and to judge the situation with equanimity = *giudicare la situazione con serenità*.

eredità, n.f. — as well as biological heredity it also means: a legacy or inheritance. Thus *lasciare in eredità*, to bequeath or leave to, and *entrare in possesso di un'eredità*, to come into an inheritance. The Italian law of succession, derived from the Napoleonic code, stipulates (———→ STIPULARE) that a proportion of any legacy must go to the surviving spouse and children who cannot be excluded from the inheritance even by a will, *un testamento*.

esagerare, v. — to exaggerate, but not always. When, e.g., *L'Espresso* (19/9/93) asked, of the media magnate Rupert Murdoch, *Sta esagerando il tycoon venuto dall'Australia?* it meant: Is the tycoon from Australian going too far? *Hai esagerato con la panna* (———→ CREMA) would mean: you've put in too much cream. *Esagerato* can be: excessive or extravagant (———→ STRAVAGANTE) as well as exaggerated, e.g. *prezzi esagerati*, excessive prices, and *lui è sempre esagerato*, he's always over the top.

esaltare, v. — sometimes to exalt or extol. Often, though, it means: to enhance (*il vapore esalta il sapore delle pietanze*, steaming enhances the flavour of dishes) or else to inflame, excite or thrill (*il complesso esalta la folla prima del concerto*, the band whip up the crowd before the concert). *Una persona esaltata* is, consequently, an over-excited or hot-headed person, and is definitely not to be confused with an exalted person = *una persona di rango/grado elevato**.

esasperato, adj. — exasperated but, occasionally, excessive, extreme or exaggerated, as in *l'esasperata ricerca di un look sempre nuovo e scioccante*, the exaggerated search for an ever new and shocking look/image.

esercizio, n.m. — exercise (although military exercises = *le esercitazioni*), but sometimes it means: a business concern, as in the term *un pubblico esercizio*, an establishment which opens to the public, applied to cafés (———→ BAR, CAFFÈ), hotels, restaurants and cinemas. Michelin guides suggest that *Alcuni esercizi meritano di essere segnalati alla Vostra attenzione per la qualità tutta particolare dei loro servizi* (———→ SERVIZIO), Some establishments deserve to be brought to your attention because of the particularly high-quality service they provide. The notice *denominazione* dell'esercizio* (followed by the name of the hotel), found on all hotel doors, is simply the name of the establishment. Since *in esercizio* is: in use, do not cross a railway track if you see the sign *binario in esercizio*, line in use. Note how ads. recommend household appliances (*gli elettrodomestici*) *per economia d'esercizio*, because of their low running costs.
———→ COMMERCIO

esibizione, n.f. — should not be mistaken for an exhibition (= *una mostra* or *un' esposizione*). It is a performance, show or display. *L'esibizione della cantante Madonna ha*

suscitato scalpore therefore means that the singer M.'s show or performance caused a furore (———→ FURORE) or scandal. *Un'esibizione di spogliarello* turns out to be a strip-tease act or show, and *un'esibizione di danze scozzesi* is a display of Scottish country dancing. Note that *fare esibizione di sè*, showing off, is not the same as making an exhibition of oneself = *rendersi ridicolo in pubblico/comportarsi in modo ridicolo*.
———→ PRODURRE, SPETTACOLO

esilarare, v. — eminently confusable with exhilarate (variously = *stimolare, appassionare* or *rendere euforico*). It actually means: to amuse, delight or cheer up, as in *lo spettacolo* ha esilarato il pubblico*, the show delighted the audience (———→ AUDIENCE). *Una scena* esilarante* is therefore a very funny or hilarious scene, whereas an exhilarating scene = *una scena stimolante* or *appassionante* (———→ ECCITANTE).
———→ ILARITÀ

eskimo, n.m. — not an Eskimo (= *un eschimese*) but a parka or warm anorak. The garment associated with Italian youth protest in the late 1960s and early 1970s. The fashionable equivalent in the nineties was the padded jacket known as *il giaccone*.

esonerare, v. — looks like to exonerate (= *discolpare*) but means: to remove from office or else to exempt. Beware, therefore, of confusing headlines such as *Il c.t. è stato esonerato*, which means that the team manager (*c.t.* = *commissario tecnico*) has been dismissed, not exonerated. *Esonerare dal servizio militare/dalle tasse scolastiche* (———→ RIFORMARE, SCOLASTICO) is: to exempt from military service or from school fees.

esplorare, v. — to explore, but *esplorare la zona*/il terreno**, if referred to the military, means: to reconnoitre or scout the area or land.
———→ RICOGNIZIONE

esponente, n.m. — not an exponent (= *un difensore, un sostenitore* or *un esperto*) but a top representative, spokesperson or leading member, e.g. *un esponente del partito conservatore ha spiegato la nuova politica* del governo*, a leading member of the Conservative party explained the government's new policy.

espresso, n.m. and adj. — express as well as the archetypal Italian black coffee. It is also used of any dish prepared for you while you wait, e.g. in some trains *la pasta* asciutta viene servita espressa*, freshly prepared pasta is served. However, do not think that *un (treno) espresso* is an express train. It is a through train, but if an express is what you need, board *un treno I.C.* (= *Inter City*) for which you will need to buy *un supplemento*, a supplement. Beware, too, of *un diretto* which, in spite of its name, is a stopping train, not a direct.
———→ CIRCOLARE, COMPARTIMENTO

espulsione, n.f. — expulsion in all senses, but it can be dismissal or sacking from work (———→ LICENZA), while in sport it is (a) sending-off. Also means: ejection, which explains the quaint sign *espulsione automatica*, automatic ejection, on tape decks and V.C.R.s. An ejector seat, however, is *un sedile eiettabile*.

estensione, n.f. — extension in the figurative sense of enlargement but also, confusingly, extent, area or size, so that *l'estensione di un problema/un paese* is likely to be the extent of a problem or the size or area of a country.
———→ ENTITÀ

estenuante, adj. — not extenuating (extenuating circumstances = *circostanze attenuanti*) but exhausting or wearing, as in *un lavoro estenuante*, (an) exhausting work/job. Italian has remained closer to the original Latin meaning of making thin, while English has only retained the figurative idea of lessening.

estetica, n.f. — aesthetics, but it also means: beauty or external appearance (———→ APPARENZA), as in *avere un senso* dell'estetica*, to have a natural feel for beauty, and *l'estetica dal centro storico* sarà danneggiata dalle nuove costruzioni* (———→ EDIFICIO), the appearance/beauty/harmony of the old city centre will be damaged by the new buildings. *Un* or *un'estetista* is not an aesthete (= *un esteta*) but a beautician.
———→ MISS

estinzione, n.f. — extinction, in all senses, but also annulment or cancellation, as in *l'estinzione di una pena/un debito*/un conto*, the annulment or cancellation of a sentence (———→ SENTENZA), a debt or an account (———→ ACCONTO). Finance companies may offer *la possibilità di estinzione anticipata* (———→ ANTICIPARE) *sul mutuo casa*, the option of redeeming the mortgage on your home before term expiry.

esuberante, adj. — usually exuberant, but be warned: it occasionally retains the original Latin meaning of excessive or over-abundant. Corrado Alvaro, in *Il nostro tempo e la speranza* (1952) ['Hope and Our Time'], wrote of *il problema meridionale, in gran parte originato da una popolazione esuberante e scarsamente qualificata*, the Southern problem stemming, in large measure, from an excessively large and poorly skilled or trained population (———→ QUALIFICATO, SCARSO).

etichetta, n.f. — etiquette or ceremony (*badare all'etichetta*, to stand on ceremony), but most often a label or price-tag, e.g. *l'etichetta di una bottiglia di vino*, the label on a bottle of wine, and *attaccare* un'etichetta*, to stick on a label or tie on a price-tag. To label a person = *etichettare qualcuno/affibbiare un'etichetta a qualcuno*.
———→ CONVENIENTE, DECORO

evadere, v. — only to evade or dodge of taxes (*evadere il fisco/le tasse* ———→ FISCALE). For everything else use *evitare*. In an office, *evadere la corrispondenza*, therefore, means not: to evade but to deal with or clear the correspondence or mail, and something *utile per chi è incaricato di ricevere ordini, evadere reclami e prestare assistenza** is useful for those whose job it is to receive orders, deal with complaints and give assistance.

eventuale, adj. — resembles eventual (= *alla fine* or *finalmente*) and tends to occur in similar situations. However, it means: possible. So avoid confusing *celebrare* un'eventuale vittoria*, celebrating a possible victory, with celebrating an eventual or ultimate victory = *celebrare una vittoria ottenuta alla fine/infine/finalmente*. *Un'eventuale alternativa* is a possible alternative, and the warning sign *non assumiamo alcuna responsabilità per eventuali furti* means: we cannot be held responsible for any thefts which may occur. Similarly, you should not be misled by the adverb *eventualmente*. *Eventualmente chiamerò*

il medico means: I'll call the doctor if it's necessary, whereas eventually I'll call the doctor
= *alla fine chiamerò il medico*.
———→ OCCORRENZA

evidentemente, adv. — is not evidently but obviously or clearly. Compare *evidentemente
hanno deciso di partire*, they've obviously decided to leave, with evidently they've decided
to leave = *a quanto pare hanno deciso di partire*. The statement: *la lira è evidentemente
sottovalutata* therefore means that the lira is clearly undervalued. Quite evidently/obviously
= *con tutta/ogni evidenza**.

evidenza, n.f. — occasionally means: evidence, e.g. *abbiamo evidenza di sintesi delle due
proteine*, we have evidence of the synthesis of the two proteins, or *arrendersi all'evidenza*,
to bow or yield to the facts or the evidence. However, police evidence or testimony = *un
indizio* or *una prova* (if evidence of a crime) or *la testimonianza/la deposizione* (if evidence
given in court). Usually *l'evidenza* means: plainness, obviousness or clarity, so that
l'evidenza di una prova means, confusingly: the obviousness, clarity or irrefutable nature of
a piece of evidence, while *negare l'evidenza* is: to deny what is plain/obvious or the plain
facts. Compare also, *mettere/porre in evidenza*, to bring or point out, and to produce as
evidence = *adurre come prova*. *Con evidenza* means: obviously or clearly. Note that *il
testimone* is the witness (an eye-witness is *un testimone oculare*).
———→ ASSOLUZIONE, EVIDENTEMENTE, PROCESSO

evoluzione, n.f. — evolution — social, cultural or Darwinian — but sometimes best
rendered by: development, as in Forecom's advert for its business courses: *I sistemi
avanzati di formazione** ... *per l'evoluzione personale e professionale*, the advanced
training systems for personal and professional development. Likewise, *un libro dedicato*
(———→ DEDICARE) *all'evoluzione storica della lingua italiana* is a book devoted to the
historical development of the Italian language, and *l'evoluzione di una malattia* is how an
illness is developing. Trickier are usages such as *l'evoluzione dei cavalieri* or *dei ginnasti*
meaning: the riders' or gymnasts' routine.

F

fabbricazione, n.f. — not fabrication but manufacture, e.g. *l'Italia è celebre per la fabbricazione di articoli in pelle*, Italy is famous for the manufacture of leather goods. *Una fabbrica* is a factory (———→ FATTORIA). The thief's story was all a fabrication = *l'alibi del ladro era tutto inventato/era tutta una bugia*.
———→ INDUSTRIA, SOCIETÀ

facile, adj. — means easy, of course, but never facile (= *superficiale* or *semplicistico*). Beware especially of *un carattere* facile*, an easy-going nature, *uno stile facile*, a flowing or accessible style, and *una donna facile*, a loose woman. While its opposite, *difficile*, is usually a straightforward equivalent of difficult, note expressions like *è difficile che lei venga/lo faccia*, she's unlikely to come or to do it.
———→ LABORIOSO

fama, n.f. — means reputation more often than fame (= *la celebrità* or *la notorietà**), e.g. *in Italia la fama di Montaigne non conosce interruzioni*, in Italy M.'s reputation has never slipped, and *un ristorante che gode di una fama internazionale*, a restaurant which enjoys an international reputation.

familiare or *famigliare*, adj. — familiar in all senses, but also family, as in *i segreti familiari*, family secrets, and *un'impresa familiare*, a family business/concern. *Una vita familiare* might be a familiar life (*nota, consueta* or *abituale* would make it absolutely clear) or else a family life. The title of Natalia Ginzburg's novel *Lessico famigliare* (1972) is translated as 'Family Sayings', and the popular magazines *Oggi* and *Gente* could be described as *i grandi settimanali familiari*, the major or big family weeklies. *Guidare* una familiare* is to drive a family saloon/U.S. sedan.
———→ PARENTE

fantasia, n.f. — fantasy, but also imagination, so that *avere molta fantasia* is: to have a good imagination, and *dare libero sfogo alla fantasia* is: to give free rein to your imagination. Note that *un tessuto fantasia* is a bold or brightly-patterned material.
———→ FANTASTICO

fantastico, adj. — fantastic, in all senses, and fantastical, but sometimes fantasy is a better rendering, as in *'Il signore degli anelli', la trilogia fantastica di J.R. Tolkien*, 'Lord of the Rings' (1954–55), J.R.T.'s fantasy trilogy.
———→ FANTASIA

fastidioso, adj. — do not be deceived by its similarity to fastidious. It actually means: bothersome or irritating, as in *una voce/una situazione/una zanzara fastidiosa*, an annoying voice, situation or mosquito. *Un bambino fastidioso* is, therefore, a tiresome child, whereas a fastidious child = *un bambino pignolo* (if finicky), *un bambino schizzinoso* (if a picky eater) and *un bambino meticoloso* (if painstaking). A fastidious palate = *un palato raffinato*.

fatale, adj. — tread carefully. Sometimes unproblematic, as in *un'imprudenza fatale*, fatal carelessness, *un errore fatale*, a fatal mistake, *una debolezza fatale*, a fatal weakness, and *un'attrazione fatale*, a fatal attraction. However, a fatal accident = *un incidente* mortale*, a

fatal blow = *un colpo mortale*, and a fatal illness = *una malattia incurabile*, while a decision that could prove fatal is *una decisione che potrebbe rivelarsi disastrosa*. *Fatale* itself can be misleading in its meaning of inevitable. Thus *un fatale declino* will sometimes be an inevitable rather than fatal decline, *una fatale conseguenza* is an inevitable consequence, and *era fatale che questo avvenisse* means: it was inevitable that this would happen. Verga in his foreword to *I Malavoglia* (1881) ['The House under the Medlar Tree'], pessimistically described *il cammino fatale, incessante, spesso faticoso e febbrile, che segue l'umanità per raggiungere la conquista del progresso*, the inevitable, endless, often wearisome and febrile road followed by humanity in its quest for progress. The pitfalls do not end here. *L'anno/il giorno/il momento fatale* will often translate as the fateful year, day and moment, while *un uomo fatale* (as Manzoni described Napoleon in his poem *Il Cinque Maggio*, 1821) is a man of destiny. On the other hand, *una donna fatale* is, straightforwardly, a femme fatale, although other expressions of this type are possible, e.g. *uno sguardo fatale*, a seductive or irresistible look.
————→ AFFASCINANTE, FATALITÀ

fatalità, n.f. — sometimes fatality, as in *il senso* di fatalità dei Siciliani*, the sense of fatality of the Sicilians, whose outlook was described by Lampedusa in a famous passage of *Il Gattopardo* (1956) ['The Leopard'] as being *condizionato da fatalità esteriori*, conditioned by events outside (our) control. *È stata una fatalità*, on the other hand, means: it was a misfortune or sheer bad luck. In Moravia's novel *La Romana*, (1960) ['The Woman of Rome'] the heroine remarks: *La fatalità … aveva voluto che io con la mia bellezza mi fossi imbattuta in uomini che non potevano procurarmi quella felicità*, As fate would have it I, for all my beauty, had come across men who could not bring me such happiness. Road fatalities may be either *incidenti mortali* (————→ ACCIDENTE, INCIDENTE), if referring to the accidents, or *i morti/le vittime* if referring to the victims.
————→ FATALE

fattoria, n.f. — a notorious false friend meaning not: a factory (= *una fabbrica*) but a farm or, sometimes, an estate. The life of a traditional northern Italian *fattoria*, with its square or rectangle of two-storey buildings grouping a number of families around a large central courtyard, was recreated by Enrico Olmi in his film *L'albero degli zoccoli* (1978), ['The Tree of the Wooden Clogs'].
————→ INDUSTRIA

festivo, adj. — rarely festive (= *gioioso, lieto, festoso* or *'di festa'*), it normally means: Sunday or holiday. On timetables and shops you will, e.g., see the notice *orario festivo*, timetable/opening times for Sundays and holidays. *Giorni feriali* or *lavorativi*, working days, contrast with *giorni festivi*, public holidays. *Un biglietto festivo* is a weekend ticket, and the paradoxical *lavoro festivo* is overtime carried out on non-working days (————→ STRAORDINARIO).

fiasco, n.m. — a fiasco or failure (*fare fiasco* is: to flop). However, besides this figurative use, of unexplained origin and borrowed by English from Italian, *un fiasco* is also a (wine) flask, as in the world-renowned, straw-covered *fiasco di Chianti* (————→ DENOMINAZIONE, SOFISTICATO).

figura, n.f. — figure in most contexts, including the human body, although here the emphasis tends to be on build, e.g. *avere una figura atletica* or *flessuosa*, to have an

athletic or lithe figure/build/physique. If the stress is on curvaciousness, use *le forme* (—————→ FORMA); if it is on slimness, choose *la linea* (an enviable figure = *una linea da fare invidia*). Note that most Italian of concepts *fare bella figura*, making a good impression in public, as opposed to losing face, *fare brutta figura*. In a book, *le figure* are plates or illustrations. Mathematical figures = *le cifre*.
—————→ SINUOSO

figurina, n.f. — a figurine, but *figurine* are much more familiar to Italian children as the picture-cards they collect in, e.g., bubble-gum packets.

finalità, n.f. — not finality (= *il carattere* definitivo*) but aim, purpose or objective, as in *le finalità d'un libro*, a book's aims, and *un'azione* svolta con finalità caritevoli*, an action performed for charitable ends or motives. Contrast *la finalità della sua decisione*, what motivated his decision, and the finality of his decision = *il carattere definitivo della sua decisione*.
—————→ SCOPO

finanziere, n.m. — may translate unproblematically as financier. It is trickier when it refers to a revenue policeman, border guard or customs officer, i.e. a member of the *Guardia di Finanza*, one of Italy's three main law-enforcement corps (—————→ AGENTE).

fiscale, adj. — sometimes simply fiscal or tax, e.g. *il codice fiscale*, the tax code, *l'evasione fiscale*, tax dodging, or *la ricevuta fiscale*, the receipted bill for tax purposes which you must be given by restaurants, cafés, hotels and all stores in Italy (when a receipt is not issued both proprietor and customer may be fined). However, note that *un medico fiscale* is a doctor who checks up on employees off on sick leave: his/her visit is *la visita fiscale*. *Essere fiscale* or *comportarsi in modo fiscale* mean: to be or act in an over-strict, petty, officious or nit-picking way. The development of these negative meanings is linked to tax-collectors and their exactions, and can be understood by reading the early sections of Silone's *Fontamara* (1933) and Carlo Levi's *Cristo si è fermato a Eboli* (1945) ['Christ stopped at Eboli'].
(—————→ ESERCIZIO)

flipper, n.m. — pinball (machine) and not a flipper (= *una pinna*), so *giocare a flipper* is: to play pinball. A false-anglicism derived from the pair of flipper-handles which propel the balls on to the pin-table.
—————→ TILT

fluente, adj. — fluent but sometimes flowing, of hair or beard: *i capelli fluenti* (or *sciolti*) or *una barba fluente*. His Italian is fluent = *parla correntemente* or *fluentemente l'italiano*, and a fluent speech = *un discorso* scorrevole, sciolto* or *fluente*.

forfait, n.m. — like forfeit occurs in the context of finance but means: lump-sum, so that *un prezzo a forfait* is a flat rate or all-inclusive price, and *un pagamento a forfait* is payment on a lump-sum basis. To pay a forfeit, on the other hand = *pagare una multa, una penalità* or *un'ammenda*. Also encountered, surprisingly, in the world of sport where *dichiarare forfait* or *forfait* is: to cry off or scratch. Pronounced as in French.

forma, n.f. — form of all kinds, except an application form = *un modulo**. Note that it can be a person's figure as in *un vestito che mette in risalto le sue forme*, a dress which shows her figure to advantage (———→ FIGURA), but also a mould in cooking, e.g. *una forma per dolci*, a cake tin or mould. Because it is made in a mould a cheese (round) is *una forma*. Stacks of *forme di Parmigiano*, Parmesan cheeses, are on display in larger Italian delicatessens (*le salumerie* or *pizzicherie*). Italian *formaggio* and French *fromage* are derived from Latin *FORMA*, too.

formazione, n.f. — formation, although it is increasingly encountered meaning: training (for work). Thus *un periodo di formazione*, a training period, and *un corso di formazione*, a job training course. The magazine *Campus* describes itself as *il giornale dell'Università, della Ricerca e della Formazione*, the journal/periodical for universities, research and training.
———→ PREPARAZIONE, STAGE

formula, n.f. — formula in many cases. However, in holiday literature it means: option, deal or package. Typical are the *F.S.* (i.e. *Ferrovie dello Stato*) Italian railway/U.S. railroad adverts for their *formula treno + bici*, train + bike option, and the national airline Alitalia's listing of its *formule che hanno fatto storia*, epoch-making holiday options. If buying an expensive item, you may be offered various *formule di pagamento*, methods of payment or repayment packages.
———→ PROPOSTA

fornitura, n.f. — not furniture (= *la mobilia* or *i mobili*) but supplies. *Le forniture d'ufficio* are, therefore, office supplies not office furniture = *i mobili d'ufficio*.

fortuna, n.f. — fortune, (often good fortune) but surprisingly it can mean: makeshift, as in *un atterraggio di fortuna*, an emergency landing, and *un lavoro di fortuna*, a job to tide you over. In a tight spot, *mezzi di fortuna* are whatever comes to hand. Equally oddly, it is often public recognition, standing or success. *La fortuna di Shakespeare in Italia risale solo ai primi dell'ottocento* therefore means that S.'s popularity in Italy only goes back to the beginning of the 19th century. Similarly, *fortunato* is both fortunate and popular/best-selling/successful, e.g. *La 'Storia d'Italia', il fortunatissimo libro dello storico inglese Dennis Mack Smith*, the 'History of Italy', the extremely successful book by the British historian D.M.S.

frase, n.f. — a grammatical or musical phrase but also, most commonly, a sentence.
———→ COMMA, PERIODO

frazione, n.f. — fraction, but on roadside signs with *frazione di ...* followed by the name of a locality it means something like: parish, township or district. Each *comune* or municipality in Italy is divided up into *frazioni* (———→ COMUNALE).

frequentare, v. — to frequent, but also to see or go out/around with. *Mi preoccupo di quale ambiente frequenta mio figlio*, is therefore: I'm worried about what kind of people my son is going around with, and *frequentare gli amici*, is: to see one's friends. It often means: to attend, though, so that *frequentare un corso d'inglese* is: to take or attend an

English course, and *è facoltativo frequentare le lezioni* means that attending or going to classes is optional.

──────→ AUDITORE, FREQUENZA, LEZIONE, LIBRETTO

frequenza, n.f. — as well as frequency or incidence (──────→ INCIDENZA), it means: attendance, e.g. *la frequenza è obbligatoria nelle scuole italiane dai 6 ai 15 anni*, attendance is compulsory in Italian schools from ages 6 to 15, after which compulsory schooling, *la scuola dell'obbligo*, ends.

──────→ AUDITORE, FREQUENTARE, INFERIORE, LEZIONE, PREVALENZA

frizione, n.f. — is friction, but its range is wider. It also means: a massage or rub-down, and is the clutch (pedal) in a motor vehicle, e.g. *innestare la frizione*, to engage the clutch.

fungo, n.m. — not only fungus in the botanical and medical senses but also mushroom. A toadstool is *un fungo velenoso*, i.e. a poisonous mushroom. *Andere a/per funghi*, mushroom-picking, is a favourite autumn pastime, *il porcino* (*boletus* or *cep*) and *il gallinaccio* (*chanterelle*) being particularly sought-after.

funzione, n.f. — function in most cases, but you may encounter it meaning: a church service, e.g. *assistere alle funzioni*, to attend services (──────→ ASSISTENZA), and *le funzioni della settimana santa/domenicali/pasquali*, Holy Week, Sunday or Easter services. Do not confuse with a social function = *un ricevimento*.

──────→ CULTO

furia, n.f. — sometimes fury (e.g. *la furia del vento*, the fury/violence of the wind, or *ha reagito con furia incontrollata*, he reacted with uncontrolled fury), but is often encountered in the phrases *essere in furia*, to be in a great hurry or rush, and *a furia di*, by dint of. To be furious is: *essere furibondo* or *furente*. These are sometimes safer to use than *essere furioso* which may suggest madness: *un pazzo furioso* is a raving madman, e.g., and the title of Ariosto's famous epic *Orlando Furioso* (1516) refers to the hero Roland who goes raging mad with jealousy. Note that *infuriare* can be to rage (*la guerra infuriava*, war was raging) as well as to infuriate (*i produttori italiani sono infuriati dall'accordo*, Italian producers have been infuriated by the agreement).

──────→ FURORE

furore, n.m. — do not confuse with furore. His film caused a furore = *il suo film ha suscitato scalpore/ha fatto chiasso*. On the other hand, *il suo film ha fatto furore* means that his film was a resounding success or was all the rage. Also fury, e.g. *il furore della folla*, the fury of the crowd, and *fu preso dal furore*, he flew into a rage (──────→ FURIA). John Steinbeck's 'The Grapes of Wrath' (1939) is simply called *Furore* in Italian. The English term is borrowed from *furore* and originally shared the sense of a popular hit.

fusione, n.f. — is fusion, but note that *il punto di fusione* of a metal is its melting point, while *la fusione di due ditte/due partiti politici* is the merger of two companies or political parties.

futile, adj. — can be futile (e.g. *un'azione futile*, a futile act) but also trivial (not *triviale**). *Un futile pretesto*, then, is a trivial pretext, and *parlare di cose futili* is: to talk about trivial things/trivialities.

──────→ BANALE

G

gadget, n.m. — as well as a gadget it can mean: a gimmick, as in *l'uso spietate di gadget durante la campagna elettorale*, the ruthless use of gimmicks during the election campaign.
——→ PRATICO

galleria, n.f. — gallery, but also a tunnel, e.g. *la galleria del San Gottardo/del Sempione*, the St Gothard and Simplon tunnels under the Alps. Used, too, for a shopping arcade, as in *la Galleria (Vittorio Emanuele II)* in the heart of Milan. In the theatre it may be the gallery but *la prima galleria* is the dress circle, and *la seconda galleria* is the upper circle or balcony. For the press or public gallery use *la tribuna*. Remember that *la galera* is jail.

generalità, n.f. pl. — generalities, but if asked for *le tue/Sue generalità* give your personal details/particulars.

generoso, adj. — is an exact equivalent of generous, although when used of a sportsman or woman it means: a wholehearted or gutsy competitor, e.g. *un ciclista generoso*, a big-hearted cyclist. *La generosità della squadra è stata ricompensata* therefore means: the team's tremendous effort was rewarded.
——→ ABBONDANTE

geniale, adj. — not genial (= *cordiale, simpatico, gioviale* or *affabile*) but brilliant, (——→ BRILLANTE) or 'of genius'. Compare *un uomo geniale*, a man of genius, and a genial man = *un uomo affabile*. *Un'idea/una soluzione* geniale* is a brilliant idea or solution. While a genius is *un genio*, an artist's genius is *la genialità d'un artista*.

gentile, adj. — kind, of course, but rarely gentle. A gentle person/smile/nature = *una persona, un sorriso* or *un carattere* dolce*, and gentle eyes = *occhi dolci*. On the other hand, a gentle movement/touch = *un movimento* or *tocco delicato*, a gentle breeze = *un venticello (leggero)*, on a gentle heat = *a fuoco/fiamma moderato/a*, a gentle hint = *un lieve accenno* or *una delicata allusione*, and a gentle warning = *un avvertimento blando**. Genteel manners are *maniere 'rispettabili', perbene* or *che hanno pretese di distinzione*.
——→ SOAVE

genuino, adj. — you may occasionally come across it meaning: genuine, e.g. *mostrare un affetto genuino*, to show genuine (or sincere or spontaneous) affection (——→ AFFEZIONATO), or *un film genuino ma semplicistico*, a genuine/sincere but simplistic film. However, a genuine Canaletto = *un C. autentico*, genuine love = *l'amore vero* or *sincero*, and genuine people = *gente sincera e onesta*. *Genuino* is commonest and trickiest when applied to food and drink, where it means: natural, authentic, wholesome or unadulterated. Thus Simmenthal advertise their canned meat as *sana, buona, genuina*, healthy, good and wholesome, Bel Paese claims to be *il genuino formaggio italiano*, the natural (or, perhaps, authentic) Italian cheese, and *prodotti genuini*, natural produce, is very much in vogue. Do not, therefore, confuse *il genuino cibo italiano*, good, wholesome Italian food, with genuine Italian food = *l'autentico cibo italiano*. With a little luck you may be introduced to *un buon vino genuino*, a good, naturally-produced wine from the local area.
——→ BIOLOGICO, INTEGRALE, SANO, SOFISTICATO, TIPICO

ginnasio, n.m. — do not confuse with gymnasium (= *una palestra*) whose Greek origins it shares. It is, in fact, the first two, preparatory years of the Italian grammar school or classically-orientated senior high school, *il liceo classico**, and follows on from the three years of junior high school, *la scuola media*.

———→ INFERIORE, MATURO, SUPERIORE

giovanile, adj. — beware of confusing it with juvenile (= *puerile* or *minorile*); it means: youthful. The *opere giovanili* of a writer are, therefore, his youthful works, and are not necessarily the same as juvenile works = *opere puerili* (———→ OPERA). *Avere l'aspetto giovanile* (———→ APPARENZA) is: to look young, and *la contestazione giovanile* (———→ MANIFESTAZIONE) is youth protest. On the other hand, juvenile delinquency = *la delinquenza* minorile*, and the juvenile court = *il tribunale* dei minorenni*.

giunta, n.f. — a much used term in Italian local government with none of the pejorative connotations of junta. *La giunta comunale*/provinciale/regionale* is the executive committee of the town, provincial or regional council. A junta, on the other hand = *un regime militare*. While the English term derives from Spanish, *giunta* is either Spanish or Venetian in origin.

———→ AMMINISTRAZIONE, ASSESSORE, PRESIDENTE

golf, n.m. — the game but also, surprisingly, a sweater, jumper or cardigan. Said to derive from English golf-coat/jacket, but there is no evidence. Not to be confused with *una colf*, a home-help (an acronym of *collaboratore** or, more usually, *collaboratrice familiare**).

———→ DOLCEVITA

gorilla, n.m. (coll.) — a gorilla, but also a body-guard or 'heavy', e.g. *il presidente* non va mai in giro senza il suo gorilla*, the President never goes out and about without his body-guard.

governare, v. — to govern, but Italian also retains the verb's original Latin meaning of to steer or handle a boat/ship, *governare una barca/nave*. It also has some surprising figurative uses, e.g. *governare la casa*, to look after the home, *governare le bestie*, to tend the animals, and *governare il vino*, to see to the wine. Note that *rigovernare* is: to wash up or do the dishes.

graduato, n.m. — confusable with graduate (= *un laureato*) but is actually an N.C.O. in the military.

———→ BOMBARDIERE, BRIGADIERE, MARESCIALLO

grandioso, adj. — does not have the negative connotations of grandiose (= *fastoso* or *pomposo*), so *un progetto grandioso*, an imposing, magnificent or breath-taking project/plan, is not necessarily a grandiose one = *un progetto pomposo* or *monumentale*. *Un grandioso panorama sulla pianura padana* is a splendid/imposing view over the Po valley.

gratuito, adj. — gratuitous, but also free or not-charged-for, e.g. *l'ingresso è gratuito*, admission is free, and *l'assistenza* medica gratuita*, free medical care.

grosso, adj. — big, large or fat, but never gross. Gross neglect = *l'estrema negligenza*, a gross mistake = *un errore madornale*, gross behaviour/language = *un comportamento/un linguaggio* volgare, grossolano* or *osceno*, and a gross person = *una persona grassa e ripugnante*. Gross salary is *lo stipendio lordo* (⎯⎯→ RETRIBUZIONE).
⎯⎯⎯→ LARGO

guidare, v. — to guide or lead, but often to drive, fly or ride a vehicle. *Guidare la macchina verso la stazione di servizio** is, therefore: to drive a car towards the service station. To guide the car would be: *dirigere la macchina*. Ford ads. for their *Fiesta* insist: *Devi proprio guidarla*, You've just got to drive it. Note that to drive to work is best rendered by *andare al lavoro in/con la macchina*.
⎯⎯⎯→ LICENZA, PATENTE, PILOTA

gusto, n.m. — taste (in all senses), flavour, liking or pleasure. Thus Lavazza coffee maintains that *A volte le pause al bar* lasciano un gusto particolare*, Sometimes breaks (from work) at the café leave a special taste. It can be tricky, though. Do not be misled, e.g., by Panvista's ad. for its language schools, with its flag-wrapped sweets and the caption: *Tutte le lingue con più gusto*, Every language with more flavour/enjoyment. With more gusto would have been: *con più entusiasmo*. Only occasionally equivalent to gusto, as in *mangiare di gusto*, to eat with gusto or relish. To sing or act with gusto = *cantare/ recitare* con grande entusiasmo, energia* or *slancio*, whereas *cantare/recitare con gusto* is: to sing or act with (good) taste. An English borrowing from Italian which like al fresco*, ballerina*, bimbo*, bravura*, casino*, confetti*, fiasco* and furore* has gone its own way.
⎯⎯⎯→ MORBIDO

I

ideale, adj. — ideal (*la bellezza ideale*, ideal beauty and *una scelta ideale*, an ideal choice), but watch out for it when it means: imaginary. *I personaggi* (———→ PERSONAGGIO) *ideali dei suoi libri* are the imaginary characters of his books, *il film è ambientato in un pianeta ideale* means: the film is set on an imaginary planet, and Western Europe has been described as *quel triangolo ideale situato tra Gibilterra, il mare Adriatico e l'Oder-Neisse*, that imaginary triangle situated between Gibraltar, the Adriatic and the Oder-Neisse. May also, occasionally, mean: 'of ideas' or spiritual, as in *una solidarietà ideale e politica tra i paesi dell'Europa*, a spiritual and political solidarity among the countries of Europe.

idioma, n.m. — never use it for idiom in the sense of figure of speech (= *un modo di dire, un idiotismo, un'espressione idiomatica* or *una locuzione*). It is a neutral, literary word for a language, tongue or variety of speech, whether national, regional or local.
———→ LINGUAGGIO

igiene, n.f. — corresponds to hygiene in, e.g., *l'igiene alimentare*, food hygiene, and *l'igiene della casa*, hygiene in the home, but it sometimes means: health or sanitation, as in *l'igiene pubblica*, public health. Note *un assorbente igienico*, a sanitary towel, and *la carta igienica*, toilet paper. *Un igienista* may be a dental hygienist but is also a health freak.
———→ INTIMO, SANITÀ

ignorare, v. — to ignore, but also to be unaware of, so *ignorava i rischi* could mean either: he ignored or was not aware of the risks.

ilarità, n.f. — hilarity, but sometimes simply gaiety, cheerfulness or good humour, as in *la loro ilarità è contagiosa*, their cheerfulness is infectious.
———→ ESILARARE

illuminazione, n.f. — illumination, but usually best rendered by lighting, as in *l'illuminazione domestica*, domestic lighting, and *il mercato europeo dell'illuminazione*, the European lighting market. *L'illuminismo*, on the other hand, is the Enlightenment, and *un despota illuminato* is an enlightened despot.
———→ LUCIDO, LUMINOSO

immaturo, adj. — immature, but sometimes there are pitfalls, e.g. *una decisione immatura* may turn out to be a premature decision, and you will want to avoid buying *frutta immatura*, unripe fruit.
———→ MATURO

impervio, adj. — not impervious (variously = *impenetrabile, impermeabile, sordo* or *indifferente*) but impassible or inaccessible. *Un sentiero impervio* is, therefore, an impassible track/path, and *una zona* particolarmente impervia* is a particularly inaccessible area.
———→ INTERROTTO, VIABILITÀ

impetuoso, adj. — impetuous or impulsive of behaviour, but also used of natural phenomena. *Un vento/un torrente impetuoso*, is a raging wind or torrent.

importo, n.m. — is a sum or amount of money, and should not be mistaken for an import = *un'importazione*. *L'importo complessivo* is, therefore, the sum total, and the word *importo* on a petrol pump indicates what you have to pay.
————→ LICENZA

impressionare, v. — rarely to impress (= *colpire favorevolmente* or *fare una buona impressione*). It means, rather: to shock, upset, affect or shake. Compare *lo spettacolo* lo ha impressionato*, he was shocked, (awe)struck by the show (or the show made a strong impression on him), and he was impressed by the show, *lo spettacolo l'ha colpito favorevolmente/gli ha fatto una buona* or *un'ottima impressione*. *Impressione* is impression, but note that *quel film d'orrore fa veramente impressione* means: that horror film is really frightening, while *i serpenti mi fanno impressione* means that snakes disgust me (————→ SENSO) or give me the shivers.
————→ SUSCETTIBILE

inabilità, n.f. — seldom inability (= *l'incapacità*); more often disability or unfitness, as in *l'inabilità al lavoro*, unfitness for work, and *un'inabilità temporanea*, a temporary disability.
————→ ABILITÀ, INVALIDO, MUTILATO

inaccessibile, adj. — inaccessible, but it can also apply to people, in which case it means: indifferent (to) or unmoved (by), e.g. *il re è rimasto inaccessibile alle sue preghiere*, the king was unmoved by his pleas.

inchiesta, n.f. — does mean: inquest (*un'inchiesta guidiziaria in caso di morte improvvisa*, lit. a judicial enquiry in cases of unexpected death) but, more commonly, it is an enquiry, an investigation or a survey. Thus *la polizia/i giudici allarga(no) l'inchiesta*, the police or judges are widening their enquiry, *una commissione* d'inchiesta*, a committee of enquiry, *i politici sotto inchiesta*, (the) politicians under investigation, and *un'inchiesta sulle abitudini alimentari degli Italiani*, a survey into the Italians' eating habits.

incidente, n.m. — as likely to be encountered meaning an accident (————→ ACCIDENTE) as an incident. Thus *un incidente stradale/ferroviario*, a road or rail accident. A diplomatic incident is *un incidente diplomatico*, and the security forces fear incidents may occur is: *le forze dell'ordine temono incidenti*. However, an amusing incident = *un episodio divertente*.

incidenza, n.f. — rarely incidence (= *la frequenza** or *la ricorrenza**) but, rather, impact or effect. Compare *l'incidenza delle malattie cardiache sulla popolazione*, the impact of heart disease on the population, and the incidence of heart disease in the population = *la frequenza/la ricorrenza* delle malattie cardiache nella popolazione*. *Il linguaggio* sportivo ha una rilevante* incidenza sull'uso linguistico italiano* means: sporting language has a significant impact on Italian usage.

incisione, n.f. — an incision, but an etching, engraving or lithograph, as well. *L'incisione di un disco* is the recording of a disc. Writing of the violinist Nigel Kennedy, *La Repubblica* (12/11/91) remarked: *la sua incisione delle 'Quattro Stagioni' di Vivaldi ha venduto un milione di copie nel solo 1989*, his recording of Vivaldi's 'Four Seasons' sold a million copies in 1989 alone.
————→ DISEGNO

incitamento, n.m. — incitement, but can be subtly different. The English term tends to be negative, in which case Italian prefers *l'istigazione* (e.g. incitement to crime = *l'istigazione a delinquere* ⟶ DELINQUENZA, and incitement to hatred and violence = *l'istigazione all'odio e alla violenza*). *L'incitamento* is, therefore, sometimes best translated by incentive or encouragement, as in *un incitamento allo studio**, an incentive to study, and *l'incitamento all'onestà*, encouragement to be honest.

incoerente, adj. — inconsistent not incoherent (an incoherent speech = *un discorso* sconnesso* or *slegato*). *La Repubblica* (28/4/89) quoted the Prime Minister (⟶ PRESIDENTE) as insisting: *Farò dimettere i ministri incoerenti*, I shall force ministers who are inconsistent to resign. *Un arbitro* incoerente* is, therefore, an inconsistent referee.
⟶ COERENTE, CONSISTENTE, INCONSISTENTE

incompetente, adj. — not necessarily incompetent (= *incapace*). It may simply be: not competent or else unqualified (⟶ QUALIFICATO). Thus *sono incompetente in materia di/in fatto di medicina* actually means: I am not qualified or competent to judge in medical matters.
⟶ COMPETENTE

inconsistente, adj. — not inconsistent (= *incoerente**) but flimsy or insubstantial. Compare *un ragionamento inconsistente*, a groundless, flimsy or unfounded argument (⟶ ARGOMENTO), and an inconsistent argument = *un ragionamento incoerente*.
⟶ COERENTE, CONSISTENTE

incremento, n.m. — not a salary increment (= *uno scatto*) but an increase of any kind. *Un sensibile* incremento annuale della produzione* is, therefore, an appreciable annual increase in production.

incriminare, v. — to incriminate but also to charge with a crime, e.g. *la polizia non ha indizi sufficienti per incriminarlo*, the police don't have sufficient evidence to charge him.
⟶ EVIDENZA

indicare, v. — to indicate, point out or show, but it can sometimes be puzzling. *Indicare un buon rimedio per il mal di gola*, e.g., is: to suggest a good remedy for a sore throat; *puoi indicarmi una buona farmacia?* means: can you recommend a good chemist? and *una pentola particolarmente indicata per la cottura del pesce* is a pan particularly suitable for cooking fish. Remember that *un prezzo indicativo* is an approximate (not an indicative = *rivelatore*) price.

indifferentemente, adv. — sometimes an exact equivalent of indifferently, but often means: equally well or without distinction. *Piace indifferentemente a vecchi e giovani* means that it is popular with young and old alike, and *assumere* uomini e donne indifferentemente* is: to employ men and women, without distinction. In such contexts, indifferently = *in modo mediocre*.
⟶ INDISTINTAMENTE

indistintamente, adv. — indistinctly but, confusingly, it can also mean: without distinction, equally well or indiscriminately. Thus *trattava bene tutti i prigionieri, indistintamente*, he treated all the prisoners well, without distinction; *coltivava indistintamente rapporti con il*

governo e la mafia, he nurtured links (———→ RAPPORTO) equally well with the government and the mafia; and *i terroristi colpirono indistintamente militari e civili*, the terrorists struck at soldiers and civilians, indiscriminately.
———→ DISTINTO, INDIFFERENTEMENTE

industria, n.f. — industry, but also an industrial concern. Contrast *l'industria tessile*, the textile industry, and *un'industria tessile*, a textile factory or company.
———→ SOCIETÀ

inferiore, adj. — inferior, but it also retains its basic Latin meaning of lower or lesser, in a numerical or spatial sense. Thus, *il piano inferiore*, the floor below, as opposed to *il piano superiore** which is above, and *la chiesa inferiore di S. Francesco*, the lower Church of St Francis at Assisi. *La scuola media (inferiore)* is junior high school, which all children below 15, *di età inferiore ai 15 anni*, must attend (———→ COMPRENSIVO, FREQUENZA) after primary school, *la scuola elementare**.

inflessibile, adj. — inflexible, but also uncompromising, strict or stringent. It can, therefore, be found in positive contexts, as in the Volkswagen ad. *Perché una Volkswagen sia sempre più sicura, sono necessari collaudi inflessibili*: For a VW to be safer still, uncompromising/ rigorous/stringent checks are required.
———→ CONTROLLARE, STRINGENTE

influsso, n.m. — not influx (= *un afflusso* or *un'affluenza**) but influence. Sicilian cooking shows Arabic influence, *l'influsso arabo*, while many recent borrowings into Italian show the influence of English, *l'influsso dell'inglese*.

informativo, adj. — informative (*un articolo informativo*, an informative article) but not always. *Un servizio informativo*, e.g., is a news or information service. Note, too, that *l'informazione* can be news as well as information. Italian Radio believes that the public has a right to *un'informazione corretta* (———→ CORRETTO), decent, honest or balanced news/reporting, the Veneto paper *Il Gazzettino* claims to give its readers *una informazione completa* (———→ COMPLETO) *ogni giorno*, full news every day, and Reuters is *un'agenzia d'informazioni*, a news agency.

infortunato, adj. — resembles unfortunate (= *sfortunato*) but actually means: injured (———→ INGIURIARE), as when the sports pages refer to *un giocatore infortunato*, an injured player.
———→ LESIONE

ingegnere, n.m. — is an engineer but only if he or she has a degree from an engineering faculty (*una facoltà d'ingegneria*). Thus *un ingegnere civile/elettronico*, a civil or electronics engineer. Definitely not an engineer of the type who repairs T.V. sets or telephones (= *un tecnico*). The Royal Engineers/U.S. Army Engineers = *il Genio* (———→ SPECIALITÀ). Note that *ingegnere* is commonly used as a title before the surname, in both writing and speech, as in *buongiorno Ingegner Agnelli!* Hello Mr A.; other qualifications frequently used as titles are *architetto* (architect), *ragioniere* (accountant), *geometra* (surveyor), and, of course, *dottore** (doctor, but also any graduate ———→ GRADUATO).

ingenuità, n.f. — means: ingenuousness or naivety, not ingenuity (= *l'ingegnosità*), so that *l'ingenuità degli scienziati* is the scientists' naivety.

ingiuriare, v. — remember that *ingiuriare qualcuno* is: to insult or shout abuse at someone, whereas to injure (them) = *ferire*. *Un'ingiuria* is, therefore, not an injury (= *una ferita*) but an insult, an affront (⟶ AFFRONTARE) or verbal abuse, as in the headline about the film director Lina Wertmuller: *processata* (⟶ PROCESSO) *per ingiurie a un bimbo**, put on trial for insulting a child.
⟶ INFORTUNATO, LESIONE

inibizione, n.f. — is inhibition, but it can also be a legal ban or suspension. Do not be surprised if, during a sporting scandal, you come across a headline like *Tre anni di inibizione per illecito sportivo*, Three-year suspension for sporting irregularities.

inserzione, n.f. — insertion, but a newspaper advertisement, too, e.g. *pubblicare* or *mettere un'inserzione sul giornale*, to place an ad. in the paper.
⟶ PUBBLICITÀ, STAMPA

insistere, v. — to insist, of course (*va bene, se insisti*, all right, if you insist; *insiste che è innocente*, he insists he is innocent), but also to persist. *Insiste a chiedere i suoi soldi*, he persists in asking for his money, is, therefore, different from he insists on asking for his money = *ci tiene assolutamente a chiedere i suoi soldi*, and the exasperated *non insistere!* means: don't go on! This explains why *una pioggia insistente* is persistent rain (⟶ PERSISTENTE) and *l'insistenza del maltempo* is the persistence of (the) bad weather.

insufficiente, adj. — insufficient or inadequate, but in schools it is used for fail, below average or unsatisfactory marks. Work which just passes, makes the grade, or is satisfactory receives the comment: *sufficiente* (⟶ SUFFICIENZA).
⟶ DISCRETO, VOTO

integrale, adj. — is seldom integral (it is an integral part of our plans = *è parte integrante dei nostri progetti*). Usually it means: complete, so that *un'edizione integrale*, of a book, is an unabridged edition, *un film in versione integrale* is an uncut version of a film, and *un integralista* is a (religious) fundamentalist. Of food, though, it means: wholemeal. Italy only began to acquire a preoccupation (⟶ PREOCCUPATO) with healthy eating, *il mangiare sano**, in the 1970s and especially in the 1980s, and to meet the demands (⟶ DOMANDARE) of vegetarians, *i vegetariani*, and vegans, *i vegetaliani*, for organically-grown food, *il cibo biologico**. Wholemeal spaghetti, *gli spaghetti integrali*, was therefore available in Britain, at least, when it was still unknown in Naples. Italy was slower to react to the trend because of its unbroken tradition of wholesome home cooking (⟶ GENUINO), and a relative absence of junk or fast food, *il trash/fast food*, and perhaps because of a more indifferent attitude to nature. While recent evidence points to the virtues of the traditional Mediterranean diet (⟶ DIETA), Anglo-Saxon healthy eating has made its mark. Vegetarian restaurants are to be found, and stores are full of *il pane integrale, la pasta* integrale, la farina integrale, il riso integrale* and *i biscotti integrali*, wholemeal (or brown) bread, pasta, flour, rice and biscuits.

integrare, v. — to integrate, but also to supplement or bring up to strength. The statement: *gli studenti inglesi sono costretti a prendere un prestito dal governo per integrare la borsa di studio* therefore means that British students are obliged to take out a government loan to supplement their grant. Similarly, *una pensione* integrativa* is an occupational pension (so called because it supplements the state pension), and *l'integrazione*, as well as integration, is (a) supplement: the Banca Nazionale del Lavoro offers customers *un'interessante* integrazione della liquidazione* o della pensione*, a financially-attractive way of supplementing your severance pay/golden handshake or your pension. *Essere messo in cassa integrazione* is: to be laid off or made redundant — *la cassa integrazione* is Italy's generous wage-related unemployment scheme for employees of large companies, paying out over 70% of final salary to those temporarily laid off, or to the longer-term unemployed (———→ DIPENDENTE, LICENZA, OCCUPAZIONE).

intelligenza, n.f. — usually intelligence but, occasionally, comprehension, as in *le note sono essenziali per l'intelligenza del testo*, (the) footnotes are essential for understanding the text.

intendere, v. — can be: to intend or mean, as in *uno sbaglio che non intende perdonare*, a mistake he does not intend to forgive, or *cosa intendi con questo?* what do you mean by that? However, it can mean: to understand (*ecco come l'intendo io*, this is how I understand it) or, perhaps more confusingly, to consider, see or view: Martin Dawes describe one of their mobile 'phones as *il portatile ideale* per i professionisti e le aziende che intendono il telefono come uno strumento di lavoro davvero completo**, the ideal portable 'phone for professionals and companies who see or view the telephone as an all-round work tool. Note the reflexive form; if someone says *non m'intendo*, it means: I'm no expert/I'm no judge.

interessante, adj. — interesting but, as in French, the Italian term has also come to mean: financially attractive or advantageous. This explains why ads. for second-hand cars in Italy invariably boast the expression *prezzo interessantissimo*, a give-away price. Quaintly, a woman described as *in stato interessante* is expecting a baby.
———→ CONVENIENTE, INTERESSARE, LIQUIDAZIONE, OCCASIONE

interessare, v. — to interest but also, confusingly, to concern or affect. *Una misura governativa che interessa tutti gli italiani* could, therefore, be a government measure which interests or (more likely) which affects all Italians. In a news bulletin or weather forecast, *la zona* interessata* is the affected area.
———→ INTERESSANTE

intermezzo, n.m. — a musical intermezzo, but also an interval or break at the opera, concert-hall, theatre or cinema.
———→ LIRICO, OPERA

intermittente, adj. — intermittent, but *una luce/un'insegna intermittente* is a flashing light/sign.
———→ ILLUMINAZIONE, LUMINOSO

interpretare, v. — to interpret, whether of facts, behaviour, language or the performing arts, although in the case of the latter there is sometimes a subtle difference. *Maria Callas interpretava spesso la Tosca di Puccini* is likely to mean: M.C. often played/sang the role of Tosca, *C'eravamo tanto amati di Ettore Scola, interpretato da Nino Manfredi e Vittorio Gossman*, is the film *C'eravamo tanto amati* [1981] ['We Were Once So Close'] by E. Scola,

with or starring N.M. and V.G., and *Clint Eastwood interpreta Dirty Harry* is simply: C.E. plays Dirty Harry. *Un interprete* is, therefore, an actor/actress, a singer or a performer as often as it is an interpreter.
———→ MELODRAMMA, PROTAGONISTA, RECITARE

interrogazione, n.f. — is simply questioning rather than interrogation (= *l'interrogatorio*, which is also questioning). Note, in particular, that *un'interrogazione parlamentare* is a parliamentary question, and that, in schools, *l'interrogazione* is an oral class-test: these are held regularly in all subjects and reveal the importance of the oral examination, *l'esame orale*, at every level of Italian education (———→ EDUCAZIONE). *Interrogare* is either to interrogate or to question, so that *abbiamo interrogato 100 casalinghe per l'inchiesta** means: we questioned 100 housewives for the survey.
———→ AUDIZIONE, DOMANDARE

interrotto, adj. — interrupted, but sometimes blocked, cut off or impracticable, as in the sign or headline: *strada interrotta dalla neve/dai lavori in corso*, road blocked by snow/by road works.
———→ IMPERVIO, VIABILITÀ

intervento, n.m. — is sometimes a straightforward equivalent of intervention (as in *l'intervento armato*, armed intervention), but it can be tricky. While *l'intervento del ministro*, e.g., may be the minister's intervention, it is also, according to context, his presence, participation or even his press article, speech or statement (———→ DISCORSO). Of an academic conference it is a paper. On the other hand, when Olivetti claim to make *3.000.000 di interventi annui nel mondo* they are referring to the 3 million call-outs they make to clients, world-wide, every year (———→ ASSISTENZA). In medicine, *un intervento* is an operation.

intimo, adj. — intimate, but it can pose problems. Sometimes it means: deep, as in *l'intima struttura dell'atomo*, the deep or inner structure of the atom, and *l'intimo significato di una poesia*, the deep or inner meaning of a poem. At other times it means: personal or private, so beware of *le parti intime*, private parts, *l'igiene* intima*, personal hygiene, and *la biancheria intima*, underwear (———→ SLIP). In a department store, the sign *lingerie — intimo uomo* indicates the lingerie and men's underwear counters. *L'intimità* is intimacy, in all senses, but it can be privacy, e.g. *nell'intimità della propria casa*, in the privacy of one's own home (———→ PROPRIO).

intossicazione, n.f. — if someone complains that they are suffering from the effects of *un' intossicazione*, do not get the wrong idea. It is food poisoning that is involved. Intoxication = *l'ebbrezza* or *l'ubriachezza* (———→ ASTEMIO). Similarly, *intossicare* is not to intoxicate (= *ubriacare* or *inebriare*) but to poison with bad food (*è stato intossicato da cibo avariato*, he was poisoned by food which was off), or even with chemicals (*operai intossicati dal fumo nocivo*, workers poisoned by harmful fumes). Sometimes used figuratively, too, as in *il clima dei negoziati è sempre più intossicato*, the climate of the negotiations is becoming increasingly poisoned.
———→ COSTIPAZIONE

intricato, adj. — confused, tangled or involved, but — unlike intricate — is never positive. Compare *negoziati intricati*, muddled, confused or tangled negotiations, and intricate

negotiations = *negoziati complessi e delicati/dettagliati*. An intricate motif, mechanism or style = *un motivo*/un meccanismo/uno stile complesso (e minuzioso)*.
———→ CONFUSIONE

intrigante, adj. — not intriguing (= *affascinante**) but meddlesome, interfering or scheming, so that *una persona intrigante* is definitely to be avoided.
———→ INTRIGO

intrigo, n.m. — does not always correspond to intrigue or plot. It can also be a messy business or confused/involved situation, so that *gli ho detto di non cacciarsi in quegli intrighi* means: I told him not to get mixed up in that messy business.
———→ CONFUSIONE, INTRIGANTE, PASTICCIO

invalido, n.m. and adj. — is not quite the same as (an) invalid (= *(un) infermo*). Instead it means: disabled. Thus *un invalido di guerra* is someone disabled in the war, and *un invalido del lavoro* has had to retire because of injuries sustained at work. On public transport, seats *riservati agli invalidi* are reserved for the disabled.
———→ INABILITÀ, MUTILATO

investire, v. — to invest, in all senses, but it can appear in the strangest contexts. On the weather forecast, *un'ondata di caldo ha investito l'Italia*, means: a heat-wave has struck/enveloped Italy, and on the news, *i pedoni sono stati investiti dalla corriera* is: the pedestrians were struck or run over by the coach. The statement *la riforma ... Deve investire lo Stato nel suo complesso* (*La Repubblica*, 10/7/93) means that the reforms must shake up/radically affect the state as a whole.

invidioso, adj. — shares the same root as invidious but only retains the original sense of envious. *Una scelta invidiosa* is, therefore, an envious choice, whereas an invidious choice = *una scelta antipatica* (———→ SIMPATIA) or *ingiusta*. An invidious comparison = *un paragone* odioso, antipatico* or *ingiusto*.

ipotesi, n.f. — occasionally a hypothesis (Avogadro's hypothesis is *l'ipotesi di Avogadro*). Usually best translated, though, by assumption, supposition, conjecture, suggestion, notion, idea, theory or even possibility. *Un'ipotesi sbagliata*, e.g., is a mistaken assumption, *respingere l'ipotesi di una nuova costituzione* is: to reject the idea or suggestion of a new constitution, *l'ipotesi più attendibile* is the most credible theory, and *le ipotesi sul tappeto sono due* means: there are two possibilities up for discussion. Note the expression: *nella peggior delle ipotesi*, if the worst comes to the worst.

irregolare, adj. — mostly corresponds to irregular, but sometimes means: unlawful. *Lavoratori stranieri irregolari*, e.g., are illegal immigrant workers (whose papers are not in order, *in regola*). They became a social problem in Italy in the 1990s with the sudden influx of third-world immigrants, *l'afflusso di extracomunitari* (———→ INFLUSSO).
———→ ABUSIVO

irrilevante, adj. — do not be tempted to translate it as irrelevant. It means: insignificant or negligible. Compare *un particolare irrilevante*, an insignificant detail, and an irrelevant detail = *un particolare che è fuor di proposito*. Again, *un argomento* irrilevante* is an unimportant topic or issue, whereas an irrelevant argument = *un ragionamento* or

un'argomentazione non pertinente. *Una somma/un contributo irrilevante* is a negligible sum of money/contribution.
————→ RILEVANTE

iscrizione, n.f. — inscription or inscribing, but most commonly means: enrolment in or joining an organisation. Thus *l'iscrizione all'università* is registering or matriculating at university: this involves paying the registration fee, *la tassa d'iscrizione*, which, until the 1990s, had remained very low (between £50 and £100/U.S. $75 and $150 per annum). The slogan *Sostieni il WWF con la tua iscrizione* means: Support the W.W.F. by joining/ becoming a member.
————→ DOMANDARE

isolare, v. — can be to insulate as well as to isolate, so that *una casa isolata*, an isolated/ insulated house, is potentially ambiguous. Note, too, that while *una zona* isolata* is an isolated area, *la zona è stata subito isolata* (*La Nuova Venezia*, 28/7/93) means: the area was immediately cordoned off. *L'isolamento della casa* is, therefore, both the isolation and insulation of the house. Do not be tempted to use *l'insolazione* as it means: sunstroke.

istituto, n.m. — can correspond to institute (e.g. *l'Istituto italiano di cultura*, the Italian Cultural Institute, which promotes Italy's cultural interests abroad) or institution (*un istituto d'istruzione superiore**, a higher or further education institution ————→ COLLEGIO, EDUCAZIONE). Its range is wider, though. It is used as a general term for all types of school or college, as in *istituti in sciopero* (————→ AGITAZIONE), schools/colleges on strike, and in universities it is simply a department, so that the statement *lunedì non vengo in istituto* is likely to mean: I'm not coming into the department on Monday. Note *un istituto di bellezza*, a beauty parlour (————→ ESTETICA). *Istituzionale* is institutional, but at university *un corso istituzionale* is a foundation course.

L

laborioso, adj. — can be laborious (e.g. *un parto laborioso*, a long and difficult birth, or *un'indagine laboriosa*, a laborious investigation), but it often means: hard-working. The propaganda (———→ PROPAGANDA) of the Lega Nord (the Northern League party which emerged strongly in the 1990s) characterises the inhabitants of Northern Italy as *gente laboriosa*, hard-working people. A laborious style = *uno stile pesante* (———→ FACILE).

languido, adj. — often corresponds to languid or languorous, but occasionally it simply means: listless, faint, exhausted or drained, as in *La mattina mi svegliai tutto languido e dolente* (Moravia, *Il Disprezzo*, 1953 ['Scorn']), In the morning I woke up all limp and aching.

largo, adj. — never confuse with large (variously = *grande, grosso*, ampio, vasto* or *numeroso*). It means: wide or broad, as in *una strada larga*, a wide street, and *un fiume largo*, a broad river (———→ RIVIERA). *Un vestito largo* is a loose (fitting) or full dress.

lesione, n.f. — a medical lesion, but also used for injury in a legal sense, as in *lesioni personali gravi*, grievous bodily harm. More surprisingly, it is a crack in a building, so that *le lesioni nella cupola del Brunelleschi possono essere l'effetto dell'assedio del traffico* (*La Repubblica*, 21/4/92) means that the cracks in Brunelleschi's dome (———→ DUOMO) may be due to the effects of the pounding from traffic (———→ CIRCOLAZIONE).
———→ INFORTUNATO, INGIURIARE

lettura, n.f. — not a lecture (= *una conferenza** or *una lezione**) but a reading (the original meaning of lecture), as in Luigi Russo's *Letture Critiche del Decameron* (1956) ['Critical Readings on the *Decameron*'].

lezione, n.f. — lesson in all contexts, but also used for university or college lectures, e.g. *Devo partire: ho lezione alle 11*, I've got to go: I've got a lecture at 11 o'clock.
———→ AUDITORE, CONFERENZA, DISERTARE, FREQUENTARE, LETTURA

liberty, n.m. and adj. — not liberty, of course (= *la libertà*), but art nouveau, *lo stile liberty*, as in *i rari edifici* (———→ EDIFICIO) *liberty di Charles Rennie Mackintosh*, the few art nouveau buildings by C.R.M. From Sir Arthur Liberty's well-known London Liberty stores of the 1890s. Oddly, while Italian uses an English term, English uses a French one, and French uses an English one, *le Modern Style*.

libreria, n.f. — avoid the understandable temptation to associate this with library. They have the book (*il libro*) in common, but *una libreria* is a bookshop (or bookcase), whereas a library = *una biblioteca*.
———→ AUTORE, EDITORE

libretto, n.m. — an operatic libretto (———→ LIRICO, MELODRAMMA, OPERA) but, more commonly, simply a booklet or small book. In *La Lettera all'Alvarotto* (1536) ['Letter to Alvarotto'], the great comic playwright Ruzante began his quest for eternal life by consulting his *compagni libretti*, his little companion books. *Un libretto degli assegni* is a cheque book/U.S. checkbook, *un libretto di risparmio* is a savings (account) book (———→

ACCONTO), and *un libretto delle istruzioni* is an instructions booklet. *Il libretto universitario* is the students' record book/U.S. transcripts in Italy, containing details of courses attended (⟶ FREQUENTARE) and exams taken (⟶ VOTO).

licenza, n.f. — handle with care. *Una licenza* may be a licence/U.S. license, e.g. *una licenza di caccia/di pesca/di porto d'armi/di fabbricazione**, a hunting, fishing, gun or building licence. However, a driving/U.S. driver's licence = *la patente** (*di guida*) ⟶ GUIDARE), the T.V. licence = *il canone (d'abbonamente alla T.V.)*, and an import licence = *un permesso d'importazione* (⟶ IMPORTO). More problematically, it is also military leave (*essere in licenza*, to be on leave) and a school diploma or certificate (as in *la licenza elementare**, the primary school leaving certificate). *Licenziare*, far from meaning: to license (= *autorizzare, permettere* or *accordare una licenza a*), is actually to dismiss, sack or fire from work (⟶ AGITAZIONE, ASSUMERE, DIPENDENTE, OCCUPAZIONE).

linguaggio, n.m. — language, but remember that Italian has two words for this concept. *La lingua* is invariably used for national languages, as in *la lingua italiana*, the Italian language, *parlare in lingua*, to speak in Italian (rather than in dialect, *il dialetto*), and *la lingua scritta/parlata*, the written or spoken language. Otherwise opt for *il linguaggio*, e.g. *il linguaggio degli umani/degli uccelli*, human/bird language, *il linguaggio mimico*, sign language, *il linguaggio giornalistico/politico/burocratico*, journalistic, political or bureaucratic language, and *il linguaggio di Dante*, D.'s language. Standard Italian, *l'italiano standard*, exists for the written language but is problematic to define for the spoken language. A more realistic description is *l'italiano regionale*, a form of Italian with a regional colouring in vocabulary and accent used by most speakers in this strongly regional peninsula. As dialect-speaking declines in most of the country, some of its features survive by leaving an indelible mark on regional Italian.
⟶ IDIOMA, VOCABOLARIO

liquidazione, n.f. — only means: liquidation when the winding up of a company (⟶ SOCIETÀ) is involved, e.g. *andare in liquidazione*, to go into liquidation. It can also be payment or settlement, as in *la liquidazione d'un conto/un debito**, settlement or payment of an account (⟶ ACCONTO) or debt. Perhaps most likely to be encountered, though, meaning severance pay, retirement bonus or golden handshake, e.g. *riscuotere la liquidazione*, to receive one's severance pay (⟶ INTEGRARE), or else on shop-window signs like *liquidazione di fine stagione*, end-of-season clearance sale/U.S. closing out, or *prezzi di liquidazione*, knock-down prices (⟶ CONVENIENTE, INTERESSANTE).
⟶ OCCASIONE

lirico, adj. — is sometimes lyric or lyrical (e.g. *la poesia lirica*, lyric poetry, and *uno slancio lirico*, a lyrical outburst), but can also mean: operatic. *Luciano Pavarotti è un noto* (⟶ NOTORIETÀ) *cantante lirico* therefore means that L.P. is a well-known opera singer, La Scala is *un teatro lirico* (⟶ PROSA), an opera house, and opera itself is *l'opera* lirica*. The lyrics of a song = *le parole*.
⟶ INTERMEZZO

litigare, v. — to quarrel, argue or fight, but rarely with the legal connotations of to litigate (= *essere in causa* or *in lite*). Thus *i protagonisti di 'Chi ha paura di Virginia Woolf?'*

litigano senza tregua, the main characters (⎯⎯⎯→ PERSONAGGIO, PROTAGONISTA) of 'Who's Afraid of V.W.?' argue incessantly.
⎯⎯⎯→ ARGOMENTO, DISCUSSIONE

lucido, adj. — is occasionally lucid (*una mente lucida*, a lucid mind), and sometimes clear (*una spiegazione lucida*, a clear explanation). Often, though, it keeps its etymological sense of bright, gleaming or shiny, as in *i capelli lucidi*, shiny hair, *le scarpe lucide*, polished shoes, *il pelo lucido*, glossy coat (of animals), *un pavimento* lucido*, a gleaming floor, and *gli occhi lucidi*, bright or shiny eyes.
⎯⎯⎯→ BRILLANTE, LUMINOSO, SCINTILLANTE

luminoso, adj. — do not assume that it is always: luminous. *Una stella luminosa* is a shining star, *una giornata luminosa* is a clear, bright day, *un'idea luminosa* is a bright idea (Greenpeace describe their energy-saving lightbulb as *un'idea luminosa per accendere di speranza il nostro futuro*, a bright idea to light up our future with hope), *un'insegna luminosa* is an illuminated sign, and *un aspetto/uno sguardo luminoso* is a radiant look. Of interiors, it means: light-filled, well-lit, bright or sunny, as when Velux promise to *trasformare il Vostro vecchio sottotetto in un ambiente luminoso e invitante*, convert your old attic (⎯⎯⎯→ ATTICO) or loft into a light-filled and inviting environment. Student notice-boards will carry ads. for *appartamenti luminosi*, sunny or light-filled flats/U.S. apartments.
⎯⎯⎯→ ILLUMINAZIONE, LUCIDO, SCINTILLANTE

lunatico, n.m. and adj. — not (a) lunatic but cranky, moody, erratic or changeable. *Una persona lunatica* or *un lunatico*, a changeable person, is decidedly not the same as a lunatic = *un pazzo, un matto* or, more medically, *un alienato* or *una persona mentalmente inferma*. Lunatic behaviour = *un comportamento pazzo/da pazzi, scemo* or *idiota*, a lunatic asylum = *un manicomio* (⎯⎯⎯→ ASILO), and a lunatic fringe = *una frangia estremista*. Lunatic and *lunatico* have the moon, *la luna*, in common.
⎯⎯⎯→ MANIACO

lurido, adj. — looks like lurid but means very dirty or filthy, both literally and figuratively. Thus *avere le mani luride*, to have filthy hands, *un individuo lurido*, a disgusting or foul individual, and *una faccenda lurida*, a filthy business. On the other hand, a lurid sky = *un cielo spettrale*, and the lurid details of the article = *i particolari scandalosi/sensazionali dell'articolo*.

lussuria, n.f. — should not be confused with luxury (= *il lusso*). It actually means lust, as in *Non fu la lussuria a spingere Enrico VIII a cambiare per sei volte moglie* (*La Repubblica*, 15/12/93), It was not lust which moved Henry VIII to change wives six times. Aretino's *Sonetti lussuriosi* (c. 1525) are, therefore, his lustful or bawdy sonnets.
⎯⎯⎯→ VIZIOSO

M

macchina, n.f. — a machine, but remember that it is also a car, that *una macchina fotografica* is a camera, and that *una macchina da scrivere* is a typewriter.

maestro, n.m. — a maestro (except in sport, where you would tend to use *un fuoriclasse*) but also, more broadly, a master. Used, above all, of primary/U.S. elementary school teachers. Since most of the latter are women, the commoner form is *la maestra*. *Maestri/e* receive their teacher-training (———→ ABILITÀ, FORMAZIONE) while still at secondary school, in a special branch of senior high school (———→ SUPERIORE) called *l'istituto* magistrale* or, in everyday parlance, *le magistrali*. To qualify, they must take a competitive examination, *il concorso magistrale*. Italian children have traditionally kept the same teacher throughout their primary schooling. Note that *un master* is an M.A. or Master's degree.
———→ PROFESSORE, PUPILLO, SCOLARO

maggiore, adj. — is not always major. *Una somma maggiore*, e.g., is a greater sum, whereas a major sum = *una somma importantissima* or *molto cospicua* (———→ COSPICUO). The poet Eugenio Montale described Italo Svevo as *il maggior romanziere che l'Italia abbia dato dai tempi di Verga ad oggi*, the greatest novelist (———→ ROMANZO) Italy has produced since V. A major novelist, on the other hand = *un romanziere di prim'ordine*. *Il mio fratello maggiore* is: my older or elder brother, *per maggiori informazioni* means: for further information or details (———→ INFORMATIVO, ULTERIORE), and *una moda che va per la maggiore* is a fashion which is all the rage (———→ FURORE).
———→ MINIMO

magistrato, n.m.— is easily confusable with a magistrate (= *un pretore*) but is in fact a judge (also *un giudice*) or member of the judiciary (*la magistratura*). Italian judges are career civil servants (———→ AMMINISTRAZIONE), and Italy has a plural bench system with three *magistrati* sitting in judgement (———→ PROCESSO, TRIBUNALE).
———→ CONCILIATORE, MANDATO

malizia, n.f. — occasionally the equivalent of malice (more commonly = *la cattiveria, la malevolenza, l'animosità, la malignità* or *la malvagità*) but usually means: mischief or else cunning or guile. *Parole piene di malizia* are, therefore, likely to be very mischievous or artful/cunning words, whereas words full of malice = *parole piene di animosità* or *di malignità*. *Uno sguardo pieno di malizia* is a look which is roguish, or full of mischief/ devilment, but *le malizie del mestiere* are the tricks of the trade. It follows that *un bambino malizioso* is much more likely to be a mischievous, roguish, artful or 'fly' child than a malicious one (= *un bambino malvagio, maligno* or *che ha cattive intenzioni*). A malicious crime = *un delitto doloso*.

mandato, n.m. — a mandate, but watch out for it in legal contexts where *un mandato di comparizione* is a summons, *un mandato di perquisizione/estradizione* is a search/ extradition warrant, and *un mandato d'arresto* is a warrant for someone's arrest.
———→ MAGISTRATO, PROCESSO, TRIBUNALE

maneggiare, v. — does not mean: to manage. To manage a company = *gestire, amministrare* or *dirigere un'azienda* (————→ AMMINISTRAZIONE, DIRETTORE, SOCIETÀ); I managed to do it = *sono riuscito a farlo*; and are you managing? = *ti arrangi?* (————→ ARRANGIARE) or *ce la fai? Maneggiare*, on the other hand, is: to handle. *Un dizionario troppo pesante e difficile da maneggiare* is, therefore, a dictionary that is too heavy and hard to handle, *maneggiare con cura* (————→ CURARE) is: handle with care, *maneggiare le armi* is: to handle or wield weapons, and *la capacità di maneggiare l'italiano* means: the ability (————→ ABILITÀ) to handle Italian.

maniaco, n.m. — can be a maniac (more usually = *un pazzo* or *un matto*), e.g. *un maniaco sessuale*, a sex maniac. Usually applied to someone obsessively keen on or finicky (————→ FASTIDIOSO) about something, or who is too much of a perfectionist. Thus *un maniaco della pulizia/dell'ordine*, a cleanliness or tidiness freak, and *un maniaco del calcio*, a football fanatic. The shoe manufacturers Campanile claim in their ads.: *Siamo più maniaci di voi*, We're more obsessively fussy or perfectionist than you are.
————→ LUNATICO

manifestazione, n.f. — may be a manifestation or display, but not always. On the one hand, it can be a cultural event, as in *un programma di manifestazioni per commemorare Cristoforo Colombo*, a programme (————→ PROGRAMMARE) of events to commemorate Columbus. On the other hand, it is sometimes a political demonstration, *una manifestazione politica*. The late 1960s and the 1970s was a period marked by demonstrations and youth protest (*la contestazione giovanile**) in Italy. Student revolts, trade union activism (————→ MILITANTE, SINDACATO), the emergence of feminism, as well as terrorism of left and right, led to marches in the streets, *cortei in piazza*.
————→ POLITICA

manifesto, n.m. — is particularly confusing. It can be a manifesto, either artistic (as in Marinetti's Futurist Manifesto, *il Manifesto futurista*, of 1909) or political (*il Manifesto del Partito Comunista*, the Communist Manifesto, of 1848). However, it also means a bill (*attaccare* un manifesto*, to post up a bill) or else a poster. *Un manifesto elettorale* or *democristiano* may, therefore, mean: an election/Christian Democrat poster or manifesto. To avoid ambiguity, use *un programma elettorale/democristiano* (————→ PROGRAMMARE) for an election or Christian Democrat manifesto. Italian political posters, of sophisticated design (————→ DISEGNO, SOFISTICATO) and lavishly produced, play a larger part in elections than they do in Britain and the U.S. At election times parties are provided with billboards (*i tabelloni*) in town centres to display their graphic propaganda (————→ PROPAGANDA).
————→ VOTO

manipolato, adj. — manipulated but, surprisingly, *un vino/un cibo manipolato* is an adulterated wine/food.
————→ ALTERARE, SOFISTICATO

manovra, n.f. — manoeuvre, but you will often encounter it in the media meaning: budget or economic measures. Typical are: *pronta la manovra su casa, benzina e sanità** (*La Repubblica*, 3/2/92), the new economic measures on housing, petrol/U.S. gas, and health are ready, *agitazioni in atto in tutta Italia contro la manovra economica del governo* (*La Repubblica*, 11/10/92), industrial action (————→ AGITAZIONE) nationwide to protest

against the government's budget, and *La manovra non si tocca* (*La Repubblica*, 22/9/92), Hands off the budget proposals! Italy's annual budget, also called *la (legge) finanziaria*, is usually presented to Parliament at the end of September.
———→ PACCHETTO

mansione, n.f. — not a mansion (= *una casa/residenza signorile*) but, surprisingly, a duty, as in *le mansioni del direttore**, the manager's duties, and *le mansioni didattiche del nuovo professore**, the new teacher's duties (———→ DIDATTICO). These are genuine cognates, but Italian has undergone an even more radical semantic shift, here, than English from the original meaning of stopping-off place.

maresciallo, n.m. — does not correspond to the rank of marshal in the army or air force (= *l'ufficiale* generale comandante*). It is a warrant officer in the army, a chief petty officer in the navy, or a sergeant in the *carabinieri*.
———→ BRIGADIERE, MASSACRARE, MONTGOMERY

marina, n.f. — is not a marina (= *un porticciolo*) but a coast(line), shore or seaboard, as when Francesca in Dante's *Inferno* V (98) says that she was born on *la terra ... sulla marina dove 'l Po discende*, the land ... on the shore where the Po flows out. Also means: the navy.
———→ COSTA, RIVIERA

marmellata, n.f. — is not necessarily marmalade (which is uncommon in Italy). It is any kind of jam, as in *la marmellata di albicocche/ciliegie*, apricot or cherry jam.
———→ MOSTARDA, VASO

marrone, adj. — is brown or chestnut, not maroon (= *marrone rossiccio*), so *una giacca marron(e)* is a brown jacket. Translating brown can be tricky in Italian. For garments or objects, stick to *marron(e)*. For eyes, both *marron(e)* and *castano* can be used. For hair, choose *castano* or *bruno*, while for skin or complexion, *scuro, bruno* and *moro* are best. Brown rice, on the other hand = *il riso integrale**, and brown sugar = *lo zucchero greggio*.

massacrare, v. — to massacre, but not necessarily. Sometimes to murder, slay or gun down are more appropriate, especially as it can equally well apply to individuals. The headline *Massacrato ad Agrigento maresciallo* anti-Piovra* (*La Repubblica*, 5–6/4/92) means: anti-Mafia sergeant slain at Agrigento.

materiale, n.m. — material (*il materiale per un articolo*, the material for an article) or materials (*il materiale da costruzione*, building materials). However, it is never fabric material (= *il tessuto* or *la stoffa**).
———→ MORBIDO

matrimonio, n.m. — the wedding (ceremony) itself as well as marriage or matrimony. The Italian state, unlike the French, recognises the church wedding, *il matrimonio religioso*, on its own as legal. The registry-office ceremony (*il matrimonio civile*) accounted for around 15%–20% of weddings in the 1990s. Divorce became legal in Italy following the law of

1970 and the historic confirmation by referendum in 1974. *Un letto matrimoniale* is simply a double bed.
———→ CELIBE, CONFETTI, NUBILE

maturo, adj. — mature, but has two surprising further meanings. On the one hand, it is ripe, of fruit (*compro l'uva quand'è matura e dolce*, I buy grapes when they're ripe and sweet). On the other, it describes a senior high school student who has passed the final leaving certificate examination, *la maturità*. This is a broadly-based exam like the French *baccalauréat*, is taken in a number of specialist schools (*il liceo classico*, scientifico, linguistico, musicale* or *artistico*) and confers the right to automatic university entrance.
———→ GINNASIO, PROFESSORE, SUPERIORE

medicazione, n.f. — can be medication in the case of treatment but not of medicines (= *i medicinali*). Also a dressing, as in *medicazioni adesive per ferite*, adhesive wound dressings.
———→ CURARE, DROGA

melodramma, n.m. — melodrama, but it also retains its original meaning of opera (i.e. music drama), as in *Muti è un interprete* (———→ INTERPRETARE) *straordinario* del melodramma, di Verdi in particolare* (*La Repubblica*, 3–4/10/93), Riccardo Muti is an extraordinary conductor (or interpreter) of opera, and of V. in particular. The melodramatic plots of most operas have spawned the figurative sense.
———→ DRAMMA, OPERA, OPERETTA, LIRICO

memoriale, n.m. — looks like memorial but means memoirs. One of the first and most important *memoriali* in Italian is Benvenuto Cellini's *Vita* (1558–66) ['Autobiography']. A war memorial = *un monumento* ai caduti*, and a memorial plaque = *una targa/lapide commemorativa*.

milionario, n.m. — do not be tempted to use this now out-of-date term for someone who is very rich or a millionaire = *un miliardario*. Given lira inflation, *un milione* is nowadays a relatively small sum.

militante, n.m. and adj. — rarely has the negative connotations of militant (= *(un) estremista*) so is often best rendered by activist, e.g. *i militanti di un partito politico*, party activists.
———→ AGITAZIONE, MANIFESTAZIONE

minimo, adj. — minimum (or minimal) is not always the right rendering. *Non ha il minimo dubbio*, e.g., is: he has not the slightest doubt, *non ho la minima intenzione d'andarci* means: I haven't the slightest intention of going, *un prezzo minimo* can be a very low price, and *tutti i minimi particolari* is: every last detail. Similarly, while its opposite, *massimo*, is maximum it can also be greatest or major, as in the title of Galileo's fundamental work *I due massimi sistemi del mondo* (1632) ['The Two Major World Systems'].
———→ MAGGIORE

miseria, n.f. — hardly ever means: misery in the sense of great unhappiness (= *la sofferenza, il tormento* or *l'infelicità*). *Vivere nella miseria* is: to live in dire poverty, indigence (or misery), and when Silone wrote of the villagers of *Fontamara* (1930) living in *la solita miseria: la miseria ricevuta dai padri che l'avevano ereditata dai nonni*, he meant:

the same old poverty: the poverty handed down from the fathers who had inherited it from their fathers (⎯⎯⎯→ EREDITÀ). If someone's salary is described as *una miseria*, then it is a pittance.

miss, n.f. — has not usurped *signorina*. It is, instead, a beauty-queen and is taken from titles like *Miss Italia*. Italian has no equivalent of Ms.
⎯⎯⎯→ ESTETICA

mistura, n.f. — is indeed a mixture but in the pejorative sense of a concoction, e.g. *un cocktail mal preparato* è una mistura*, a badly-prepared cocktail is a disgusting brew. During the Falklands conflict in the 1980s some Italian journalists were convinced that the British despised *quella mistura di Spagnoli e d'Italiani che è l'Argentina*, that hotch-potch of Spaniards and Italians who make up Argentina. Neutral words for mixture = *una miscela* (for liquids), *un misto* (for foods) and, generally, *un miscuglio* or *una mescolanza*.

mitico, adj. — mythical, but frequently it means legendary. Typical are *i mitici anni sessanti*, the legendary sixties, and the Waterman ad: *Un nome mitico che simboleggia uno dei più grandi successi della storia della penna*, A legendary name symbolising one of the greatest success-stories in the history of the pen.

mobile, adj. — mobile, moving or movable, but of character (⎯⎯⎯→ CARATTERE) it means either: quick (*un ingegno mobile*, a quick or lively mind ⎯⎯⎯→ VIVACE) or inconstant/fickle, as in the aria *La donna è mobile, qual piuma al vento*, Woman is as inconstant as a feather in the wind, from Act III of Verdi's *Rigoletto* (1851).
⎯⎯⎯→ VOLUBILE

modulo, n.m. — a module, but also a form, so that *compilare* un modulo* is: to fill in/U.S. out a form, *un modulo di domanda* is an application form (⎯⎯⎯→ DOMANDARE), and *un modulo d'iscrizione** is an enrolment form.

momentaneamente, adv. — is not momentarily (= *per/in un attimo* or *da un momento all'altro*) but at the moment or at present. *Momentaneamente si trova in vacanza* therefore means: he is on holiday at the moment/minute/present time.

mondano, adj. — not mundane but 'society'. Compare *una riunione* mondana*, a society gathering, and a mundane meeting, *una riunione banale**. *La vita mondana* is (high) society life, whereas a mundane life = *un'esistenza banale*.

montgomery, n.m. — curiously, this false anglicism means a duffel coat. The garment became synonymous with the British Field Marshal Montgomery (⎯⎯⎯→ MARESCIALLO) as he advanced through Italy with the Eighth Army in the Second World War. For other clothes with odd English names ⎯⎯⎯→ GOLF, SLIP, TIGHT.

monumento, n.m. — a monument or memorial (⎯⎯⎯→ MEMORIALE), but note that *visitare i monumenti della città* is often best translated by: to visit the sights of the city. *Il quartiere monumentale* of a town will, therefore, be its historic centre or the area where its historic buildings are concentrated.
⎯⎯⎯→ EDIFICIO, PALAZZO

morbido, adj. — should never be confused with morbid (= *morboso*). It means soft, e.g. *un letto morbido*, a soft bed, *una stoffa* morbida*, a soft material (———→ MATERIALE), *un atterraggio morbido*, a soft landing, and *un approccio morbido*, a softly, softly approach. The narrator (———→ NARRATORE) of the mock pastoral *La Nencia da Barberino* (c. 1470), attributed to Lorenzo de' Medici, described his loved one's face as *morbido e bianco, che pare un sugnaccio*, soft and white like a lump of lard. Also smooth, as in *un'introduzione morbida al nuovo lavoro*, a smooth or gentle introduction to the new job, and in the Nescafé ad. *Il piacere di un gusto* più morbido*, the pleasure of a smoother taste. In cooking, *un piatto morbido* may be a moist dish (———→ UMIDO). Illness (Latin, *MORBUM*) is the linking concept, developing into the meanings of *morbido* via the idea of limpness.

mostarda, n.f. — you would get a surprise if you confused this with mustard (= *la senape*). It is, in fact, a sweet and sour relish, containing candied and pickled fruit, as well as a hint of mustard, eaten in wintertime on its own or with dishes such as *il bollito misto*, boiled meat(s) and vegetables.
———→ MARMELLATA

motivo, n.m. — rarely motive, and usually best rendered by reason, cause or grounds. Thus *un motivo in più per combattere l'AIDS*, one more reason for fighting AIDS, *non hai nessun motivo per deprimerti*, there's no reason for you to get depressed, *non c'è motivo di preoccuparsi*, there's no cause for concern, and *motivo di licenziamento*, grounds for dismissal (———→ LICENZA). Criminal motive = *il movente*, so *senza movente* would be: without a motive, whereas *senza motivo* just means: for no reason. A person's unconscious motives = *le motivazioni inconsc(i)e* (———→ COSCIENZA). Note that *un motivo* is also a motif, pattern or design (———→ DISEGNO), while in the arts it is a leitmotif, theme or even (in music) a number or track, as in *uno dei motivi più belli dell'ultimo* ellepì di Bob Dylan*, one of the finest tracks from B.D.'s latest album.

motto, n.m. — does mean a motto, e.g. *Credere, Obbedire, Combattere: uno dei motti del fascismo*, Believe, Obey, Fight: one of the mottoes of Fascism. However, it can also be a proverb, as in Padron 'Ntoni's dictum in *I Malavoglia* (1881) ['The House under the Medlar Tree'], *il motto degli antichi mai mentì*, the proverbs of the ancients (———→ ANTICO, ANZIANO) were never false. Can be a witticism or quip, too: the sixth day of Boccaccio's *Decameron* (1349–51) is dedicated to stories of those who have successfully extricated themselves from trouble by the use of a prompt reply or clever witticism (*leggiadro motto*).
———→ SPIRITO

mutilato, n.m. and adj. — mutilated (person, text or object), but often best-rendered by disabled, crippled or handicapped (person), e.g. *un mutilato di guerra* is a disabled ex-serviceman, and *un mutilato civile* has lost a limb through illness or injury.
———→ INVALIDO

N

narrativa, n.f. — not the narrative of a novel or story (= *la parte narrativa* or *la narrazione*) but prose fiction itself. Thus *la narrativa italiana dell'ottocento* is 19th-century Italian fiction. Best-seller lists are headed *narrativa italiana/straniera, saggistica*, and *varia*, Italian and foreign fiction, non-fiction and miscellaneous.
———→ NARRATORE, PROSA, ROMANZO, VARIO

narratore, n.m. — narrator in a work of fiction (———→ NARRATIVA), but take care. It may sometimes be a storyteller (*un buon narratore*, a good storyteller), while on other occasions it can, even more confusingly, be a writer of fiction or a novelist. An article about *i giovani narratori italiani di oggi* is likely, therefore, to be about young, contemporary Italian novelists/prose writers (———→ PROSA, ROMANZO).

naturalistico, adj. — naturalistic, but also (of) nature, so that *il rischio di distruggere una zona* di enorme valore naturalistico* is the risk of destroying an area of enormous natural value, and *un paradiso naturalistico* is a nature or wildlife paradise.
———→ OASI

navigato, adj. — navigated or shipped, but *una persona navigata* has lots of experience and is worldy-wise.

nazionale, adj. — national, of course, but, at an airport, watch out for *biglietti/arrivi/voli/ coincidenze nazionali*: these are domestic or internal tickets, arrivals, flights and connections (———→ COINCIDENZA). *La nazionale* is the Italian national team; all sportsmen and women representing Italy wear blue (because it was the royal colour) and are, therefore, known as *gli azzurri*.
———→ PRESENZA

nervoso, adj. — nervous, nervy or edgy, but of limbs it means: sinewy, and of style it is: spare and incisive: *uno stile nervoso*. Note *una macchina nervosa*, a responsive, highly-strung car.

night, n.m. — not a night (= *una notte*), of course, but a night-club, so the statement *vado a ballare in un night*, actually means: I'm going dancing in a night club.

nominare, v. — can be: to nominate in the senses of to appoint, designate or propose. Often, though, it means: to name, call or mention, so that *un amico che non voglio nominare* is a friend I don't wish to name, *Angelo Beolco, nominato 'Ruzante'* is the Renaissance playwright A.B., called/known as Ruzante, and *è stato nominato nella prefazione del libro* means: he was mentioned in the foreword to the book. Note the expressions *non nominare il nome di Dio invano*, Thou shalt not take the name of the Lord thy God in vain, and the very common, *mai sentito nominare*, never heard of it (or him)!
———→ NOMINATIVO

nominativo, n.m. — is not restricted to the nominative case. It is also the official word for a person's full name, as in the SEAT ad. *Per trovare nuovi clienti [SEAT] interroga* (———→ INTERROGAZIONE) *banche dati e utilizza liste di nominativi*, To find new clients

or customers S. searches through data banks and uses lists of names. *I nominativi dei titolari e dirigenti delle aziende italiane più significative*, means: the full names of the owners and directors of Italy's leading companies (————→ SOCIETÀ).
————→ NOMINARE

notes, n.m. — or *block-notes* is a slightly confusing false gallicism meaning not notes (= *gli appunti, le note* or *i bigliettini*) but a notebook or notepad. So *portare un notes alle lezioni* is: to take a notepad to lectures (————→ LEZIONE), whereas to take notes at lectures = *prendere appunti alle lezioni*, and footnotes = *le note (a piè di pagina)*. A computer notebook is *un notebook* (————→ PERSONAL).

notizia, n.f. — is never (a) notice (variously = *un annuncio, un avvertimento, un avviso, un preavviso, l'attenzione* or *una recensione*). On the one hand, it can mean: (a piece of) news, as in *una cattiva notizia*, bad news, *le ultime notizie*, the latest news (————→ ULTIMO), *le notizie sportive*, sports news, and in expressions like *sono rimasto senza notizie di lui*, I've had no word/news of, or from, him. On the other hand, it means: information, e.g. *le notizie contenute in questo dépliant sono rivolte agli studenti stranieri*, the information contained in this brochure is addressed to foreign students, and *notizie biografiche*, biographical data.

notorietà, n.f. — particularly treacherous because, like notoriety (= *la (cattiva) fama**), it refers to fame. However, it does not usually have negative overtones, so that *la notorietà mondiale di un regista* is a film director's world-wide renown or reputation, and the statement *gli scrittori adorano essere tradotti — è qualcosa che accresce la loro notorietà* means: writers love to be translated — it's something that increases their fame/makes them better-known.

nozione, n.f. — looks like notion (= *l'idea, il concetto*, l'opinione* or *la vaga convinzione*) but actually means: the sense of something (————→ SENSO) or else the elements, fundamentals or rudiments of a discipline. So *perdere la nozione del tempo* is: to lose the sense of time, while *imparare le (prime) nozioni di disegno*, di musica o di fisica* is: to learn the basics of drawing, music or physics, and *le nozioni più rilevanti* (————→ RILEVANTE) *della linguistica* are the most significant elements of linguistics.

nubile, adj. — beware. A woman described as *nubile* (single or unmarried) is not necessarily nubile (= *giovane e attraente*). This explains apparently odd statements of the type: *il 23% delle donne nella comunità europea sono nubili*, 23% of women in the European Community are unmarried, and *La guida delle nubili agli uomini disponibili di Washington* (*La Repubblica*, 16/3/93), Single woman's guide to the eligible men in W. The male equivalent is the similarly unreliable *celibe**.
————→ MATRIMONIO, SINGOLO

O

oasi, n.f. — an oasis in the desert or of peace, but also a wildlife haven, so that *oasi e riserve protette dal WWF* are W.W.F. protected areas and reserves.
———→ NATURALISTICO

obbligazione, n.f. — is only obligation in the legal sense (otherwise use *l'obbligo*). Can be confusing when it means: bond or debenture, as in *un'obbligazione dello Stato*, a government bond, and *un'obbligazione garantita*, a secured bond.
———→ AZIONE, TITOLO

occasionale, adj. — is seldom occasional. You are liable to encounter it meaning: fortuitous or casual (———→ CASUALE), so that *un incontro occasionale*, a chance meeting, is not the same as an occasional meeting = *un incontro saltuario* or *che avviene ogni tanto*. The anti-AIDS ad. *Evitiamo rapporti sessuali occasionali con degli sconosciuti* urges us to avoid casual relations (———→ RAPPORTO) with strangers, while *uno scrittore occasionale* is a spare-time writer. On the other hand, I enjoy the occasional drink = *ogni tanto mi bevo un bicchiere*, occasional showers = *piogge sporadiche*, and occasional verses = *versi d'occasione**.

occasione, n.f. — occasion, both in the sense of opportunity (*un'occasione unica*, a unique opportunity ———→ OPPORTUNITÀ, UNICO) and event. More surprisingly, it also means: a bargain. *Una vera occasione* is, therefore, a real bargain, *un prezzo d'occasione* is a bargain price, while *un'auto d'occasione* is a second-hand car (———→ MACCHINA).
———→ CONVENIENTE, INTERESSANTE, OCCASIONALE

occorrenza, n.f. — resembles an occurrence (= *un evento, un avvenimento, un fatto* or *un caso*) but means: an eventuality (———→ EVENTUALE), as in *essere pronti per/ad ogni occorrenza*, to be ready for any eventuality. *All'occorrenza, chiamami* means: call me if necessary or if need be.

occulto, adj. — corresponds to occult but is often used in the sense of hidden, secret or illicit. *Il finanziamento occulto dei partiti politici* is: secret or unlawful payments to political parties, and *il potere di persuasione — più o meno occulto — concentrato nelle mani di un solo soggetto** (*La Repubblica*, 16/3/93) means: the more or less covert power of persuasion concentrated in the hands of a single individual. Italia Radio claims to provide *un'informazione libera da legami occulti*, news that is independent of hidden interests/ interest groups.

occupato, adj. — while *la fabbrica è occupata dagli scioperanti* indicates that the factory (———→ FATTORIA) is occupied by the strikers, and *sono occupato oggi pomeriggio* is: I'm occupied or busy this afternoon, be on your guard. Of a seat it means: taken, and of a 'phone or lavatory it means: engaged.
———→ OCCUPAZIONE

occupazione, n.f. — used of work, but it is employment in general and not an occupation (= *un mestiere, una professione* or *un impiego*) in particular. Thus the headline *Crisi* dell'occupazione*, Employment Crisis (unemployment is *la disoccupazione*), and the

statement in June 1993 from the Governor of the Bank of Italy: *la nostra vera sfida sarà l'occupazione*, our real challenge is going to be employment. Use *l'occupazione*, too, for the occupation of a factory or school, and for a spare time activity (also *un passatempo*). The statement *le donne occupate nel Comune di Milano rappresentano la maggioranza del personale in organico** means: the women employed by the Milan City Council (———→ COMUNALE) constitute a majority on the payroll.
———→ OCCUPATO

omaggio, n.m. — homage or tribute, but commonly also a free gift. So *comprando la rivista avrete il C.D. in omaggio* means that when you buy the magazine you get the C.D. free. Publishers often send teachers *libri in omaggio*, free copies of books.
———→ COMPLIMENTI

opera, n.f. — more wide-ranging than opera. *Un'opera di Donizetti* is an opera by D., but *le opere di Piero della Francesca* are Piero's works, paintings or output, and *l'opera completa di Machiavelli* is simply M.'s complete works. Also work(s) in general, e.g. *opere pubbliche*, public works, and *un'opera della natura/dell'uomo*, a work of nature or of man. Beware, too, of *l'opera universitaria*: it is not a university opera group, but the students' welfare office. Note that while an opera is *un'opera lirica*, an opera house or singer is *un teatro/un cantante lirico**.
———→ LIBRETTO, MELODRAMMA, OPERETTA

operatore, n.m. — generally a safe equivalent of operator (e.g. *un operatore turistico*, a tour operator) but note that *un operatore di borsa* is a stockbroker or dealer (———→ AZIONE, TITOLO), *un operatore cinematografico* (like Alfredo in Tornatore's 1988 film *Cinema Paradiso*), is a film projectionist, while *un operatore pedagogico* would be someone working in the field of teaching or education. Sometimes it means: operative, though, as in *un operatore sanitario* (———→ SANITÀ), a health worker, and in the pricelessly euphemistic *un operatore ecologico* (lit. an ecological operative), a dustman or refuse/U.S. garbage collector.

operetta, n.f. — operetta, but also a small or slight literary work, as in Leopardi's *Operette Morali* (1824) ['Moral Tales', lit. 'Minor Moral Works'].
———→ OPERA

opportunamente, adv. — may be opportunely (also = *tempestivamente*) but is likely to mean: suitably or appropriately, as in the statement *opportunamente usati, i tuoi soldi possono migliorare il mondo*, used in the right way, your money can improve the world.
———→ OPPORTUNITÀ

opportunità, n.f. — a partial false friend. On the one hand, it is (an) opportunity, e.g. *approfittare dell'opportunità*, to take advantage of the opportunity, *le pari opportunità*, equal opportunities, and *le opportunità d'investimento*, investment opportunities. On the other hand, it can mean appropriateness, advisability or rightness, as in *il primario ha espresso seri dubbi sull'opportunità dell'intervento*, the consultant has expressed serious reservations about whether the operation is appropriate/advisable; and *ridiscutere l'utilità e l'opportunità di studiare il latino*, to reopen the debate on whether it is useful or right to study Latin.
———→ OCCASIONE, OPPORTUNAMENTE

oratore, n.m. — orator, but often simply a public speaker, as in *un buon/mediocre oratore*, a good or poor public speaker. *Un buon parlatore* speaks well but may also be a chatterbox. The speaker of the lower house of the Italian parliament = *il presidente* della camera dei deputati*. Oddly, *uno speaker* is a T.V. announcer.

ordinario, adj. — is not as innocuous as it looks. On occasion it is straightforward, as in *la posta ordinaria*, ordinary-rate postage, *un azionista ordinario*, an ordinary shareholder (———→ AZIONE), and *fuori dell'ordinario*, out of the ordinary. Often, though, another rendering is called for, e.g. *un biglietto ordinario*, a full-fare or standard ticket, *la tariffa* ordinaria*, standard fare/rate (———→ RATA), *il lavoro ordinario*, work paid at the standard rate (as opposed to overtime, *il lavoro straordinario**), and *cose di ordinaria amministrazione**, routine business. Its secondary meaning of: common or vulgar often makes other adjectives preferable. An ordinary or nondescript person = *una persona normale* or *qualunque* and is very different from *una persona ordinaria*, a 'common' or vulgar person. So ordinary people = *la gente comune/normale*, ordinary problems = *i problemi d'ogni giorno*, his ordinary voice = *la sua voce normale* or *consueta*, ordinary paper = *la carta comune*, and ordinary, of a performance or work or art = *banale** or *mediocre*. Beware, especially, of confusing *un professore* ordinario* (or *un ordinario*) with an ordinary teacher = *un professore normale* or (if pejorative) *mediocre*: it is a full university professor, e.g. *Manlio Cortelazzo, ordinario di Dialettologia Italiana all' Università di Padova*, M.C., Professor of Italian Dialectology at the University of Padua.

ordinazione, n.f. — is both religious ordination and a commercial order, as in *ricevere* or *cancellare un'ordinazione*, to receive or cancel an order, and *(fatto) su ordinazione*, made to order/U.S. custom made.

organico, adj. and n.m. — organic, but also organised, structured or integrated. The publishers Mondadori (———→ EDITORE) describe their popular *Oscar* paperbacks as *la biblioteca per tutti: la più completa, la più organica, la più economica*, the library (———→ LIBRERIA) for all: the most wide-ranging, the most systematic and the cheapest. The tax magazine *Il Fisco* (———→ FISCALE) claims to provide *informazione organica e qualificata* (———→ QUALIFICATO), structured and expert information (———→ INFORMATIVO), while *un piano organico per le regioni* is an integrated plan for the regions. *L'organico* is the staff or roll of employees, so that a firm which is under-staffed is *sotto organico*; *un'amministrazione* che vuole diminuire l'organico* is an administration looking to shed staff; and *in organico* means: on the payroll. Organic food = *il cibo biologico**.

originale, adj. — is not always a trustworthy friend. *Il peccato originale* is original sin, *un'idea originale* is an original idea (———→ CONCETTO, NOZIONE), and *un (dipinto) originale* is an original (painting). If the emphasis is on origins, though, *originario* tends to be used. Thus *l'aspetto originario della casa*, the original appearance (———→ APPARENZA) of the house, and *il significato originario della parola*, the original meaning of the word. The problem is that *originale* can be: eccentric, so that *è un tipo un po' originale* means: he's a bit of an eccentric/oddball.

osservazione, n.f. — is not always as neutral as observation. *Gli ho fatto un'osservazione sullo stato della cucina* is likely to mean: I criticised him/made a critical remark to him about the state of the kitchen, and *un professore* che fa continuamente delle osservazioni a un alunno* is a teacher who is constantly criticising a pupil.

P

pacchetto, n.m. — a pack(et) but also a commercial package. *Un pacchetto vacanze* is a holiday package, *un pacchetto turistico* is a tourist package, and Ford offer *un Super Pacchetto Assistenza**, a Super After-Sales Package. *Un pacchetto software* (⟶ PERSONAL) is a software package.
⟶ CONFEZIONE

palazzo, n.m. — is deceptive on two counts. It may be an (apartment) building or block of flats as well as a palace. Thus *abito in un palazzo al centro di Roma* is likely to mean: I live in an apartment block in the centre of Rome, especially as most Italians rent or own a flat/U.S. apartment rather than a house. Not a surprising semantic development given the high frequency of palaces in the older parts of Italian cities (⟶ EDIFICIO, MONUMENTO). With a capital letter it is used (rather pejoratively) for the Italian political establishment, as in the headline *È crollato il Palazzo* (*La Repubblica*, 20/4/93), The Establishment in collapse. This is so because most Italian centres of power are housed in palaces: in Rome, *palazzo Chigi* is the Prime Minister's residence, the seat of the President (⟶ PRESIDENTE) is *palazzo del Quirinale*, the Chamber of Deputies is in *palazzo Montecitorio*, and the Senate sits in *palazzo Madama*.

paragone, n.m. — ignore the similarity to paragon (= *un modello*, so that a paragon of virtue = *un modello di virtù*); it means: a comparison. Thus *non c'è paragone tra questi due prodotti*, there's no comparison between these two products, and *un paragone odioso*, an invidious (⟶ INVIDIOSO) comparison.

parco, n.m. — a park, but do not take it for granted. *Il parco rotabile* is railway/U.S. railroad rolling stock, *il parco veicoli* or *circolante* is the total number of vehicles on the road, and *il parco abitazione* is the housing stock. Note that the strange false anglicism *una luna park* is a fairground or fun-fair. A car park or parking lot = *un parcheggio*.

parente, n.m. — eminently confusable with parent, but it means: a relative or relation. Do not, therefore, take *i parenti*, relatives, for parents (= *i genitori*). Family ties may remain important in an Italy characterised by an uncaring and inefficient state (⟶ ARRANGIARE) but the traditional extended family (*la famiglia patriarcale* or *estesa*) has largely been replaced by the nuclear family (*la famiglia nucleare*) with one of the lowest birthrates in the world.
⟶ FAMILIARE, RELAZIONE

parziale, adj. — partial (*un successo/un'eclissi parziale*, a partial success/eclipse) but, sometimes, biased. So *un arbitro** *parziale* is a biased referee or umpire, *un giudice parziale* is a biased judge (⟶ MAGISTRATO), and the complaint *sei troppi parziale nei suoi confronti* means: you're too biased towards him. I'm partial to cream, on the other hand = *ho un debole per la panna* (⟶ CREMA).
⟶ PREGIUDIZIO

pasta, n.f. — more wide-ranging than pasta. It is also dough or pastry (*la pasta frolla*, short-crust pastry, *la pasta sfoglia*, puff pastry), as well as a small cake (hence *una pasticceria*, a cake shop) and a paste (*la pasta di acciughe* is anchovy paste and *la pasta di* *mandorle* is marzipan). Italians call a dish of pasta *la pastasciutta* (lit. dry pasta) to distinguish it from *pasta in brodo* which is pasta in broth.

pasticcio, n.m. — is not a pastiche (= *un pastiche*, e.g. the style of Umberto Eco's *Il nome della rosa* (1980) ['The Name of the Rose'] is a pastiche of a medieval monk's, *un pastiche dello stile d'un monaco medievale*). *Un pasticcio* is a pie, as in *pasticcio di lasagne*, lasagne pie. By extension it is a mess, as in *hai combinato* (———→ COMBINARE) *un bel pasticcio*, a fine mess you've made of things, so that the title of C.E. Gadda's novel *Quel pasticciaccio brutto di via Merulana* (1957) means: 'That awful mess-up in Via Merulana'. The French term was borrowed from Italian, in the sense of a hotch-potch.
———→ INTRIGO

patente, n.f. — is confusable with patent (= *un brevetto*) but is actually the driving licence/U.S. driver's license, *la patente (di guida)*. This is obtained following the driving test, *l'esame di guida* (———→ GUIDARE) or *per la patente*, and often, lessons with *una scuola guida*, a driving school. *Il ritiro* or *la sospensione della patente* is the withdrawal of the driving licence.

pavimento, n.m. — easily mistaken for pavement/U.S. sidewalk (= *il marciapiede*), but it actually means: floor.

peculiarità, n.f. — never peculiarity in the sense of oddness (= *la stranezza, la singolarità* or *la bizzarria*) but only when it means: distinctiveness or uniqueness. So *il programma valorizza la peculiarità di ciascun paese* (*Campus*, 9/9/92) means that the programme stresses the uniqueness of each country, and a statement like *la peculiarità del Cattolicesimo italiano* only refers to the distinctiveness or special nature of Italian Catholicism.

periodo, n.m. — a period, but not in punctuation: that is *(un) punto (fermo)*. Watch out for it meaning: a (usually complex) sentence, e.g. *uno stile asciutto e semplice con periodi brevi e pochissimi aggettivi*, a spare, simple style with short sentences and very few adjectives.
———→ COMMA, FRASE

permanenza, n.f. — occasionally permanence (note, especially, *in permanenza*, continuously), but usually encountered meaning: a stay in a place. The paradoxical *una breve permanenza in Italia* is a short stay in Italy, *non posso prolungare la mia permanenza* means: I can't stay any longer, and the exhortation *buona permanenza!* is the same as: enjoy your stay!

permutare, v. — to permute but also to exchange, as in ad. claims of the type: *vi diamo la possibilità di permutare il vostro telefono usato per un modello nuovo*, we give you the opportunity of exchanging your existing 'phone for a new one.

perplesso, adj. — handle with care. It does not always mean: perplexed. *All'inizio era un po' perplesso ma poi ha preso la decisione* is just as likely to mean: to start with he was a little hesitant/uncertain/undecided, but then he made up his mind.

persistente, adj. — persistent but also long-lasting. The sign of a good sparkling wine (*uno spumante*) like Prosecco is *un perlage finissimo e persistente*, tiny, long-lasting bubbles. Similarly, *la persistenza* can occasionally mean: survival as well as persistence, as in *la*

persistenza di una lingua/una razza/un genere letterario, the survival of a language, a race or a literary genre.
———→ INSISTERE, PREGIUDIZIO

personaggio, n.m. — a personage, but it is far commoner, and tends to mean: a personality or big name (———→ BIG), e.g. *un personaggio della cultura/del mondo politico*, an important figure in the field of culture or in the political world. Also a character in a book, film or play, as in *i personaggi di una commedia* di Goldoni*, the characters in a Goldoni play.
———→ CARATTERE, PROTAGONISTA

personal, n.m. — is used, oddly, as a noun, and means not: a personal (stereo) (= *un walkman*) but a personal computer. Also known as *un personal computer* or *un P.C.* IBM promise to help you solve *qualsiasi problema tu possa incontrare con l'uso del tuo personal*, any problem you encounter when using your P.C., Casio describe one of their computers as *un personal con la vocazione all'insegnamento*, a P.C. with a teaching vocation, and the magazine *Software* offers *Per il tuo personal una vasta scelta di oltre 1000 programmi*, A vast choice of over 1000 programs for your P.C. Italian has borrowed English computing terminology wholesale, including *il computer, il hardware, il software, il floppy disk* and *il mouse*.

perturbare, v. — is to disturb rather than to perturb (= *turbare* or *allarmare*), as in *perturbare l'ordine pubblico*, to disturb public order, and *perturbare la coscienza* di qualcuno*, to disturb someone's conscience. Note that in a weather forecast the warning: *il tempo si perturberà dopo Natale* means that the weather will deteriorate after Christmas.
———→ ANNOIARE

perverso, adj. — not perverse but perverted or wicked, so do not confuse *un bambino perverso*, a depraved child, with a perverse child = *un bambino che contraddice per il gusto* di contraddire. Avere gusti perversi* is: to have perverted tastes.
———→ VIZIOSO

petrolio, n.m. — irresistibly like petrol/U.S. gas(oline) (= *la benzina*) but it means: petroleum or oil, as in *una raffineria di petrolio*, an oil refinery, and *il (petrolio) greggio*, crude (oil). Note that *una stufa a petrolio* is a paraffin heater. Italy is heavily reliant on oil imports for its energy needs, so that the 1973 oil shortage, *la crisi* del petrolio*, led to a ban on Sunday driving and to a (short-lived) expansion of its nuclear capacity.
———→ CARBONE, ENERGETICO

phon, n.m. — *usare il phon* or *il fon* is not the same as using the 'phone. It means: using the hairdryer. From the *Föhn*, the hot, dry Alpine wind.
———→ CABINA, DUPLEX

pietà, n.f. — piety, but often compassion, pity or sympathy (———→ SIMPATIA), as in *provare pietà per qualcuno*, to feel pity or compassion for someone. Sometimes used pejoratively, e.g. *le sue scuse fanno pietà*, his excuses are pitiful or pathetic.
———→ DEVOZIONE

pilota, n.m. — a pilot, but also, rather unexpectedly, a racing driver, e.g. *un pilota di formula* uno*, a Formula One driver.
———→ GUIDARE

pirata, n.m. — pirate, but it can turn up in unexpected places. *Un pirata (dell'aria)* is a plane hijacker, while *un'auto pirata* is a car involved in a hit-and-run accident (———→ ACCIDENTE, INCIDENTE).

plebiscito, n.m. — plebiscite (as in the series of referenda by which the various regions of the peninsula joined the new Italy after 1860), but also an overwhelming or unanimous vote of approval. *L'elezione del presidente* è stato un plebiscito* therefore means that the president was elected on a landslide.
———→ VOTO

pocket, n.m. — or *pocket-book* is neither a pocket (= *una tasca*) nor a pocket-book (= *un taccuino* or *un portafoglio*). It is a false anglicism meaning: a (cheap) paperback.

poema, n.m. — confined to a long, usually epic, poem such as Ariosto's *Orlando Furioso* (1516), Tasso's *Gerusalemme Liberata* (1581) or even Dante's *Commedia* (c.1314–21). A poem = *una poesia*.
———→ PROSA

polemica, n.f. — a polemic, but as often as not it simply means: controversy or dispute. So *un'antica polemica* (———→ ANTICO) is an old or ancient dispute, and *'Il Mercante di Venezia' è un'opera* che ha sempre suscitato scalpore e polemiche* means that 'The Merchant of Venice' is a work which has always aroused scandals and controversies.
———→ FURORE

politica, n.f. — politics, of course, but often policy. *La politica estera* or *sociale* del governo* is, therefore, the government's foreign or social policy, the title of Gabriella Klein's book *La politica linguistica del fascismo* (1986) means: 'The Linguistic Policy of Fascism', and *la politica editoriale* (———→ EDITORE) is editorial policy. *Un politico* is a politician, and *un partito (politico)* is a (political) party.
———→ URNA, VOTO

polluzione, n.f. — treat with caution. The normal word for pollution is *l'inquinamento*. *La polluzione notturna* is a wet dream.

polso, n.m. — pulse (*un polso irregolare*, an irregular pulse), but Italian has evolved the two extended meanings of wrist (*slogarsi il polso* to dislocate one's wrist ———→ DISLOCARE), and cuff (*i polsi sfilacciati*, frayed cuffs). *Un uomo di polso* is a man of energy or character.

ponderoso, adj. — do not take *un volume/uno studio* ponderoso*, a weighty tome or study, for a ponderous or laboured one (= *pesante* or *ampolloso*).

popolare, adj. — popular (*un programma popolare*, a popular programme, and *la cultura popolare*, popular culture), but sometimes 'of the (common) people', as in *le tradizioni popolari*, folk traditions. Note, in particular, *un quartiere popolare*, a working-class district, *le case popolari*, council or local authority housing, and the left-wing term *le masse popolari*, the mass of the common people or the working masses.

portico, n.m. — a portico or porch but also a colonnade or arcade, as in the extensive *portici* in Turin and Bologna where one can window-shop, sheltered from sun or rain.

portoghese, n.m. — a citizen of Portugal but also a gatecrasher. In the 18th century the Portuguese embassy in Rome is said to have laid on a lavish theatrical gala for which no tickets were issued; only Portuguese were admitted free. This may be why *fare il portoghese* is: to gatecrash.

praticare, v. — to practise/U.S. practice, but not of sport (= *allenarsi*) where it means: to take part in, engage in or play. Thus *praticando uno sport si migliora la propria salute*, by taking part in or 'doing' a sport, you improve your health, and *pratica regolarmente il tennis*, he plays tennis regularly.

pratico, adj. — practical, but also handy or convenient (———→ CONVENIENTE), e.g. *un aggeggio pratico*, a handy gadget (———→ GADGET), and *è pratico far la spesa al supermercato*, it's convenient to do the shopping at the supermarket. *Pratico di* means: well-versed in, so that *una segretaria pratica del mestiere* is a secretary thoroughly acquainted with the job. Tourists may find the phrase *non sono pratico di questa città* (I don't know my way about this town) useful. A practical joke = *un tiro mancino*.

precedenza, n.f. — precedence, but most commonly means: right-of-way or priority on the roads. So *avere la precedenza*, to have right-of-way, and *dare la precedenza*, to give way. In Italy vehicles approaching from the right have right-of-way, *i veicoli provenienti da destra hanno la precedenza*.
———→ CIRCOLAZIONE, GUIDARE, PATENTE

preferire, v. — to prefer, but not in every case. *Invece di bere l'acqua del rubinetto, preferite l'acqua minerale* means: instead of drinking tap/U.S. faucet water, stick to mineral water, and the advice: *in ogni regione d'Italia sarà meglio preferire i vini locali* suggests that in each region of Italy the best idea is to stick to local wines.

pregiudizio, n.m. — prejudice or bias, but can sometimes mean: superstition, as in *la persistenza* di pregiudizi popolari* (———→ POPOLARE) *come il malocchio*, the survival of popular superstitions like the evil eye (particularly prevalent in Italy).
———→ PARZIALE, PREVENZIONE

preoccupato, adj. — is seldom an exact equivalent of preoccupied (= *soprappensiero/ sovrappensiero, assorto* or *distratto*). Usually it means: anxious, troubled, worried or concerned, as in *sono preoccupato per mio figlio*, I am worried/concerned/anxious about my son, and *ti vedo preoccupato*, you look worried/troubled to me.

preparato, adj. — prepared or ready, but often encountered meaning: well-trained, qualified (———→ QUALIFICATO) or informed. *Amministrazioni preparate che sanno utilizzare la sapienza di ecologi* are well-informed local authorities/administrations (———→ AMMINISTRAZIONE, COMUNALE) which know how to use the wisdom of ecologists. The Istituto Italiano di Previdenza calls its insurance agents (———→ AGENTE) *professionisti preparati e cortesi*, well-trained/qualified and well-mannered professionals. *Preparazione*, as well as preparation, can also mean: qualification, training or background. A course boasting of *l'eccezionale preparazione degli insegnanti* is claiming that its teachers are exceptionally well-qualified or trained, and a job ad. stipulating that *i requisiti richiesti sono: preparazione culturale e spirito* imprenditoriali* means: the prerequisites we are seeking are: a good cultural background/training/grounding and an enterprising outlook. *La preparazione necessaria per svolgere il lavoro* is: the necessary qualifications for the job.

presenza, n.f. — (a) presence, but also appearance, in two very different senses. *Una persona di bella presenza* is someone of smart appearance/who presents well, but *ha 30 presenze nella nazionale** means: he's made 30 appearances for the national team.
————→ APPARENZA

preservativo, n.m. — provides a very different kind of protection from a preservative (= *un conservante*; contains no artificial colours or preservatives = *non contiene né coloranti né conservanti artificiali*). *Un preservativo* is a condom, as in the government anti-AIDS ad. *Imbarazzante il preservativo? Nessuno è ancora morto per l'imbarazzo*, Find the condom embarrassing? Nobody has ever died of embarrassment.
————→ CASINO, RAPPORTO

presidente, n.m. — president (*il presidente della Repubblica*, the President of Italy, and *il presidente degli Stati Uniti*, the U.S. President), but also Chairman/person. The Italian Prime Minister is called *il presidente del consiglio (dei ministri)* because he chairs the cabinet. *Il presidente del consiglio d'amministrazione** is the Chairman of the board of directors (so *Gianni Agnelli, presidente della FIAT* means: G.A., chairman of FIAT). Consequently, *la presidenza* will often mean: chair(manship), as in *la presidenza di una commissione* parlamentare*, the chairmanship of a parliamentary committee. *Un preside* is a headteacher in a school.
————→ DIRETTORE, PALAZZO

pretendere, v. — looks like to pretend (= *fare finta*) but means: to claim, insist or expect. You should, therefore, distinguish carefully between *pretendere che qualcosa sia vero*, claiming that something is true, and pretending that it is true = *far(e) finta che qualcosa sia vero*. *Gli piacciano le caramelle* (————→ CARAMELLA) *ma le pretende senza zucchero* means: he likes sweets/U.S. candy but insists on them/it being sugar-free; *non puoi pretendere che gli altri siano sempre d'accordo con te* is: you can't expect others always to agree with you; and the exasperated *cosa pretendi?* means: what do you expect? Pretender to the throne and pretentious(ness) retain a vestige of these meanings.

prevalenza, n.f. — in spite of appearances, has nothing to do with prevalence (= *la frequenza** or *la (larga) diffusione* ————→ DIFFUSO). It means preponderance or superiority, as in *la prevalenza della popolazione di lingua tedesca nella provincia di Bolzano*, the preponderance of German-speakers in the province of Bolzano (in Italy's semi-autonomous northern region of Alto Adige). *Una prevalenza numerica* is numerical superiority.

preventivo, adj. — preventive (*la medicina preventiva*, preventive medicine) but also estimated, so if you're applying to take a course in Italy you may wish to write: *Le sarei grato se potesse farmi sapere il costo preventivo del corso*, I would be grateful if you could let me know the estimated cost of the course. *Un preventivo* is an estimate (————→ QUOTAZIONE).

prevenzione, n.f. — prevention, but also bias, prejudice or preconceived idea, e.g. *l'idea che l'aglio fa parte di tutti i piatti italiani è una prevenzione*, the idea that all Italian dishes contain garlic is a (popular) preconception, and *nutrire prevenzioni contro qualcuno*, to be biased against someone.
————→ PARZIALE, PREGIUDIZIO

processo, n.m. — can be a process (e.g. *un processo di mutazione che è già in atto*, a process of change which is already underway), but you are likely to encounter it meaning: (a) trial. Thus *un processo penale*, a criminal trial, and *un maxiprocesso*, a (mafia or terrorist) supertrial. Also used figuratively, so that *processo all'autostrada* means: motorways/ U.S. freeways or turnpikes on trial, and the headline *Torna la gonna lunga e merita un processo* (*Il Venerdì della Repubblica*, 9/4/93) proclaims: the long skirt is back and deserves to be put on trial. Similarly, *processare* is not: to process (= *esaminare (attentamente)* or *elaborare*) but to try or prosecute. At the height of the political scandals of the 1990s *La Repubblica* (24/10/93) announced: *Tutti gli onorevoli inquisiti potranno essere processati*, All the 'right honourables' under investigation can be tried.
————→ MAGISTRATO, TRIBUNALE

produrre, v. — to produce, but not in show business (= *mettere in scena*). The reflexive form can be confusing: *una cantante che si produce in uno spettacolo** actually means: a singer appearing in a show.
————→ ESIBIZIONE, RECITARE

professore, n.m. — not necessarily a university professor (= *un (professore) ordinario**). It is the normal word for a secondary school teacher as opposed to a primary/U.S. elementary teacher (*un maestro**).
————→ GINNASIO, INFERIORE, MATURO, SUPERIORE

profondo, adj. — profound but also deep, as in *l'acqua profonda*, deep water, *una ferita profonda*, a deep wound, and *il profondo Sud*, the deep South. Note that, like French, Italian has no specific word for shallow: you simply use *poco profondo*.

profumo, n.m. — perfume or scent, but also an appetising food smell or aroma. *Il buon profumo del sugo* is the delicious smell of the stew or gravy, and *il profumo dell'olio d'oliva è inconfondibile* means: the aroma of olive oil is unmistakable.
————→ AROMA

programmare, v. — to program(me) a computer or appliance (*il timer 24 ore per programmare l'ora e la durata del funzionamento*, the 24-hour timer to program(me) when and how long it comes on), but also, frequently, to plan. The Ansaldo group claims: *C'è un'Italia che, dopo aver programmato lo sviluppo industriale, oggi vuole respirare meglio*, there is a part of Italy which, now that industrial development has been planned out, wants to have a breather. Stiassi business diaries (————→ AGENDA) target *il moderno manager che programma ogni minuto della propria giornata*, today's manager who plans every minute of his day. *Programmare un viaggio* is, therefore: to plan a journey, and *il programma* is a program(me) in all senses, but it can simply be a plan, too. Thus the Touring Club Italiano call Spring: *tempo di programmi, viaggi, weekend,* a time for plans, journeys and weekend breaks. Also a school or university syllabus, e.g. *qualsiasi proposta* di variazione* del programma va discussa con il docente,* any proposal to alter (———→ ALTERARE) the syllabus must be discussed with the lecturer concerned, or *una scuola difficile con programmi tradizionali,* a difficult school with traditional syllabuses.

promiscuo, adj. — its bark is worse than its bite. It has lately taken on the sense of promiscuous, although *sessuale* is added. Thus *una persona sessualmente promiscua/che ha molti partner sessuali* is a promiscuous person. However, the word's core meaning remains: mixed. Odd though they appear, *un matrimonio* promiscuo* is a mixed marriage, and *una scuola promiscua* is a co-ed. school. Mixed farming, *la coltura promiscua,* provides the attractive patchwork of small fields which characterises Tuscany.

pronto, adv. and interj. — not pronto (= *subito*) but ready, so that *il pranzo sarà pronto subito* means that the dinner will be ready right away. Italians exclaim *pronto!* when they pick up the 'phone.

propaganda, n.f. — not necessarily as pejorative as propaganda. Do not be surprised to see official billboards at election times with the notice (———→ NOTIZIA): *Propaganda degli enti e delle associazioni,* Advertising material by public bodies and associations. *Fare propaganda,* therefore, may simply be: to publicise, so that *una ditta che fa molta propaganda in America* is a firm doing a lot of advertising in the U.S., and *spese di propaganda* are publicity or advertising expenses.
———→ CONGREGAZIONE, MANIFESTO, PUBBLICITÀ

proposta, n.f. — a proposal or suggestion, but much used in advertising to mean: an offer, e.g. *una vasta scelta di proposte convenienti* (———→ CONVENIENTE), a wide range of value-for-money offers.
———→ FORMULA, SOLUZIONE

proprietario, n.m. — proprietor but often simply an owner or else a landlord, so *la polizia ha interrogato il proprietario della macchina*,* the police questioned (———→ INTERROGAZIONE) the owner of the car; *sono proprietari della casa in cui abitano,* they own their own home; and *il proprietario ha stabilito l'affitto con gli inquilini,* the landlord has set the rent with his tenants.

proprio, adj. — while *un nome proprio* is a proper noun, and *un vero e proprio lazzarone* is a proper rascal, it most commonly means: one's own, e.g. *ognuno deve comprarsi i propri libri,* everyone must buy their own books. The proper (i.e. correct) books = *i libri giusti/appropriati.* Proper, of behaviour or people = *perbene, rispettabile* or *decoroso* (———→ DECORO), while a proper examination of the issue = *un serio esame/un esame esauriente dell'argomento*.*

prosa, n.f. — prose, of course, but also, curiously, theatre or drama (———→ DRAMMA). *Preferire la prosa all'opera** is: to prefer theatre to opera, *un attore/un festival di prosa* are a theatre actor and festival, and *una compagnia di prosa* is a drama company.
———→ LIRICO

protagonista, n.m. or f. — is a protagonist, both in the sense of main character in a book, film or play, and of a chief participant in an event or cause. Thus *'Super Mario' ha per*

protagonista un idraulico italiano, the hero of *S.M.* is an Italian plumber, and *Germaine Greer una delle protagoniste del femminismo inglese*, G.G. one of the protagonists of British feminism. Frequently used, though, simply to mean: a big name or major force, so that *il Milan e Napoli, i due protagonisti della stagione* is: A.C. Milan and Naples, the two major forces of the football season; *i protagonisti attuali* (⎯⎯→ ATTUALE) *della T.V.* are the big T.V. personalities of the moment (⎯⎯→ BIG); and *se tornerà in Italia, lo farà solo da protagonista*, means: if he returns to Italy it will only be in a major role. The exhortation *partecipa da protagonista!* urges you to take part and make your presence felt! *Il protagonismo* is the politics of personality and/or ambition.
⎯⎯→ CARATTERE, PERSONAGGIO

protocollo, n.m. — protocol, but it has bureaucratic as well as diplomatic meanings. *Un protocollo* is a register or ledger, so that *seguire il protocollo* is: to go by the book. *Un numero di protocollo* is a reference number, and *carta protocollo* is foolscap paper.
⎯⎯→ AMMINISTRAZIONE, DIPLOMATO

provvidenza, n.f. — can be divine Providence, but you will generally encounter it meaning: (emergency) measure(s), e.g. *provvidenze per i senzatetto/i disoccupati/i profughi*, emergency measures to help the homeless, the unemployed or the refugees. *Provvidenze per proteggere i prodotti interni dalla concorrenza* are measures to protect home-produced goods from competition.

psicosi, n.f. — may be the clinical condition of psychosis but, in ordinary usage, it is a climate of terror. The headline *Psicosi dopo gli attentati* means: State of fear following the terrorist attacks, while *la psicosi degli esami* is exam fever.

pubblicità, n.f. — publicity, but also, more specifically, advertising or an advertisement, e.g. *la pubblicità Benetton ha suscitato scalpore* could mean that the Benetton advert (in particular) or its advertising (in general) caused a furore (⎯⎯→ FURORE). A T.V. ad. is called *uno spot*.
⎯⎯→ AUDIENCE, PROPAGANDA

pullman, n.m. — can be a Pullman car, but, far more commonly, it is a coach/U.S. bus. So *fare una gita in pullman* is: to go on a coach trip. The diminutive, *un pulmino*, is a mini-bus.

puntuale, adj. — does mean: punctual (*essere puntuale*, to be on time) but can reserve surprises. *Una descrizione puntuale del libro* is a careful or accurate description of the book (⎯⎯→ ACCURATO), and *per ogni testo il curatore* fornisce un puntuale commento** means: the editor provides a point-by-point commentary on each text. Garzanti dictionaries claim to provide *la traduzione puntuale di ogni termine*, the precise/exact translation of every term. On a very different tack, *un intestino puntuale* or *regolare* is (a) regular intestine or bowels (⎯⎯→ COSTIPAZIONE). *Puntualmente*, as well as meaning: punctually, can be: accurately, fully or in detail, e.g. *'Campus' ti aggiorna puntualmente sulle opportunità* di viaggi e borse di studio*, 'C.' keeps you fully up-to-date (⎯⎯→ AGGIORNAMENTO) with travel and scholarship opportunities, and *rispondere puntualmente a tutte le critiche*, to answer all criticisms in detail.

puntura, n.f. — as in puncture (= *la foratura*; I've had a puncture = *ho forato la gomma*), the idea of pricking is present. *Una puntura*, though, is an insect sting/bite, a prick from a sharp object, or else an injection or jab/U.S. shot.

pupillo, n.m. — looks like a (school) pupil (= *un alunno, un allievo* or *uno scolaro**) but is in fact a ward of court and, by extension, a favourite or protegé. *Il pupillo della maestra* (⟶ MAESTRO) is, therefore, the teacher's favourite/pet, and the politician's disclaimer *Ma non è stato un mio pupillo* (*La Repubblica*, 27/10/93) means: He was not a protegé of mine. The pupil of the eye = *la pupilla*. All are diminutives of Latin *PUPA* (baby or doll), including the eye (perhaps because people are reflected small in it).

Q

qualificato, adj. — occasionally means: qualified (especially in phrases like *è il più qualificato per il posto*, he's best qualified for the post), although *abilitato* is used in precise contexts, e.g. *un professore* abilitato* (———→ ABILITÀ), a qualified teacher. Confusingly, *qualificato* can range in meaning from: expert, through high quality to skilled. Thus *personale qualificato* is expert staff, *un servizio* di assistenza* altamente qualificato* is a high quality or expert after-sales service, *disponibile nei punti di vendita più qualificati* means: available at the best retailers/sales outlets, *un qualificato servizio d'informazione* is a well-informed information or news service (———→ INFORMATIVO), while *un operaio qualificato* is a skilled worker. As well as to qualify, *qualificare* is, sometimes: to train, skill or or upgrade. *Qualificare la manodopera*, e.g., is to train/skill the workforce, and *i nuovi laboratori qualificheranno ulteriormente l'ospedale* means that the new labs will further upgrade the hospital. Similarly, *la qualificazione* can be upgrading as well as qualification, as in *la qualificazione delle città termali come grandi centri salutistici*, the upgrading of spa towns to major health centres.

qualità, n.f. — quality, but sometimes value judgement is not involved. A shop *che vi offre diverse qualità di formaggi e vini* is, therefore, really offering you various (———→ DIVERSO) types or varieties of cheeses and wines, while *persone di ogni qualità* are people of all types.

questione, n.f. — is only a question in the sense of a topic that needs to be discussed (*un sondaggio della Doxa sulle questioni scottanti del momento*, an opinion poll by Doxa — the Italian equivalent of Gallup — on the burning issues of the moment), or else a problem that needs to be solved (e.g. Gramsci's essay *La questione meridionale* (1930) ['The Problem of the South'], and Italy's perennial language question/dispute, *la questione della lingua* ———→ LINGUAGGIO). A question requiring an answer is *una domanda*, and to ask a question is *fare una domanda* (———→ DOMANDARE).
———→ RILEVANTE

quota, n.f. — (a) quota (*una quota di immigrazione*, an immigration quota), but do not count on it. Sometimes it means: share (*ho versato la mia quota*, I've paid my share), rate (*la quota fissa per ogni medicinale prescritta crescerà a tremila lire*, the fixed rate for every prescription will rise to 3,000 lire ———→ TICKET), fee: *la quota (di partecipazione) per il corso è centomila lire* states that the fee for the course is 100,000 lire, or level (*L'Europa ha la quota più alta di disoccupazione giovanile**, Europe has the highest level of youth unemployment). More surprisingly, it means: height above sea-level or else altitude. Thus *sono nato nelle Dolomiti a quota 1000m.*, I was born 1000m. up in the Dolomites, and *volare ad alta/bassa quota*, to fly at high or low altitude.

quotato, adj. — not quoted (= *citato* ———→ CITAZIONE, QUOTAZIONE), except on the stock exchange (*titoli quotati in borsa* are listed securities). Otherwise it means: highly regarded, so that *un giovane romanziere* (———→ ROMANZO) *molto quotato* is, despite appearances, a young novelist who is very highly thought of, and *il corso più quotato, affidabile ed economico esistente sul mercato* is the most highly-rated, reliable and cheapest course on the market.
———→ AZIONE, TITOLO

quotazione, n.f. — a quotation on the stock market (———→ AZIONE, TITOLO) but never of someone's words = *una citazione**. *Un attore che ha un'ottima quotazione* is an actor who is highly regarded (———→ QUOTATO), *la quotazione d'un cavallo* is a horse's betting odds in a race, while *le quotazioni della zona* centrale di Milano sono colate a picco* means: house prices in the central area/district of Milan have plummeted. On the other hand, a quotation or estimate for a house or for work to be done = *un preventivo**.

R

raccomandazione, n.f. — recommendation for a job, but with rather special overtones of influence and protection. Either written or verbal, *la raccomandazione* from someone influential — in politics, the church or business — has traditionally smoothed the path to employment. Its importance is explicable in a country distrustful of official mechanisms, reliant on person-to-person dealings, where (at time of writing) the spoils and patron-client system were only starting to be dismantled (————→ CONCUSSIONE), and where the reference (*la referenza*) is invariably only an open testimonial. The practice is amusingly described in Moravia's short story 'La Raccomandazione' in *Nuovi Racconti Romani* (1959) ['New Roman Tales']. A term also associated with anxious mothers, in which case it means: exhortation or urging, e.g. *ignorò le raccomandazioni della madre di mettersi il cappotto*, he ignored his mother's pleas for him to wear his coat; the mother's words, frequently heard in Italy, would be: *mi raccomando, mettiti il cappotto*, be sure to/don't forget to put your coat on, eh? The committee's recommendations to the government are ... = *la commissione* ha suggerito al/consigliato al governo di ...* Note that *raccomandare una lettera* is to register a letter (————→ REGISTRARE).

radiazione, n.f. — corresponds, mostly, to radiation but crops up unexpectedly meaning: the striking off/U.S. taking a license from a doctor, *la radiazione d'un medico*, or the banning of a sportsperson, *la radiazione d'uno sportivo*.

radicchio, n.m. — shares its origins with radish but is actually a type of chicory. Best known outside Italy is the large red variety from Treviso, *il radicchio rosso di Treviso*.

rapire, v. — appears, confusingly, in crime reports, but means not: to rape (= *stuprare* or *violentare*) but to kidnap or abduct, so *i quattro giovani hanno rapito l'infermiera nel centro di Roma* actually means that the four youths abducted the nurse in the centre of Rome.
————→ SEQUESTRARE

rapporto, n.m. — may simply be a rapport (*un buon rapporto tra medico e paziente*, a good rapport between a doctor and his patients) or relationship (*essere in buoni rapporti con i genitori*, to get on well with one's parents ————→ PARENTE). On the other hand, it can be a report (*il rapporto annuale della Banca mondiale*, the annual report of the World Bank) or — more trickily — the sexual act. *L'età del primo rapporto* is the age at which young people first have sex, *i rapporti prematrimoniali* (————→ MATRIMONIO) is pre-marital sex, and the advert (————→ PUBBLICITÀ): *L'AIDS non si trasmette vivendo una normale vita sessuale ma attraverso rapporti con persone già infette* means that AIDS is transmitted not through a normal sex life, but by having sex with people who are already infected (————→ PROMISCUO).
————→ OCCASIONALE, PRESERVATIVO

rata, n.f. — occurs in the context of finance. However, it means not: rate but instalment, e.g. *ripagare l'ipoteca in 12 rate mensili*, to pay off the mortgage in 12 monthly instalments. The exchange/interest rate = *il tasso di cambio/d'interesse*, an hourly rate = *una tariffa* oraria*, and a fast rate = *un ritmo veloce*.

realizzare, v. — to realise profits, projects, hopes or dreams, but also to make. *Un film realizzato da Fellini*, is a film made by F., *un prodotto realizzato in materiale* resistente* (⟶ RESISTENZA) *e impermeabile*, is a product made in a durable, waterproof substance, *una società* che studia, progetta e realizza reti di telecomunicazioni* means: a company which devises, plans and sets up/puts in place telecommunications networks, and *una guida completa realizzata in inglese* is a complete guide written in English. On the football field, *realizzare un gol* is: to score a goal. Do you realise what you are doing? = *ti rendi conto di quello che fai?* On film credits, *realizzazione di* means: directed by.
⟶ STUDIARE

realtà, n.f. — reality, but it may not always be so straightforward. *Un attento osservatore di tutte le realtà sociali della città*, e.g., is a careful observer of all the social situations or problems of the city, and *un prete che è vicino alla realtà giovanile** is a priest close to the problems of the young.

recitare, v. — is occasionally: to recite (*recitare una poesia*, to recite a poem ⟶ POEMA), but mainly to act or play a part on stage or in film, e.g. *recitare la parte di Ofelia*, to play the part of Ophelia, *si recitano poco le commedie del Cinquecento*, 16th-century plays (⟶ COMMEDIA) are rarely acted, and *Claudia Schiffer ha appena finito di recitare se stessa in un film … dedicato* (⟶ DEDICARE) *alla sua vita* (*Panorama*, 5/9/93), C.S. has just finished playing herself in a film devoted to her life. *Recitare a soggetto** is: to improvise, as in the title of Pirandello's play *Questa sera si recita a soggetto* (1930) ['This Evening We're Improvising']. Disconcertingly, it also means: to state, in official documents, e.g. *l'articolo 16 della Costituzione recita che …*, article 16 of the Constitution states that. As well as recitation (⟶ DIZIONE), *la recitazione* is acting, so that *una recitazione sofferta* is intense acting.
⟶ INTERPRETARE, SCENA

recordman, n.m. — not a disc jockey (= *un disc-jockey* or *digei*, i.e. D.J.) but a record-holder in sport. Italy's best sprinter of the 1970s, Pietro Mennea, was *recordman del mondo dei 200m.*, world record-holder over 200 m. The female equivalent is the even more bizarre false anglicism *una recordwoman*.
⟶ SPRINT

registrare, v. — occasionally to register (*registrare un veicolo*, to register a car) but mainly to record, e.g. *il termometro ha registrato temperature altissime quest'estate*, the thermometer has recorded exceptionally high temperatures this summer, and *questo dizionario registra sistematicamente i neologismi*, this dictionary systematically records or lists neologisms. You are bound to come across it most frequently in the context of sound recording, as in *registrare una canzone* or *una conversazione*, to record a song or a conversation, or in the ad. for the Italian telephone service's answer-phones: *Telefoni risponditori S.I.P. Registri la tua voce e rispondono per te*, S.I.P. answer-phones. You record your voice, and they answer for you. To register for a course = *iscriversi* (⟶ ISCRIZIONE), to register a birth = *denunciare**, and to register a letter = *raccomandare* (⟶ RACCOMANDAZIONE).

relazione, n.f. — relation or relationship (*relazioni diplomatiche*, diplomatic relations, *relazioni pubbliche*, public relations, and *stabilire una relazione*, to establish a relationship), but also a paper or report. Thus *presentare una relazione al convegno* is: to give a paper at the conference (⟶ CONFERENZA), and *la consueta relazione del 31 maggio del* *governatore della Banca d'Italia* is the usual report (———→ RAPPORTO) on 31 May by/from the governor of the Bank of Italy. A family relation = *un parente**.

replica, n.f. — can correspond to a replica (*la replica d'una statua*, the replica of a statue). You may be puzzled, though, by the comment: *la commedia*/lo spettacolo* ha avuto 50 repliche* or *molte repliche*, the play/show had fifty performances, or had a long run. *Il diritto di replica* is the right of reply.

resistenza, n.f. — resistance in all senses, but stamina, endurance or toughness, too, so that *avere una grande resistenza (fisica)* is: to have tremendous endurance, while *la resistenza di una stoffa** is the toughness or durability of a fabric. Note that *colori resistenti* are fast colours, and that *una porta che resiste* is a door which will not give or budge.

retribuzione, n.f. — is never punitive retribution (= *la punizione* or *il castigo*; divine retribution = *la giustizia divina*) but only remuneration or salary. The ambiguous-looking statement *la scarsa retribuzione degli insegnanti* is, therefore, only referring to the poor pay levels (———→ SCARSO) of teachers.

revisione, n.f. — is the revision of a contract, of a timetable or of a piece of writing. However, it is also an overhaul (*una revisione del motore*, an overhaul of the engine), or a service (*la revisione del riscaldamento centrale* or *della macchina**, the servicing of the central heating or of the car). Revision for an examination = *un ripasso*.

riciclare, v. — to recycle waste, but also used figuratively meaning: to launder money, as in *riciclare i guadagni illeciti della Mafia*, laundering the Mafia's illegal earnings.
———→ RICUPERARE

ricognizione, n.f. — resembles recognition (= *il riconoscimento*) but means: reconnaissance, as in *un'approfondita ricognizione dei sistemi missilistici del nemico*, in-depth reconnaissance of the enemy's missile systems. However, *la ricognizione di un cadavere* is the identification of a body.
———→ ESPLORARE

ricorrenza, n.f. — recurrence but also, rather oddly, a festivity, feast day or holiday, as in *festeggiare una ricorrenza*, to celebrate (———→ CELEBRARE) an anniversary, *la ricorrenza del 2 novembre*, Remembrance Day, and *nella ricorrenza del tuo compleanno*, on the occasion of your birthday.

ricoverare, v. — perversely close in context to recover (= *guarire, rimettersi* or *ristabilirsi* of health, or *ricuperare** of objects), it really means: to admit/send to hospital or to hospitalise. Compare *è stato ricoverato (in ospedale) d'urgenza*, he was rushed to hospital, and he recovered in hospital = *si è rimesso in ospedale*. Can also mean: to take in, care for or look after, as in *I piccoli barbagianni caduti dal nido sono ricoverati al centro della L.I.P.U.*, Baby owls fallen from the nest are cared for at the L.I.P.U. centre (Italy's bird-protection organisation). *Una casa di ricovero* or *di riposo* is an old people's home.
———→ CURARE

ricuperare, v. — to recuperate costs or expenses (*ricuperare il denaro speso*, to recuperate or recover the money spent), but not to recuperate from an injury or illness (= *rimettersi* or *ristabilirsi* ———→ RICOVERARE). Can also pose problems when it means: to salvage or recover (*i corpi sono stati ricuperati dalle macerie*, the bodies were recovered from the rubble), to play a postponed match (*ricuperare una partita*), to rehabilitate (*ricuperare gli handicappati e i tossicodipendenti*, to rehabilitate handicapped people and drug addicts), or to re-use/recycle (*il comune ricupera il vetro*, the town council recycles glass ———→ RICICLARE).

riduzione, n.f. — is reduction, but it can be treacherous when it means: adaptation. *La riduzione cinematografica di un romanzo**, e.g., is the screen adaptation of a novel, while the Taviani brothers' film *Kaos* (1984) could be described as *la libera riduzione di una serie di novelle di Pirandello*, the free adaptation of a series of P.'s short stories.

riferire, v. — when reflexive, is: to refer (*a che cosa ti riferisci?* what are you referring to?). Otherwise it means: to report, tell or communicate, so do not confuse *riferisco soltanto quello che ho sentito*, I'm only reporting/repeating what I heard, and I'm only referring to what I heard = *faccio solo riferimento a quello che ho sentito*. I referred him to a good lawyer = *l'ho indirizzato a/gli ho indicato un avvocato in gamba*.
———→ RIPORTARE

riformare, v. — to reform, but also to declare unfit/to exempt from military service, *il servizio militare* or *la naia* (coll.), which in Italy is compulsory and lasts for one year. To be rejected, *riformato* or *esonerato* (———→ ESONERARE), you must either be in poor health, be below 1m. 50 in height, be the eldest of at least seven children, be the son of a pensioner, or the only child of a widow. Students may defer (*rinviare*) their call up (*la leva*) till age 26.
———→ DISLOCARE

rigido, adj. — is rigid, but it crops up unexpectedly in the context of weather, meaning: very cold, so that *un clima rigido* is a harsh climate, and *temperature troppo rigide per l'uomo* are temperatures which are too severe for man.

riguardo, n.m. — not regard (= *la considerazione* ———→ CONSIDERATO, or *la stima*) but respect or care. Traditionally, Italians treat the old with respect, *trattano gli anziani* (———→ ANZIANO) *con riguardo*. An inconsiderate person is, therefore, *una persona senza riguardi*, while *gli ospiti di riguardo* are distinguished guests (———→ DISTINTO). My regards to the family = *(tanti) saluti alla famiglia*.

rilasciare, v. — to release a person (*rilasciare gli ostaggi*, to release the hostages) or information (*rilasciare la notizia**, to release the news), but also to issue or give. *Rilasciare un passaporto* is, therefore: to issue a passport, and *rilasciare un'intervista* is: to give or grant an interview. To release a film = *distribuire un film*.

rilevante, adj. — deceptively similar to relevant in appearance and context, it actually means: significant. *Una questione* rilevante*, an important issue is, therefore, not the same as a relevant question = *una domanda* (———→ DOMANDARE) *pertinente*. Similarly, *informazioni rilevanti* is: significant or noteworthy information or news (———→ INFORMATIVO), whereas all the relevant information = *tutte le relative informazioni*. A relevant course (of study) = *un corso utile*, this is not relevant to my needs = *questo è estraneo a* or *non ha niente a che fare con le mie esigenze*, and what he wrote is still relevant = *quel che ha*

scritto rimane sempre valido/attuale*. Similarly, *la rilevanza* is not relevance (= *la pertinenza*) but significance or importance, so that *personaggi di grande rilevanza* are personages or characters (————→ PERSONAGGIO) of great significance/consequence.
————→ INCIDENZA, IRRELEVANTE

rimuovere, v. — to remove but also, in psychoanalysis, to repress, as in *rimuovere ricordi penosi*, to repress painful memories. This is a main theme of Primo Levi's meditation on Holocaust survival, *I Sommersi e i Salvati* (1986) ['The Drowned and the Saved'].

rinunciare, v. — does correspond to renounce but, more mundanely (————→ MONDANO), it is often just: to give up, say no to or do without, e.g. *Per paura di prendere l'aereo Sylvester Stallone rinuncia alla vacanza a St Moritz* (*Noidonne*, March 1991), Because of his fear of flying, S.S. says no to his holiday in St Moritz, and *ho rinunciato a capire questo libro*, I've given up trying to understand this book.

riparare, v. — to repair an object or a wrong, but also to shelter or protect, e.g. *una polizza che ripara la famiglia da eventuali perdite*, an insurance policy protecting the family from losses which may occur (————→ EVENTUALE). To repair (to a place) = *recarsi a*.
————→ AGGIUSTARE, RIPARAZIONE

riparazione, n.f. — reparation (*le riparazioni di guerra*, war reparations) but often, simply, repair, e.g. *una casa in riparazione*, a house that is undergoing repairs, and *un vestito che ha bisogno di riparazioni*, a dress that needs mending (————→ AGGIUSTARE). Note, in particular, *l'esame di riparazione*, the Autumn resit exam taken by school pupils who fail a subject in the Summer examination (————→ VOTO).
————→ RIPARARE

ripetizione, n.f. — repetition, but watch out for it meaning: a private lesson, e.g. *prendere ripetizioni d'inglese*, to take private English lessons. Since the Italian school day finishes early and parents (————→ PARENTE) tend to be very keen on their children doing well at school, *dare ripetizioni*, coaching, is common in the afternoons.

riportare, v. — in journalism, is not: to report but to carry or publish, as when *Campus* (3/3/92) described 'What's on in London' and 'Time Out' as *i due giornali che riportano settimanalmente il calendario di concerti e spettacoli* (————→ SPETTACOLO) *teatrali*, the two papers which carry/publish weekly listings of concerts and theatre shows. '*Novella Duemila' riporta interviste con vedettes del mondo dello spettacolo* means: *Novella Duemila* (a popular scandal and tit-bits magazine) carries interviews with show-business stars. On the other hand, the newspaper reported the event = *il giornale ha pubblicato* or *dedicato* (————→ DEDICARE) *un servizio*/un reportage sull'/all'evento*, or alternatively: *ha fatto il resoconto/la cronaca dell'evento*. To further complicate matters, *riportare* can also mean: to quote, as in *l'articolo riporta per esteso i giudizi dei critici*, the article quotes the critics' views at length (————→ CITAZIONE).
————→ RIFERIRE

riservato, adj. — reserved in all senses, but also confidential, as in *un documento/uno studio* riservato*, a confidential document or study.

ristorazione, n.f. — looks like restoration (= *il restauro*, of a building or work of art, and *la restaurazione*, of a monarchy) but means: catering (from *ristorante*, restaurant). *Una ristorazione efficiente e economica* is, therefore, efficient, cheap catering. The root concept underlying all of these terms is the return to normality.
———→ CONSERVATIVO

ristrutturare, v. — may simply be: to restructure (*ristrutturare un'organizzazione/un' azienda*, to restructure an organisation or a firm), but the word's original, literal meaning of to renovate or refurbish persists, so that the ad. *vendesi appartamento completamente ristrutturato* means: for sale — flat/U.S. apartment, entirely renovated.

ritirare, v. — not to retire from work (= *andare in pensione*) but to withdraw, pick up or collect. *Ritirare soldi da un conto corrente* is: to withdraw money from a current account (———→ ACCONTO), *ritirare lo stipendio* is: to draw one's salary (———→ RETRIBUZIONE), and *ritirare la posta* is: to collect the post or mail. Italians retire at 60 (men) and 55 (women), and their pension provision, at 70% of the average national wage, was the highest in Europe in the early 1990s.

riunione, n.f. — reunion (*una riunione di famiglia*, a family reunion), but often simply a meeting, e.g. *una riunione del personale*, a staff meeting, *una riunione del consiglio dei ministri*, a Cabinet meeting, and *una riunione d'atletica*, an athletics meet. *Il direttore* è in riunione* means: the manager or boss is in a meeting (———→ AGENDA).

riverenza, n.f. — reverence, but *fare una riverenza* is: to make a bow or drop a curtsey.

riviera, n.f. — not the riviera or Côte d'Azur (= *la costa* azzurra*). It is any coast(line), e.g. *la riviera adriatica*, the Adriatic coast, taking in the resorts of Rimini, Riccione and Cattolica. The Italian riviera is called *la riviera ligure* (i.e. Ligurian coast) or *la riviera di levante* (for the stretch east of Genoa) and *la riviera di ponente* (for the part west of Genoa). The coast around San Remo is known as *la riviera dei fiori* as flowers are a major crop. Remember that a river = *un fiume*.
———→ MARINA, STAZIONE

rodeo, n.m. — a rodeo but, by extension, *un rodeo automobilistico* is a joyride or joyriding.

romanesco, n.m. and adj. — is not the architectural style, Romanesque (= *lo stile romanico*, as in the jewel-like Badia in Fiesole, above Florence), but the working-class dialect of Rome, employed by the poet G.G. Belli (1791–1863), and much in evidence in the post-war neo-realist films of De Sica and Rossellini. *L'accento romanesco* (Italy's cockney) has characterised popular actors like Nino Manfredi and Anna Magnani.

romanzo, n.m. — not (a) romance but a novel, e.g. *i romanzi storici di Walter Scott hanno influenzato il romanticismo italiano*, W.S.'s historical novels influenced Italian Romanticism. *Un (romanzo) giallo* (lit. a yellow novel) is a thriller or detective novel, because of the yellow covers of an early popular crime series. Similarly, a sentimental novel or Harlequin Romance is *un (romanzo) rosa** (lit. a pink novel). He was searching for romance =

cercava l'avventura*, while their romance was brief = *il loro idillio/flirt dùrò poco*. The Romance languages are *le lingue romanze*.
————→ NARRATIVA

rosa, n.f. — rose, of course, but the odd-looking *rosa dei candidati* is the group or list of candidates, *la rosa dei nomi* is the shortlist, and *la rosa dei favoriti* is the group of favourites (for a post or selection). Note that *un film rosa* is a romantic film, and *un romanzo* rosa* is a 'Mills and Boon'-type novel or Harlequin Romance.

rude, adj. — looks like rude (= *maleducato* ————→ EDUCAZIONE) but means: rough or brusque of behaviour. So *un tipo rude ma simpatico* (————→ SIMPATIA), a 'rough diamond', is rather different from a rude type = *un tipo maleducato*.

ruffiano, n.m. — in spite of appearances, has nothing to do with ruffian (= *un bruto*, *un ribaldo* or *una canaglia*). It is a pimp (also *un puttaniere*, *un pappone* or *un magnaccia*) and, by extension, a crawler or bootlicker, as in *fa il ruffiano con i superiori*, he sucks up to the bosses. Ruffian derives from *ruffiano*, via French, but popular etymology associated *ruff-* with rough, and eventually altered its meaning.
————→ CASINO, PRESERVATIVO

rumore, n.m. — has nothing to do with rumour (= *una voce*; a rumour is going around = *corre voce*). It is, instead, a noise, as in *il rumore insopportabile del traffico*, the unbearable noise of the traffic (————→ SOPPORTARE).

S

salutare, v. — to salute but also, of course, to greet, e.g. *ho salutato gli amici prima di partire*, I said goodbye to my friends before leaving, and *salutami tuo padre*, say hello to your father for me. *Un saluto* is a greeting as well as a salute, as in *tanti saluti!* best wishes/all the best!

sanità, n.f. — can be sanity (*la sanità mentale* or *di mente*), although sanity should prevail in the end = *alla fine il buon senso* dovrebbe trionfare*, and he regained his sanity might be: *ha ristabilito/riacquisito l'equilibrio mentale/psicologico. La sanità* is most commonly encountered, however, meaning: health, in general. The statement: *proteggere la sanità morale e mentale dei bambini* is urging us to protect children's moral and mental health, while the headline *Sanità, il governo nel caos dei ticket** (*L'Espresso*, 16/4/89) means: Health — the government in a mess over (health) charges, and *tagliare la spesa nei settori più costosi: sanità e prevedenza* is: cost-cutting in the most expensive areas — health and benefits. Note in particular *il Ministero della sanità*, the Ministry of Health, *la sanità pubblica*, public health, and *l'Organizzazione mondiale della sanità*, the W.H.O. *Sanitario* is: sanitary (although a sanitary towel/napkin = *un assorbente igienico* ——→ IGIENE), but usually it means: 'health', as in *la programmazione sanitaria*, health planning (——→ PROGRAMMARE), *l'assistenza* sanitaria*, health care, and *il Servizio Sanitario Nazionale*, the National Health Service. Treatment in Italy is obtained via the local U.S.L. (*Unità sanitaria locale*) health clinic.
——→ CURARE, SANO, TILT

sano, adj. — not only mentally sane (= *sano di mente*) but physically healthy. *Il mangiar sano*, healthy eating, is fashionable. The pasta manufacturer Barilla urges consumers with the ad.: *mangia sano, torna alla natura*, eat healthy, go back to nature, and Convagri (the Italian fruit and vegetable growers' association) boasts of: *Una tradizione buona, intelligente, sana. Mangiare all'italiana*, A good, intelligent, healthy tradition. Eating — Italian style. A sane attitude or approach = *un atteggiamento* or *un approccio sensato/ pieno di buon senso*/equilibrato* (——→ SENSIBILE).
——→ DIETA, GENUINO, INTEGRALE, SANITÀ

sanzione, n.f. — sanction (*le sanzioni economiche*, economic sanctions, and *dare la propria sanzione a*, to give one's sanction to), but also a legal penalty, punishment or measure. The statement: *limiti obbligatori a 50 e 40 km/h quando c'è scarsa* (——→ SCARSO) *visibilità, con pesanti sanzioni per i trasgressori* means: obligatory speed limits of 50 and 40 km.p.h., with heavy penalties/fines for offenders.

scarso, adj. — indicates a lack, but is seldom a direct equivalent of scarce. *La scarsa visibilità*, e.g., is poor visibility, *mostrare uno scarso interesse* is: to show little interest, *con scarsi risultati/successo* is: with little result/success, *un anno scarso per gli affari* is a poor year for business (——→ AFFARE), *un'esistenza di scarse soddisfazioni* is a life of few rewards, and *le porzioni erano scarse* means: the portions were meagre or small. Shopkeepers weighing out goods for you will announce: *sono due chili scarsi*, that's just under 2kg. (——→ ABBONDANTE). On the other hand, sugar is scarce this year = *c'è una penuria di zucchero quest'anno*, while the recommendation: Water is scarce — don't waste it = *L'acqua è poca: non sprecarla. Scarsamente* is rarely the same as scarcely (=

appena, a stento, a malapena or *non ... certo*), so compare *un'operazione utile ma scarsamente efficace*, a useful operation but of limited effectiveness, with a useful but scarcely effective operation = *un'operazione utile ma non certo efficace*.

scena, n.f. — corresponds to scene in virtually all contexts, theatrical or otherwise, but it also means: the stage itself, so that *il lato destro della scena* is: stage right, *entrare in scena* is: to come on stage, and *mettere in scena una commedia** is: to stage a play.
———→ DRAMMA, PROSA, STAGE

scenario, n.m. — a scenario both in the sense of a film or play outline, and of a future sequence of events (*dopo le recenti elezioni ci sono due possibili scenari*, there are two possible scenarios after the recent elections). Be on your guard, though. It can also be stage scenery/decor/set, or a (natural) backdrop/setting, e.g. *ha contribuito al successo dell'Otello lo stupendo scenario del Palazzo Ducale*, the magnificent backdrop of the Doge's Palace contributed to the success of *Othello*; *il fascino di una natura selvaggia e la suggestione* di scenari unici al mondo*, the charms or attractions of untamed nature and the spell of settings/scenery which is/are unique (———→ UNICO); and *un servizio* con commenti* (———→ COMMENTO), *analisi* e previsioni sullo scenario italiano e internazionale*, a report with comments, analyses and forecasts against an Italian and international background.
———→ DECORO, SCENA

scientifico, adj. — scientific, but should not be taken for granted. It may also mean: scholarly, rigorous or objective. *Criteri scientifici*, e.g., are objective criteria, and *pubblicazioni scientifiche*, scholarly publications, stand opposed to *pubblicazioni divulgative*, popular(ising) books (———→ DIVULGARE). When reading newspaper crime-reports (*la cronaca nera*) you will bump into *la (squadra/la polizia) scientifica*, the police forensic unit.

scintillante, adj. — scintillating (*idee scintillanti*, scintillating ideas), but also, commonly, shining or gleaming. *Gli occhi scintillanti* are, therefore, bright/shining eyes, and *uno scintillante vaso* di bronzo* is a gleaming bronze jar. The opening lines of Grazia Deledda's novel *Canne al Vento* (1913) ['Canes in the Wind'] describe the Sardinian landscape as *scintillante d'acqua nel crepuscolo*, gleaming with water in the twilight.
———→ BRILLANTE

sciroppo, n.m. — syrup/U.S. sirup, but also the fruit cordial, of various flavours, sold in all cafés (———→ BAR, CAFFÈ) diluted with mineral or soda water. *Lo sciroppo* and crushed or slush ice are the ingredients of the popular and refreshing *granita* or *granatina*. *Uno sciroppo per la tosse* is a cough-mixture.

scolaro, n.m. — not as grand as a scholar (= *uno studioso*); it is only a school pupil (also *un alunno* or *un allievo*).
———→ SCOLASTICO

scolastico, adj. — is only rarely scholastic. It almost always means: 'school', 'of school' or 'educational', as in *il sistema scolastico*, the school or education system, *i libri scolastici*, school books, and *la riforma scolastica*, educational reform.
———→ DIDATTICO, EDUCAZIONE, SCOLARO

scopo, n.m. — not scope (= *i termini di riferimento, la portata, l'occasione*, il margine di manovra**, or *il raggio d'azione**) but aim or intention. Compare *lo scopo di quest' inchiesta**, the aim of this enquiry, and the scope of this enquiry = *la portata* or *i termini di referimento di quest'inchiesta. Lo scopo della mia vita* is: my aim in life, *l'inglese per scopi speciali* is English for special purposes, while the expression *a scopo di lucro* means: purely for financial gain.
———→ FINALITÀ

scorno, n.m. — resembles scorn (= *il disprezzo*) but means humiliation or shame, as in the satirical cartoon (———→ VIGNETTA) by Forattini in *L'Espresso* in August 1993 showing Italian troops being kicked out of Somalia over the punning caption: *scorno d'Africa*, African humiliation/horn (i.e. *corno*) of Africa.
———→ SMACCO

scotch, n.m. — not just the whisky but the sticky tape. *Mi serve lo scotch* will almost certainly mean: I need the sellotape.

scrupolo, n.m. — scruple (*gente senza scrupoli* are unscrupulous people), but also great or meticulous care, so that *un lavoro fatto con scrupolo* is a job done meticulously.
———→ ACCURATO

scrutinio, n.m. — not scrutiny (= *l'esame critico/minuzioso*) but election ballot/poll (*uno scrutinio segreto*, a secret ballot) or count (*effettuare lo scrutinio*, to count the votes). Also the examining board of secondary-school teachers (———→ PROFESSORE) meeting at the end of the term or year to award marks/grades to a class (———→ VOTO), e.g. *lunedì si fà lo scrutinio del trimestre*, we're meeting on Monday to assign this term's marks or grades.
———→ URNA

secolare, adj. — secular (*il potere secolare*, secular power), but also centuries-old or age-old, e.g. *un albero secolare*, a centuries-old tree, and *la rassegnazione secolare dei contadini*, the age-old resignation of (the) peasants.

sedato, adj. — sedated, of pain, but also put down, of unrest. *Disordini sedati dalle forze dell'ordine* are riots quelled by the security forces, and *le sue proteste hanno scatenato una rissa sedata solo con l'intervento* della polizia* means: his protests sparked off a row/a fracas only put down when the police intervened.

semaforo, n.m. — a different type of signalling from semaphore (= *il sistema di comunicazione con le bandierine*). It is in fact the traffic lights, so that *il traffico si è fermato al semaforo* means: the traffic stopped at the lights.
———→ CIRCOLAZIONE

sensibile, adj. — an almost irresistible deceptive cognate meaning not: sensible (= *sensato* or *dotato di buon senso*/di giudizio*) but sensitive. It is tempting to take *un bambino sensibile*, a sensitive child, for a sensible one = *un bambino sensato/di giudizio*. The statement *mi piacciono gli uomini di carattere*, ma che siano anche sensibili*, therefore means: I like men to have character, but also to be sensitive, and *avere la pelle sensibile* is: to have sensitive skin. Note that *un amico sensibile ai miei problemi* is a friend who is sympathetic/responsive to my problems. It can mean: appreciable, noticeable or tangible, too, though. Do not be taken in by *un sensibile incremento* annuale*: it is an appreciable annual increase, while the assertion by Olivetti that *lo sviluppo tecnologico ha modificato in modo sempre più sensibile l'organizzazione lavorativa delle imprese* maintains that technological change has modified, in an increasingly tangible way, companies' working practices. Mind the adverb as well — *il canone del duplex* è sensibilmente inferiore** means: the rental for a shared 'phone-line is appreciably lower. As for *sensibilizzare*, it means: to make aware, e.g. *una campagna per sensibilizzare l'opinione pubblica ai problemi ambientali*, a campaign to raise public awareness/consciousness of environmental problems.

senso, n.m. — sense, whether of meaning (*capire il senso della frase**, to understand the meaning/sense of the sentence, and *questo non ha senso*, this makes no sense), judgement (*mi fido del tuo buon senso*, I trust in your good sense), the body (*i cinque sensi*, the five senses), or the feelings (*provare un senso di colpa*, to have a sense/feeling of guilt). However, it is also direction or way, so that the *senso unico** road-sign means: one way, and *in senso orario* is: clockwise. More surprisingly, it means: disgust or repugnance, as in *il sangue/i topi mi fa(nno) senso*, blood/mice disgust(s) me, and in the title of Visconti's film *Senso* (1954), set in the Risorgimento period.
———→ SENSIBILE, SENTIMENTO

sentenza, n.f. — rather tricky since it occurs in the same legal contexts as sentence (= *una condanna* ———→ CONDANNARE, DENUNCIARE) but means: a verdict or decision. *La sentenza del tribunale** is, therefore, the court's verdict, *una sentenza controversa* is a controversial verdict or decision, and *il primo processo* fu nel 1978, l'ultima* (———→ ULTIMO) *sentenza nel 1992* means: the first trial was in 1978, the last verdict in 1992 (the last sentence, on the other hand = *l'ultima condanna*). A grammatical sentence = *una frase**.

sentimento, n.m. — is generally best rendered by feeling, as in *ho espresso i miei sentimenti*, I've expressed my feelings/spoken my mind, and *i demagoghi che strumentalizzano i sentimenti del pubblico*, the demagogues who manipulate the public's feelings. *Provare un sentimento di gratitudine/gioia* is: to feel gratitude or joy. It can mean: sense, too, e.g. *ha poco sentimento*, he's lacking in good sense (———→ SENSO). *Questi sono pure i miei sentimenti* corresponds to: these are my sentiments/feelings, as well, and *il sentimento è importante quanto la razionalità* states that sentiment is as important as reason. However, if derogatory, use *il sentimentalismo*, e.g. a love story full of (cloying) sentiment = *una storia d'amore piena di sentimentalismo*.

sequestrare, v. — to sequestrate, seize, confiscate or impound but also, less predictably, to kidnap, e.g. *Aldo Moro fu sequestrato e assassinato dalle BR nel 1978*, A.M. was kidnapped and murdered/assassinated (———→ ASSASSINARE) by the Red Brigades in 1978.
———→ RAPIRE

serenità, n.f. — serenity, but usually more appropriately rendered by peace of mind, as in the UNIPUL insurance ad.: *la serenità di una donna e la sicurezza di una famiglia meritano più attenzione*, a woman's peace of mind and a family's security deserve more attention.
———→ EQUANIMITÀ

serio, adj. — may simply be serious (*un problema serio*, a serious problem, and *uno sguardo serio*, a serious look), but it often means: honest, reliable or hardworking. Compare *uno studente serio*, a committed student, or one who takes his or her work seriously, and *uno studente serioso*, an earnest student who may lack a sense of humour. *Una ditta seria* is a reputable firm.

servizio, n.m. — straightforwardly: service in most cases. It may cause problems, though, when it means: a report or feature in the media, or else a bathroom/toilet. Thus *il telegiornale riporta* (⟶ RIPORTARE) *regolarmente un servizio da Montecitorio*, the T.V. news carries/features regular reports on proceedings in parliament (⟶ PALAZZO), and *un appartamento con doppi servizi*, a flat/U.S. apartment with two bathrooms.

simile, n.m. — not a simile (= *una similitudine*) but a fellow human being. *Amare e rispettare i propri simili* is: to love and respect one's fellow man, while the proverb *ogni simile ama il suo simile* means: birds of a feather flock together.

simpatia, n.f. — not sympathy but liking or attraction for somebody. Contrast *provo simpatia per lui*, I like him/I find him likeable, and I feel sympathy for him = *provo compassione, pietà*, commiserazione* or (if shared feeling) *comprensione per lui*. Alitalia seek to create *un'atmosfera tipicamente italiana, con tutta la sua tradizionale simpatia*, a typically Italian atmosphere, with all its traditional likeableness. From *simpatia* is derived that key word *simpatico*, as Italian as its rough equivalent, nice, in English. *Una persona simpatica* is more than nice, though; they are attractively likeable. Note *mi è simpatico*, I like him, and its opposite *mi è antipatico*, I dislike or can't stand him.

sindacato, n.m. — can be a business syndicate (also = *un consorzio*), but you will invariably encounter it meaning: trade union. Italian unions, with around 10 million members in the early 1990s, have traditionally been formed around political rather than trade affiliations, and were at their strongest in the 1970s, achieving automatic wage-indexing (*la scala mobile*) and some of the best employment protection rights in Europe. Their decline in the 1980s and 1990s led to the scrapping of indexing and to the emergence of independent unions (*i sindacati autonomi* ⟶ AUTONOMIA) with no party affiliations. These are known by the acronym *Cobas* (i.e. *Comitati di base*, Grassroots Committees) and are particularly strong in education, transport/U.S. transportation, and the civil service. A press syndicate = *un'agenzia di stampa**, while a crime syndicate = *una racket*. Remember that *un sindaco* is a mayor.
⟶ AGITAZIONE, CATEGORIA, OCCUPAZIONE

singolo, adj. — although *una camera singola* is a single room, and *una facciata singola* is a single side (of paper), it usually means: individual, and should not be confused with single (= *unico*, solo, senza eccezione*, or *semplice*). When Rolex claim, of their watches, that *ogni singolo elemento è esaminato con cura* (⟶ CURARE), they mean that every individual element/component is carefully examined. Every single element, on the other hand = *ogni elemento senza eccezione*. Similarly, *la posologia corretta* (⟶ CORRETTO) *per ogni singolo paziente* is the correct dosage for each individual patient, and the observation *ogni singola regione d'Italia ha il suo dialetto o dialetti* states that every individual region of Italy has its dialect(s). He did everything in a single day = *ha fatto tutto in una sola giornata*, and Titian's masterpieces brought together in a single volume =

i capolavori di Tiziano raccolti in un unico volume. A single/U.S. one-way ticket = *un biglietto di sola andata*, while a single person = *un(a) single* or *una persona non sposata* (———→ CELIBE, NUBILE). *Un singolo* is an individual or else a tennis singles.

sinistro, adj. — sinister, but also 'on the left' (*il lato sinistro del viale*, the left side of the avenue). By extension, it also means: awful or 'sad', as in the assertion *Le zampe d'elefante e gli zatteroni: due delle più sinistre mode degli anni Settanta*, flares and platform soles: two of the 'saddest' 70s fashions. The left (*la sinistra*) has negative connotations in many languages.

sintetico, adj. — synthetic, but beware. It often means: concise or pithy, as when Collins Mondadori describe their range of dictionaries as *Pratici da consultare, precisi e sintetici*, Handy (———→ PRATICO) to consult, accurate (———→ ACCURATO) and concise. *Scrivere in modo sintetico ed efficace* therefore means: to write in a pithy and effective manner. Similarly, *descrivere una situazione sinteticamente* is: to describe a situation concisely. *La sintesi* is synthesis; however, if on your T.V. listings you find: *alle 23,30 Wimbledon: sintesi-replica**, then at 11.30 p.m. they are showing recorded highlights of Wimbledon.
———→ AGILE

sinuoso, adj. — sinuous or winding, but also curvaceous of a figure (———→ FIGURA), e.g. *un'attrice affascinante* e sinuosa*, a bewitching actress with a sexy figure.

slip, n.m. — not a slip (= *una sottoveste* or *una sottana*) and not worn exclusively by women. It is briefs, (under)pants or panties, but also bathing trunks or a bikini bottom. Boxer shorts are *un boxer*. The slip, chit or receipt you are given in shops when you make a purchase = *lo scontrino*.
———→ INTIMO

smacco, n.m. — not literally a smack or slap (= *uno schiaffo* or *una sberla*), although it is a figurative slap in the face. So *subire/patire uno smacco* is to suffer a let-down, blow or humiliation, and *il rifiuto del governo di trattare è stato un grave smacco per i terroristi* means: that the government's refusal to negotiate was a real slap in the face or serious blow/humiliation for the terrorists.
———→ SCORNO

soave, adj. — shares the idea of smoothness with suave, but without pejorative connotations. *Modi soavi* are, therefore, sweet or gentle manners, and should not be confused with suave manners = *modi insinuanti*. The headline in *La Repubblica* (8/4/93): *Abbado a Salisburgo ... Soave Brahms, ma senza applausi* means: Claudio A. in Salzburg ... Smooth/sweet-sounding Brahms, but the audience unenthusiastic. In the love-duet at the end of Act I of Puccini's *La Bohème* (1896), Rodolfo calls Mimì *soave fanciulla*, sweet maiden. The world-famous white wine, Soave, comes from the area near Verona in the western Veneto.
———→ GENTILE

sociale, adj. — is far from being restricted to social. As the adjective from *socio* (member, partner or associate) it is a widespread commercial term. The following are particularly useful: *il capitale sociale*, authorised or share capital, *la sede sociale*, company headquarters, *una quota** sociale*, a membership fee, and *i libri sociali*, a trader's books. Do not be misled by *una cantina* sociale*: it is a wine(grower's) co-operative. *Un pensionato sociale* is a pensioner on basic state pension.

società, n.f. — (a) society of any type, but you will come across it meaning: a commercial company, too. Thus una *Società per Azioni (S.p.A.)*, a Public Limited Company (P.L.C.), and the potentially more misleading *una società multinazionale*, a multinational company. Oddly enough, it is also a football club (————→ CIRCOLO).
————→ AZIONE, QUOTAZIONE, SOCIALE

sofisticato, adj. — lays two traps for the unwary. While *una tecnologia sofisticata* is sophisticated technology, *una persona* or *una moda sofisticata* are sometimes best rendered by: an affected person and an affected/fussy style. A sophisticated person or fashion = *una persona* or *una moda raffinata/chic/elegante*. Bewilderingly, it also means: doctored of food and drink, so that *un vino* or *un cibo sofisticato* will invariably be a doctored/adulterated wine or food.

soggetto, n.m. — can be the subject of a discussion, a painting or a sentence. However, a school/university subject = *una materia*, and the subject of a state = *un suddito*. Can also mean: an individual, as in *i soggetti psicologicamente più influenzabili sono i bambini*, the individuals/persons most easily influenced psychologically are children, and *lo stesso soggetto non può essere titolare di più di una licenza**, the same individual cannot hold more than one licence. Note that in the theatre *recitare* a soggetto* is: to improvise.
————→ ARGOMENTO

soluzione, n.f. — is any kind of solution. Sometimes, though, it simply means: an idea (————→ CONCETTO, IDEALE), as in the Lamy pen ad.: *Esclusiva ... per le soluzioni innovative come la clip*, Unique (————→ UNICO) ... with its innovative ideas like the clip. Trickier still, it can mean: payment, e.g. *rimborsiamo le tue spese in un'unica soluzione oppure gradualmente*, we refund your expenses in a single payment (————→ SINGOLO) or else over a period of time. Of high-tech equipment it means: resolution. Thus Sony advertise *il 20-bit, con la soluzione significativamente migliore*, 20-bit sound, with its significantly higher resolution. Note that *senza soluzione di continuità* is: without a break.

sopportare, v. — is not to support victims (= *confortare*), a weight, theory, cause (= *sostenere**), a family (= *mantenere*) or an organisation (= *sovvenzionare* or *finanziare*). It means: to put up with, bear, endure or stand, so do not mistake *non sopporto il nazionalismo* (I can't stand/abide nationalism) for I don't support nationalism (= *non sostengo/non sono d'accordo con il nazionalismo*). *Non sopporta i latticini* means: he can't take dairy products, while *una pianta capace di sopportare il freddo* is a plant able to withstand the cold. To support a team = *fare il tifo per/tifare per una squadra*. The recent anglicism *supportare* is beginning to be used for: to support or back a person or organisation.

sorpassare, v. — to surpass, exceed or overtake, but also used literally, as in the warning: *è vietato sorpassare in curva**, no overtaking on bends.

sostenere, v. — to sustain, but also to support (*l'ho sostenuto col braccio/col denaro*, I supported or backed him with my arm/with money, and *sostenere un partito*, to support or back a political party). Watch out for it, especially, when it means: to maintain or assert, e.g. *come fai a sostenere una cosa del genere?* how can you maintain/assert such a thing?

and *lui sostiene il contrario*, he maintains that the opposite is true. To sustain a loss = *subire una perdita*.

———→ SOPPORTARE

specialità, n.f. — a speciality in all senses, but also a military term meaning a special unit, e.g. *una specialità del Genio*, a special unit of the Royal Engineers/U.S. Army Engineers (———→ INGEGNERE).

spettacolo, n.m. — a spectacle or sight, but also, simply a show, e.g. *allestire uno spettacolo*, to put on a show, and *il pubblico ha assistito, numeroso, allo spettacolo*, the public attended (———→ ASSISTENZA) the show in large numbers. *Spettacolare* is: spectacular, but the statement *il Cinquecento è il secolo più grande della nostra cultura spettacolare* means: the 16th century is the most important century for our theatre culture.

———→ ESIBIZIONE, SCENA, STAGE

spia, n.f. — a spy or even a sneak, but also, in other contexts, a pilot-light, night-light, or a peephole in a door. By extension, it is a tell-tale sign or indication, so that *l'aumento della disoccupazione è una spia della crisi** means that rising unemployment is a tell-tale sign of recession.

spina, n.f. — is spine (both of the back, *la spina dosale*, and of plant needles), but it is also a thorn (*non c'è rosa senza spine*, there are no roses without thorns), a fishbone, and — because of its pins — a plug (*attaccare* la spina*, to plug in). In a beer-parlour (*una birreria*) you can get *birra alla spina*, draught beer, while the expression, *stare sulle spine* means: to be on tenterhooks.

spirito, n.m. — mostly corresponds to spirit, but can also mean: wit, so that *una persona di spirito* or *una persona spiritosa* is a witty person, and the ironical *che spirito di patata!* means: oh, very funny! *La presenza* di spirito*, though, is presence of mind. Alcoholic spirits = *i superalcolici*. Note *una casa spiritata*, a haunted house, and the expression *ha la faccia spiritata*, he looks as if he's seen a ghost, or he has a wild look on his face.

sprint, n.m. — a sprint (———→ RECORDMAN), but also the pick up or acceleration of a car. *Una berlina che manca di sprint* is, therefore, a saloon/U.S. sedan which is rather sluggish.

squillare, v. — avoid the temptation of equating it with to squeal (= *stridere* or *strillare*). It means: to ring, of a 'phone or doorbell, e.g. *il telefono ha squillato in continuazione*, the 'phone never stopped ringing. Note *una vittoria squillante*, a resounding victory. *Lo squillo del campanello* is the ring of the doorbell, but *una ragazza squillo* is a call-girl (———→ CASINO, RUFFIANO).

stabile, adj. — does mean stable (*un governo stabile*, stable government, *prezzi stabili*, stable prices), but not always. *Un impiego/lavoro/posto stabile* is a steady job, *essere in pianta stabile* is: to be employed on a permanent basis, while *un teatro/una compagnia/ un'orchestra stabile* are a permanent theatre, theatre company or orchestra. Similarly, *un'isola abitata stabilmente* is an island inhabited on a permanent basis.

stage, n.m. — has nothing to do with the stage. It is a training course or a period of work experience. Thus *gli stage, della durata di tre settimane, si svolgeranno ...* means: the training courses, lasting three weeks, will be held ..., and *corsi di lingua e stage d'apprendimento all'estero* are language courses and organised stays or placements abroad. *Uno stage internazionale di Commedia dell'arte* is an international workshop on Commedia dell'Arte. Pronounced as in French. The (theatre) stage = *il palcoscenico, la scena** or *il teatro*, a stage in a process/life = *uno stadio, un punto* or *un periodo**, and a stage in a cycle race = *una tappa*.
———→ FORMAZIONE, PREPARATO

stampa, n.f. — not a stamp (= *un (franco)bollo*) but a print (*una vecchia stampa*, an old print), printing (*un errore di stampa*, a printing error, and *la stampa è stata inventata nel 400*, printing was invented in the 15th century), or else the press (*la stampa quotidiana/settimanale*, the daily or weekly press). Italy's daily press is largely regional rather than national, with most papers providing a mix of local, regional and national news. There is no equivalent of the British popular or tabloid press (*la stampa popolare* inglese*), that market being satisfied by illustrated weekly magazines (*i rotocalchi*) such as *Oggi, Gente* and *Novella Duemila*.

stazione, n.f. — is not always a station. It may be a holiday resort, as in *una stazione invernale/sciistica*, a winter-sports/ski resort.

stick, n.m. — not a wooden stick (= *un bastone*) but a tube of deodorant, a lipstick (*uno stick di rossetto*), a stick of shaving cream, or a packet/tube of sweets/U.S. candy (*uno stick di caramelle* ———→ CARAMELLA). The cognate *una stecca*, on the other hand, is a slat in blinds, a billiard or pool cue, or a carton of cigarettes (*una stecca di sigarette*).

stiletto, n.m. — the dagger not the heels. Stiletto heels = *i tacchi a spillo*.

stipulare, v. — looks like to stipulate (= *precisare* or *stabilire come condizione*) but means: to draft. Most common are *stipulare un contratto* or *un accordo*, to draw up/draft a contract or agreement.

stoffa, n.f. — not stuff (= *la roba*) but material, fabric or cloth, so do not confuse *che tipo di stoffa è?* what kind of material is it?, and what kind of stuff is it? = *che tipo di roba è?* However, *non ha la stoffa di un pilota*/un artista* does mean: he's not the stuff pilots/artists are made of.

stop, n.m. — not a bus or train stop (= *una fermata*) but a stop-sign or signal on the road (*rispettare lo stop*, to obey the stop-sign), or else a brake-light on a vehicle (*ha gli stop che non funzionano*, his brake-lights are faulty). Note the false anglicism *l'autostop*, hitch-hiking.

storico, adj. — historic(al) but also 'all-time', or 'founding', as in *l'inflazione è a livelli storici*, inflation is at an all-time high, and *Renato Curcio, il leader storico delle Brigate Rosse*, R.C., the founding father/original leader of the Red Brigades.

straordinario, adj. — can be extraordinary (*una bellezza straordinaria*, extraordinary beauty, *un avvenimento straordinario*, an extraordinary event, and *un'assemblea straordinaria*, an extraordinary general meeting), but do not count on it. *Un'edizione* straordinaria* is a special edition, *un treno straordinario* is an extra or special train, *una recita straordinaria* is a special performance (⟶ RECITARE), and on film or T.V. credits *con la partecipazione straordinaria di …* means: special guest appearance by … Be particularly careful with *un dipendente* straordinario*, a temporary employee, and with *il lavoro straordinario*, overtime work.

stravagante, adj. — occasionally means: extravagant (*un abbigliamento stravagante*, extravagant dress), but is usually: odd(ball), weird or cranky. Compare *un comportamento stravagante*, odd, weird or excentric behaviour, with extravagant behaviour = *un comportamento esagerato* (⟶ ESAGERARE). The comment: *'Blazing Saddles', un film stravagante di Mel Brooks* means: 'Blazing Saddles', an oddball film by M.B. He is very extravagant with his money = *è molto spendereccio*; it was extravagant to buy that ring = *è stata una pazzia comprare quell'anello*; and extravagant prices = *prezzi eccessivi/ esagerati*. *Una stravaganza* is an extravagance, whereas a theatrical extravaganza = *una produzione spettacolare*, and a music extravaganza = *una composizione fantastica* (⟶ FANTASTICO).

stringente, adj. — convincing or compelling, but never stringent in the sense of strict (= *severo, rigoroso* or *inflessibile**, e.g. stringent rules = *regolamenti severi*, and stringent checks = *controlli inflessibili* ⟶ CONTROLLARE). *Un parallelo stringente* is a convincing parallel, and *un'osservazione* stringente* is a compelling or convincing remark/ observation.

studiare, v. — to study or examine. However, in advertising, especially, it is a key false friend meaning: to research, formulate, elaborate, design or devise. Thus the Sirti company *studia, progetta, realizza reti di telecomunicazioni*, researches, plans and builds (⟶ REALIZZARE) telecommunications networks. The coffee manufacturer Lavazza provides *miscele speciali che il leader italiano del caffè* studia espressamente* (⟶ ESPRESSO) *per i bar**, special blends (⟶ MISTURA) which the Italian market leader in coffee formulates/elaborates just for cafés. The *Campus* student credit card is, punningly, *la carta di credito studiata per chi studia*, the credit card devised/designed for those who study. ⟶ DISEGNO

studio, n.m. — study or studio in all senses, but also the office of any professional, so that *lo studio notarile/del notaio* is the solicitor's office, and *lo studio medico/del medico* is the doctor's office or consulting room. A recording studio = *una sala di incisione**.

succedere. v. — only to succeed someone in a post. To succeed or be successful = *riuscire* or *avere successo*. Most commonly encountered meaning: to happen, as in *queste cose succedono*, these things happen.

successivo, adj. — not the same as successive (= *consecutivo* or *di seguito*). *Nei tre libri successivi*, in the three books which followed, is not, therefore, in three consecutive books = *in tre libri consecutivi*, while *negli anni successivi* means: in subsequent years.

sufficienza, n.f. — (a) sufficiency (*hai mangiato a sufficienza?* have you had enough to eat?), but it can be deceptive. On the one hand, *ha ottenuto la sufficienza* means: he has obtained a pass/the pass mark (———→ INSUFFICIENTE). On the other hand, *un'aria di sufficienza* is a smug/conceited look, or a superior air.

suggestione, n.f. — far from being a suggestion (= *un suggerimento*) it is actually influence/intellectual dominance or, in other contexts, charm, evocativeness or irresistible attraction. *Negli anni 80 i governi hanno subito la suggestione delle idee monetariste* means: in the 80s governments fell under the influence of monetarist ideas, and *da giovane subiva la suggestione dei compagni di scuola* means that as a young man he was under the influence or dominance of his school friends. On the other hand, the magazine *AD* offers its readers *Occasioni, tentazioni, suggestioni*, Bargains (———→ OCCASIONE), tempting offers, irresistible attractions; *un turismo di intimi valori e di naturali suggestioni*, is tourism based on intimate values and natural charms; and *la suggestione di un paesaggio alpino* is the evocativeness, special/magic atmosphere or spell of an Alpine landscape.
———→ SUGGESTIVO

suggestivo, adj. — this stock word of tourist literature and artistic and literary criticism never means: sexually suggestive (= *allusivo, scorretto, sconveniente* or *spinto*). *Un itinerario/paesaggio/panorama suggestivo* is a charming, fascinating or evocative route/ landscape/view, and *una descrizione suggestiva* is an evocative or atmospheric description. Confusingly, *un'ipotesi* suggestiva* is a fascinating suggestion.
———→ AFFASCINANTE, SUGGESTIONE

superbo, adj. — occasionally means: superb (also = *splendido, eccezionale, magnifico* or *geniale**) but is usually: haughtily proud or arrogant. So *un professore* superbo* is sure to be an arrogant teacher, rather than a superb one = *un professore eccezionale, in gambissima* (coll.) or *geniale*. Superiority is the underlying concept.

superiore, adj. — can be superior (*un articolo di qualità* superiore*, a superior-quality article/item), but very often it simply means: higher. *Il piano superiore* is, therefore, the floor or story above (as opposed to the one below, *il piano inferiore**), *una somma superiore* is a higher or greater amount, *un grado superiore* is a higher rank/grade/degree, while *la scuola media superiore* is senior high school.

suscettibile, adj. — is easily mistaken for susceptible, but actually means: touchy or over-sensitive. *Una persona suscettibile*, a touchy person, is therefore not the same as a susceptible person = *una persona impressionabile* (———→ IMPRESSIONARE).

T

tappo, n.m. — not the sink tap/U.S. faucet (= *il rubinetto*) but the plug, instead. Also a bottle-top or stopper of any kind, e.g. *un tappo (di sughero)*, a cork. The origins of *tappo* and tap are identical but the Italian term stresses the containment, not the release, of the liquid.
————→ CAPSULA

tariffa, n.f. — is a trade or hotel tariff but also simply a rate, fare or charge, so that *le tariffe di abbonamento del 1994 rimangono le stesse del 1993* means: the 1994 subscription rates remain the same as 1993's, and *le tariffe ferroviarie* are rail or train fares. The telecommunications company ItalCable promises *ulteriori* (————→ ULTERIORE) *riduzioni sulle tariffe intercontinentali*, further reductions on intercontinental charges.
————→ CONVENIENTE

tastare, v. — shares its origins with to taste (= *assaggiare*) but means: to touch or feel with the fingers, as in *tastare una stoffa**, to feel a fabric. Note *tastare il polso**, to take the pulse, and *tastare il terreno**, to get the lie of the land.

terreno, n.m. — can be terrain (*un terreno montuoso*, mountainous terrain) but also plot, land, or even playing field. The sign *vendite terreni* means: building plots for sale, *le imposte sui terreni* is tax on building land, *il terreno coltivabile/arabile* is arable land, and *scendere sul terreno* is: to take the field. Note the expressions *guadagnare terreno*, to gain ground, and *tastare* il terreno*, to get the lie of the land.
————→ TERRITORIO

territorio, n.m. — A far from helpful friend. Apart from the space defended by animals or the enemy, it can rarely be translated as territory. *Una giornata calda sull'insieme del territorio (nazionale)* means: a hot day over the whole country/nationwide; *le Alpi Marittime — un territorio ancora poco conosciuto dai turisti* is: the Maritime Alps, a region still little known to tourists, and *il territorio del comune di Pesaro* is the area around the town of P. Trickier still, *territorio e urbanizzazione* is town and country planning, and *la sistemazione del territorio nazionale* is roughly equivalent to national and regional development. Surprisingly, *la trasformazione del territorio* means: changes to the (living and working) environment, and a debate on *lavoro e territorio* is about work and the environment.
————→ TERRENO

ticket, n.m. — occurs frequently in media reports, but has nothing to do with ticket (= *un biglietto*). It is, in fact, the prescription charge on medicines (around 50% of their actual cost in the early 1990s), or else the part of health-treatment costs which a patient must pay. This explains headlines like *Tutti pagheranno il ticket* (*La Repubblica*, 3/7/92), Everybody to pay health charges, and *Il caos sui ticket si somma ai disservizi cronici di Usl e ospedali* (*La Repubblica*, 5/4/89), the mess over health charges aggravates the chronic malfunctioning (————→ DISSERVIZIO) of Local Health Clinics (————→ SANITÀ) and hospitals.

tight, n.m. — is worn by men and has nothing to do with tights (*la calzamaglia* or *il collant*). It is (a) morning coat/dress. Revealingly, other items of formal dress are also (false) anglicisms in Italian. A dinner jacket/U.S. tux(edo) is *uno smoking*, and a frock-coat or tail-coat is *un frac*.

————→ GOLF

tilt, n.m. — not a tilt (= *una pendenza* or *un'inclinazione*) but a standstill. *La Repubblica* (3–4/10/93) proclaimed on its front page banner headline (*il titolone*): *Nubifragi: Italia in tilt*, Downpours: Italy at a standstill. If, because of a strike, *la città è andata in tilt*, or a government decision *ha mandato la sanità* in tilt*, it means that the city and the health services have been brought to a halt/standstill (————→ BLOCCARE) or put out of commission (————→ COMMISSIONE). A curious false anglicism deriving from the tilt effect on the pinball machine (————→ FLIPPER) which brings the game to a temporary stop.

tipico, adj. — typical, but watch out for it in the context of food and drink where it means: local, characteristic (————→ CARATTERISTICO) or authentic. Restaurants boast of *vini tipici*, characteristic local wines, and *cucina tipica*, authentic local cuisine or dishes. *Bagna cauda*, a garlic and anchovy dip from the Monferrato area of Piedmont could be described as *uno dei più tipici piatti locali*, one of the most authentic local dishes (————→ GENUINO).

titolo, n.m. — a title, but confusable on three counts. It may be a headline, as in *i titoli del telegiornale delle 20*, the 8 p.m. news headlines, and *i grossi titoli dei giornali*, the main newspaper headlines. It may also be a stock or security on the stockmarket, so that *titoli di stato* is government stock (————→ AZIONE, OBBLIGAZIONE). Also an educational qualification, *un titolo di stato*. The main ones are *la licenza* elementare**, the primary school leaving certificate; *la licenza media*, awarded (————→ RILASCIARE) at 15, at the end of compulsory schooling (————→ INFERIORE, SUPERIORE); *il diploma secondario* (of which by far the most important is *la maturità* ————→ MATURO); and the university degree, *la laurea* (————→ VOTO). Somebody with no qualifications is *senza titolo*.

toast, n.m. — do not be misled. If in a café (————→ BAR, CAFFÈ) you ask for *un toast* you will be given not toast (= *il pane tostato*) but a toasted sandwich with ham and cheese, like the French *croque-monsieur*.

toga, n.f. — appears in modern as well as ancient Rome. It is simply a judge's or lawyer's robes, or else a teacher's gown.

————→ MAGISTRATO, TRIBUNALE

trampolino, n.m. — shares the idea of springing with trampoline (= *un tappeto elastico*), but is really a diving board/springboard or a ski-jump.

trasformare, v. — to transform, but note that in rugby *trasformare una meta* is to convert a try, and in football (soccer) *trasformare un rigore* or *una punizione* is to score from a penalty or free-kick.

tremendo, adj. — occasionally corresponds to tremendous, when size or impressiveness are involved (*un temporale tremendo*, a tremendous storm), although a tremendous difference = *una differenza enorme*, a tremendous speed = *una velocità straordinaria*, and a tremendous success = *un successo eccezionale/straordinario**. The main point to remember is that whereas tremendous is often positive, *tremendo* tends to be negative (and thus remains closer to its original sense of fear-inducing). A tremendous experience (= *un'esperienza* *meravigliosa* or *eccezionale*) stands in contrast to *un'esperienza tremenda* (a terrible/ awful/traumatic experience). *Un bambino tremendo* is, consequently, a dreadful child, *una paura tremenda* is a terrible scare, and *un professore* veramente tremendo* means: a ferociously strict teacher. When the pop singer Adriano Celentano sang *Con tutte le ragazze io sono tremendo*, he really meant that he was a terror with all the girls. Words about terror often acquire, like tremendous, the opposite meaning: it is happening to awesome in English and has happened to *terrible* (= great or marvellous) in French.

tribunale, n.m. — is a tribunal but also a court, so that *il tribunale civile* or *penale* is the civil or criminal court(s), and *il tribunale dei minorenni* is the juvenile court (———→ GIOVANILE). The term *la corte* is reserved for higher courts such as *la Corte d'appello*, the Court of Appeal, and *la Corte costituzionale*, the Constitutional Court.
———→ CONCILIATORE, MAGISTRATO, PROCESSO, TOGA

triviale, adj. — is very untrustworthy. Avoid mistaking it for trivial (= *banale** or *insignificante*) as it actually means: vulgar, coarse or obscene. *Un'espressione triviale*, an obscene expression, is not at all the same as a trivial expression, *un'espressione banale*. *Un linguaggio* triviale* is coarse or vulgar language, and the abbreviation *triv.* beside a dictionary headword indicates a vulgarism. *La trivialità* is, therefore, not triviality (= *la banalità*) but vulgarity, as in *provare fastidio per la trivialità di certi costumi da bagno*, to get annoyed (———→ ANNOIARE) by the vulgarity of certain bathing costumes (———→ COSTUME).

tubo, n.m. — not just a tube but a pipe, as in *il tubo di scarico*, the drain-pipe, *il tubo di scappamento*, the exhaust pipe, and *un tubo di gomma* or *un tubo flessibile*, a hose-pipe. Note the expression *non vale/capisce un tubo* (coll.), it's not worth a bean/he doesn't understand a damn thing. *La tubatura* is the plumbing of a building, and is repaired (———→ AGGIUSTARE) by *l'idraulico*, the plumber.

turno, n.m. — can be turn (*aspettare il proprio turno*, to await one's turn), but it is often shift, rota or duty, as in *il lavoro di turno*, shift-work, *la farmacia di turno*, the rota chemist, and *il medico di turno*, the duty doctor. Whose turn is it? = *a chi tocca?*
———→ STRAORDINARIO

U

ufficiale, n.m. — if you wish to contact an official, it is best to ask for *un funzionario*. *Un ufficiale* is usually a military officer, e.g. *un ufficiale di carriera*, a regular officer, *un allievo ufficiale*, a cadet officer, and *un ufficiale degli alpini*, an officer in the crack Alpine regiment which sports the characteristic pointed hat with feather.
————→ BRIGADIERE, MARESCIALLO

ufficioso, adj. — resembles officious (= *zelante* or *invadente*) but means: unofficial or off-the-record. Often employed in newspapers and news bulletins in expressions of the type *fonti ufficiose dichiarano*, unofficial or off-the-record sources state, and *la notizia* è ancora ufficiosa*, the news is still unofficial (as opposed to official, *ufficiale**).

ulteriore, adj. — looks like ulterior but means: further. Do not, therefore, confuse *ha ulteriori motivi per farlo*, he has further reasons (————→ MOTIVO) for doing it, and he has ulterior motives = *ha secondi fini*. *Per ulteriori informazioni rivolgersi alle autorità competenti* (————→ COMPETENTE) means: For further information, contact the relevant (————→ RILEVANTE) authorities, and *un ulteriore aggiornamento* della legislazione* is a further updating of the legislation.

ultimo, adj. — only corresponds to ultimate in the sense of fundamental, e.g. *il senso* ultimo delle sue parole ci sfugge*, the ultimate meaning of his words escapes us, and *le ultime cause dell'universo*, the ultimate origins of the universe. Otherwise it means: last or latest. Contrast *il suo ultimo successo*, his last/latest success, and his ultimate success = *il successo che ha ottenuto alla fine/infine/finalmente*. *Le ultime tendenze* are the latest trends, and *l'ultimo errore* is the last or latest mistake. The best-known epistolary novel in Italian is Ugo Foscolo's *Ultime lettere di Jacopo Ortis* (1789–1802) ['J.O.'s Final Letters']. On the other hand, the ultimate reward or sacrifice = *il compenso/sacrificio supremo*. Note that *le ultimissime* is the very latest (hot) news/gossip, and that the adverb *ultimamente* means not: ultimately (= *in definitiva, in fin dei conti, alla fine* or *in ultima analisi**) but lately or recently, e.g. *ultimamente non l'ho incontrato*, I haven't met him recently/lately.

umido, adj. — humid or damp (————→ ZONA), but in cooking it means: stewed (usually in a tomato-based sauce). *La carne in umido*, stewed beef, is a regular in Italian home-cooking (*la cucina casalinga*), providing not only the main course (*il secondo*) but also the sauce (*il sugo* or *l'intingolo*) for the pasta course (————→ PASTA).

unico, adj. — do not take for granted. It can mean unique (especially when following the noun or even detached from it), e.g. *un esemplare unico*, a unique specimen, *un' occasione* unica*, a unique opportunity, *unica fra le città d'Italia*, unique among Italian cities, and the Casio ad.: *Le Digital Diary Casio sono uniche al mondo*, C. Digital Diaries are unique. Commonly encountered, though, meaning: single, only, the (one and) only, or sole, as in *un volume unico/un unico volume*, a single volume, *una moneta unica*, a single currency, *un figlio unico*, an only son, *gli unici amici che ho*, the only friends I have, and *l'unico rappresentante del suo paese*, his country's sole representative.
————→ SINGOLO

untuoso, adj. — oily of manners (*un atteggiamento untuoso*, an unctuous attitude) but also of substances, e.g. *i capelli untuosi*, greasy hair, and *la pelle untuosa*, greasy skin.

urna, n.f. — not just the urn of Keats's ode, but also, more prosaically, an election ballot box, e.g. *deporre la scheda nell'urna*, to place one's voting paper in the ballot box. Figuratively, *andare alle urne* is: to go to the polls. In the early 1990s Italy was moving away from the extreme proportional representation system which had led, for forty years, to the wheeling and dealing of coalitions, towards the first-past-the-post system (*il sistema uninominale*), sometimes called *il voto* inglese*, the British vote.
———→ ANTICIPARE, SCRUTINIO

V

vacillare, v. — to vacillate or waver (also = *titubare*) but can mean: to stagger or totter, too. Thus *vacillare sulle gambe*, to be unsteady/wobbly on one's legs, and *vacillò per l'ubriachezza*, he staggered in his drunkenness.

variazione, n.f. — variation (*variazioni di temperatura*, variations in temperature) but also change or modification, so that *alcune variazioni d'orario* are some timetable alterations, and *una variazione nel/del programma* is a programme/syllabus change (———→ PROGRAMMARE).

vario, adj. — various or varied, but note that *vari articoli*, various or several articles/items, is not the same as *articoli vari*, sundry articles/items, and that *spese varie* are miscellaneous or sundry expenses. On best-seller lists the heading *varia* means: miscellaneous (———→ NARRATIVA).

vaso, n.m. — a vase but much more besides. It may be a flower/plant pot (*un vaso da fiori*), so that *mettere la pianta in un vaso* might be: to pot the plant or put it in a vase. *Un vaso di miele* or *di marmellata**, on the other hand, is a jar of honey or jam, while *un vaso da notte* is a chamber-pot. *Il vaso di Pandora* is Pandora's box.

vendicare, v. — not to vindicate (= *giustificare*) but to avenge, e.g. *ha vendicato l'offesa subita*, he avenged the insult he (had) suffered. *La vendetta* (vengeance) derives from this verb.

vernice, n.f. — frequently confusing since it can be both varnish or paint. *La vernice lucida/opaca/metallizzata* is gloss, matt or metallic paint, and *dare una mano di vernice* is: to apply a coat of paint.

verso, n.m. — a poetic verse, but can also be something very different: either an animal cry or call (*il verso del gatto è il miagolio*, the cry of the cat is the mew), or a human grunt (*rispondere con un verso di disprezzo*, to answer with a scornful grunt) or 'face' (*fare un verso* is: to make/pull a face).

viabilità, n.f. — is never viability (= *l'attuabilità* or *l'essere fattibile*). On the one hand, it can mean: the practicability or state of the roads, e.g. *la viabilità dell'autostrada è interrotta dalla neve*, the motorway is impassable because of snow. On the other hand, it refers to the road/transport network itself (*la regione è dotata di un'ottima viabilità*, the region is equipped with a fine road or transport/U.S. transportation system/network), or even to highway transport regulations or problems, as in *i problemi di viabilità delle grandi città*, the transport problems of the big cities, and *l'assessorato alla viabilità*, a town council's highways' department ———→ ASSESSORE.
———→ CIRCOLAZIONE, IMPERVIO, INTERROTTO

vignetta, n.f. — not a vignette (= *un ritratto/una descrizione sintetico*/a*) but a newspaper or magazine cartoon. Among the most consistently witty (———→ SPIRITO) are the laconic *vignette umoristiche* by Altan, appearing weekly in *L'Espresso*.

vile, adj. — like vile, is pejorative but it means: cowardly. *Un'azione* vile*, a cowardly act or deed is, therefore, not the same as a vile deed = *un'azione ignobile*, and *un uomo vile*, a coward, is different from a vile man = *un uomo squallido/abietto/schifoso*. *Un vile attacco alle forze dell'ordine* is a cowardly attack on the security forces. A vile cup of coffee = *un caffè* schifoso*, and vile weather = *un tempo orribile*.

villa, n.f. — a villa or country house, but also simply a detached house/U.S. one-family or single family home.
──────→ DUPLEX

villano, n.m. — shares its origins with villain (= *un mascalzone* or, in a book, play or film, *il cattivo*) but is a boor or rude person (*non fare il villano!*, don't be so rude!) or else a naughty child. The original meaning of country-dweller (i.e. villein) has evolved, from the Middle Ages onwards, into an insult, as have English peasant, French *villain* and modern Italian *cafone*.
──────→ ABUSIVO

visione, n.f. — can mean vision, both ocular and spritual, but it has its pitfalls. *Una stupenda visione sul lago di Santa Croce* is actually: a marvellous view over the lake of Santa Croce in the Dolomites; *una visione pessimista della situazione internazionale* is a pessimistic view of/outlook on the international situation, while *la prima visione di un film* is the first showing/run of a film. The comment *una colonna* sonora coerente* rende più intensa la visione di un film* suggests that a soundtrack which is appropriate to/consistent with a film makes viewing it a more intense experience. T.V. announcers end their previews with *Vi auguro una buona visione!*, a good evening's viewing to you!

vivace, adj. — is lively or vivid rather than vivacious (a vivacious girl = *una ragazza vivace e attraente/simpatica/affascinante**), and can be applied more widely. Thus *uno stile vivace*, a lively style, *un'intelligenza vivace*, a lively intelligence, *un bambino vivace*, a lively child, and *un ritratto vivace*, a vivid portrait. Can also be: colourful, as in *vivaci costumi regionali*, colourful local costumes (──────→ COSTUME). In gardening, *una pianta vivace* is a perennial.

vizioso, adj. — not to be confused with vicious (a vicious attack = *un attacco violento/ brutale*, vicious criticism = *una critica feroce*, and a vicious dog = *un cane mordace*). *Vizioso*, on the other hand, means: depraved, perverted, lewd or corrupt, so do not take *un comportamento vizioso*, 'dirty' or 'filthy' behaviour, for vicious behaviour = *un comportamento brutale*. *Un'età viziosa* is a corrupt era. A vicious circle, though, is *un circolo* vizioso*. Note that *un vizio* can be both a vice (*la lussuria* è un vizio*, lust is a vice) and a bad habit (*fumare è un vizio*, smoking is a bad habit), with the dividing line not always clear: in Pavese's poem *Verrà la morte e avrà i tuoi occhi* (1950) ['Death will come and will have your eyes'] death is called *un vizio assurdo*, an absurd habit/vice. The saying *il lupo perde il pelo ma non il vizio* is equivalent to: a leopard never changes his spots. A life of vice, however = *una vita dissoluta*, while the vice-squad = *la squadra del buon costume**. Surprisingly, *un bambino viziato* is only a spoiled child.

vocabolario, n.m. — more often dictionary (also *un dizionario*) than vocabulary (= *il lessico*). Zingarelli's *Vocabolario della Lingua Italiana* is one of the standard Italian dictionaries.

———→ LINGUAGGIO

volubile, adj. — resembles voluble, but *una persona volubile*, a changeable or fickle person, is not the same as a voluble one = *una persona loquace* or *chiacchierona*. *Un tempo volubile* is changeable or variable weather.

———→ MOBILE

voto, n.m. — a/the (political) vote, in all senses, but also a mark or grade in education, so that *prendere dei buoni/brutti voti* is: to get good or bad marks or grades. Italian marking is done on a notional basis. The school leaving-certificate exam (*la maturità* ———→ MATURO) is out of 60, with 31 the pass (*la sufficienza* ———→ INSUFFICIENTE). Degree exams are out of 110, with 110/110 being roughly equivalent to a B.A. (Hons.), II,1 in England, and 110/110 *con lode* or *cum laude* corresponding to a First/U.S. summa cum laude at Bachelor level. There are those who contend, though, that the Italian degree (*la laurea*) is actually the equivalent of an English or American M.A.

———→ SCRUTINIO, TITOLO, URNA

Z

zona, n.f. — can be zone (*la zona di guerra*, the war zone, and *la zona smilitarizzata*, the demilitarised zone), but often simply means: area. *Una zona residenziale* is a residential area/district, *una zona d'ombra* is an area of shade, *una zona vietata alla pesca* is a no-fishing area, *la zona interessata* is the affected area (——→ INTERESSARE), and *le zone del corpo più soggette all'invecchiamento* are the areas/parts of the body most liable to ageing. However, note that *una zona pedonale* is a pedestrian precinct, *una zona industriale* is an industrial estate, while *le zone umide* (——→ UMIDO) *della delta del Po* means: the wetlands of the Po delta.
——→ ISOLARE, TERRITORIO

zuppa inglese, n.f. — neither a soup (= *una zuppa* or *una minestra*) nor English. This is the Italian version of trifle, made with alcohol-soaked sponge, *zabaione* or egg custard (——→ CREMA), chocolate and whipped cream. Its unlikely name probably originates in the widespread continental preconception (——→ PREVENZIONE) about incongruous flavour combinations (——→ MISTURA) being typical of British cuisine. Anglo-Saxon revenge comes in the form of the pigeon-Italian tutti frutti ice-cream (= *il gelato con canditi* or *la cassata*).

Selective Bibliography

Italian False Friends

The two most substantial and systematic treatments of the subject are both aimed at an Italian readership:

A. D'Eugenio, *Falsi Amici Inglesi: lessico inglese ed italiano a confronto*, Atlantica Editrice, Foggia, 1984.

V. Browne, *Odd Pairs & False Friends: dizionario di false analogie e ambigue affinità fra inglese e italiano*, Zanichelli, Bologna, 1987.

For English-speaking students there is the useful workbook:

M. Sassu Frescura, *Interferenze Lessicali Italiano/Inglese*, University of Toronto Press, Toronto, Buffalo, London, 1984.

Worth consulting, too, is:

P. J. T. Glendening, *Cassell's Colloquial Italian: A handbook of idiomatic usage*, Cassell, London and New York, 1980.

A number of recent language books have devoted (a) section(s) to *falsi amici*, notably:

N. Messora, *Italian: A handbook of grammar, current usage and word power*, Cassell, London and New York, 1992, pp. 447-53.

C. P. Rosenbaum, *Italian for Educated Guessers: Shortcuts to the Language*, Forza, Menlo Park, 1985, pp. 73-9 and 165-80.

The theory and practice of false friends are explored in some recent articles:

V. Browne and G. A. Natali, 'Abusive Arguments — (Argomenti Abusivi?)', *Le Lingue del Mondo*, Jan./Feb. 1984, pp. 44-9.

C. Cona, 'I falsi amici', *Tuttitalia: the Italian Journal of the Association for Language Learning*, vol. I, June 1990, pp. 7-16.

M. Croce and W. Schoener, 'Contrastive Analysis for Italian Learners of English: an Exploration of Lexical Interference', *Rassegna Italiana di Linguistica Applicata*, vol. XIV, 1982, pp. 123-49.

S. Granger and H. Swallow, 'False Friends: a kaleidoscope of Translation Difficulties', *Le Langage et l'Homme*, vol. 23 (2), 1988, pp. 108-20.

J. Van Roey, 'Deceptive Terminology for Deceptive Cognates', in J.-P. Van Noppen and G. Debusscher (eds.), *Communiquer et Traduire — Hommage à Jean Dierickx*, Editions de l'Université de Bruxelles, Faculté de Philosophie et Lettres, XCVI, 1985, pp. 159-64.

Dictionaries (Italian Monolingual)

Italian is fortunate in being rich in monolingual dictionaries. Invaluable for further, detailed exploration of the nuances of Italian words is the monumental:

> S. Battaglia (ed.), *Grande Dizionario della Lingua Italiana*, U.T.E.T., Turin (sixteen vols. so far published).

Of the many, good, one-volume dictionaries the following, in their different ways, have proved most fruitful (the latest edition of each is assumed):

> M. Dardano (ed.), *Nuovissimo Dardano: Dizionario della Lingua Italiana*, Armando Curcio Editore, Rome.

> E. De Felice and A. Duro (eds.), *Dizionario della Lingua e della Civiltà Italiana Contemporanea*, Palumbo, Florence.

> A. Gianni (ed.), *Dizionario italiano ragionato*, G. D'Anna/Sintesi, Florence.

From the range of Italian synonym–antonym dictionaries, a handy and reliable work is:

> M. Giocondi (ed.), *Dizionario del sinonimi e dei contrari*, Editoriale Paradigma, Florence.

Dictionaries (Bilingual)

Sadly, the richness and excellence of Italian monolingual lexicography is not matched by Italian–English/English–Italian dictionaries. Students and scholars of Italian have nothing to compare with the outstanding *Collins–Robert* French dictionary. Only two are reliable, in this order:

> L. I. Caselli (ed.), *Il Nuovo Dizionario Hazon Garzanti: inglese–italiano, italiano–inglese*, Garzanti, Milan.

> V. Macchi (ed.), *Collins–Sansoni Italian Dictionary: Italian–English, English–Italian*, Sansoni, Florence.

Corpora

Corpus raw materials provide a sober and sometimes illuminating antidote both to one's own beliefs/intuitions, and to the dictionaries' fixed prescriptions about usage. The only Italian one available (as far as I know) in the U.K. is *The Corpus of Modern Italian* held in the Department of Italian Studies at the University of Birmingham.

Dictionaries (Etymological)

The often fascinating origins of Italian words can be explored in:

> M. Cortelazzo and P. Zolli, *Dizionario etimologico della lingua italiana*, Zanichelli, Bologna, 1988 (five vols.).

> E. De Felice, *Le parole d'oggi*, Mondadori, Milan, 1984.

> G. Lotti, *Perché si dice così*, Rizzoli, Milan, 1991.

For the etymologies of English cognates indispensable guides are:

J. A. Simpson and E. S. C. Weiner (eds.), *The Oxford English Dictionary*, Clarendon Press, Oxford (twenty vols.).

W. Little *et al.* (eds.), *The Shorter Oxford English Dictionary*, Clarendon Press, Oxford (two vols.).

Anglicisms and other Foreign Loan Words in Italian

The massive influx of (mainly English) borrowings into contemporary Italian, which has been a new source of false friends, is examined in:

G. S. Carpitano and G. Càsole, *Dizionario delle parole straniere in uso nella lingua italiana*, Oscar Mondadori, Milan, 1989.

I. Klein, *Influssi inglesi nella lingua italiana*, Olschki, Florence, 1972.

G. Rando, *Dizionario degli Anglicismi nell'Italiano Postunitario*, Olschki, Florence, 1987.

P. Zolli, *Le Parole Straniere*, Zanichelli, Bologna, 1991.